Black Family (Dys)Function in Novels by Jessie Fauset, Nella Larsen, & Fannie Hurst

Modern American Literature
New Approaches

Yoshinobu Hakutani
General Editor

Vol. 27

PETER LANG
New York • Washington, D.C./Baltimore • Bern
Frankfurt am Main • Berlin • Brussels • Vienna • Oxford

Licia Morrow Calloway

Black Family (Dys)Function in Novels by Jessie Fauset, Nella Larsen, & Fannie Hurst

PETER LANG
New York • Washington, D.C./Baltimore • Bern
Frankfurt am Main • Berlin • Brussels • Vienna • Oxford

Library of Congress Cataloging-in-Publication Data

Calloway, Licia Morrow:
Black family (dys)function in novels by Jessie Fauset, Nella Larsen,
and Fannie Hurst / Licia Morrow Calloway.
p. cm. — (Modern American literature; vol. 27)
Includes bibliographical references and index.
1. Domestic fiction, American—History and criticism. 2. American fiction—Women
authors—History and criticism. 3. Women and literature—United States—History—
20th century. 4. American fiction—Afro-American authors—History and criticism.
5. American fiction—20th century—History and criticism. 6. Hurst, Fannie, 1889–1968—
Criticism and interpretation. 7, Fauset, Jessie Redmon—Criticism and interpretation.
8. Larsen, Nella—Criticism and interpretation. 9. Afro-American families in literature.
10. Problem families in literature. 11. Afro-Americans in literature.
I. Title. II. Modern American literature (New York, N.Y.) ; vol. 27.
PS374.D57 C35   813'.5209355—dc21   00-048774
ISBN 0-8204-5159-2
ISSN 1078-0521

Die Deutsche Bibliothek-CIP-Einheitsaufnahme

Calloway, Licia Morrow:
Black family (dys)function in novels by Jessie Fauset, Nella Larsen, and Fannie Hurst / Licia
Morrow Calloway. –New York; Washington, D.C./Baltimore; Bern; Frankfurt am Main;
Berlin; Brussels; Vienna; Oxford: Lang.
(Modern American literature; Vol. 27)
ISBN 0-8204-5159-2

Cover design by Joni Holst

The paper in this book meets the guidelines for permanence and durability
of the Committee on Production Guidelines for Book Longevity
of the Council of Library Resources.

© 2003 Peter Lang Publishing, Inc., New York
275 Seventh Avenue, 28th Floor, New York, NY 10001
www.peterlangusa.com

All rights reserved.
Reprint or reproduction, even partially, in all forms such as microfilm, xerography,
microfiche, microcard, and offset strictly prohibited.

Printed in the United States of America

For Jacqueline Ann,
Micayla Denise,
and Erica Joy Calloway

Table of Contents

Acknowledgments ix
Introduction: Representational Shifts and Homemade Family Values 1

1 Conceiving Class and Culture: A Contextual Retrospective 11
    Conceiving 12
    Class 22
    Culture 30

2 Revising the Victorian Maternal Ideal in Jessie Fauset's
There Is Confusion 39
    The Endorsement of Black Patriarchal Authority 42
    Confronting the Bourgeois Sensibility 47
    Revisiting the Tragic Mulatto 52
    Celebrating Motherhood and Domesticity 61
    Finding Narrative Closure 71

3 Elite Rejection of Maternity in Nella Larsen's *Quicksand* and *Passing* 81
    Maternal Effacement in *Quicksand* 86
    Sexual Repression and Race Confusion in *Quicksand* and *Passing* 93
    Maternity and Domestic Entrapment in *Passing* 101

4 The Stereotypical Mammy in Fannie Hurst's *Imitation of Life* 111
    The Cultural Significance of the Mammy 113
    Mammy as the Liberator of the White "New Woman" 120
    Passing as the Modern Black Rejection of the Mammy 126

Notes 139
Bibliography 157
Index 169

Acknowledgments

In the fall of 1999 I received a manuscript solicitation letter from Dr. Heidi Burns, Senior Editor of Peter Lang Publishing, in which she expressed an interest in publishing my recently filed dissertation as a book. I remember that I was in the midst of teaching an introductory composition class at the University of Michigan and working as a faculty consultant in the university's Sweetland Writing Center, frenetically coordinating my schedule with my husband's so that one of us could nearly always be at home with our three young daughters. I had no idea what a publishing company would want with me, so I assumed that the envelope from Peter Lang contained some sort of direct mail sales flyer sent to the entire membership of the Modern Language Association. The letter found its way to the floorboard of my car and lay there for upwards of a week among weekly circulars from the area grocery stores, a scattering of expired coupons, several days' worth of my oldest daughter's incessant second grade classroom correspondence, and a haphazard collection of cassette tapes and infant toys. During my weekend cleaning of the car, I casually tore open the envelope, mildly curious to enlighten myself with the list of Lang's latest offerings. When I read of Dr. Burns' interest in my project, based upon having read the abstract contained in *Dissertation Abstracts International*, I was thrilled, but astonished; I had no idea that publishing my first book would be so easy.

Publishing my first book has been anything *but* easy. Perhaps securing the contract required little exertion on my part, but the process of editing, rearranging, reformatting, and revisiting the intellectual material which had occupied what had seemed to be my every waking moment (lucid or otherwise) for the previous several years, was taxing indeed. Fortunately, there have been a number of individuals who have, consciously or unwittingly, facilitated things for me. Because this book has its origins in a doctoral dissertation written in partial fulfillment of the degree requirements of the Horace H. Rackham School of Graduate Studies at the University of

Michigan, first acknowledgments must be extended to my committee, jointly chaired by Sandra Gunning and June Howard of the Department of English Language and Literature, and rounded out by Marlon Ross, and the History department's Michele Mitchell, who served as the outside reader. As a young mother, I was quite a non-traditional student, and I am very grateful for their understanding, flexibility, and guidance throughout the arduous process of combining the rigors of scholarship with my commitment to my family. I am also indebted to the generosity of two major fellowships which sustained me economically throughout my tenure as a graduate student: my Committee on Institutional Cooperation and Rackham Merit Fellowships ensured that financing my education was never a source of concern.

I owe an immeasurable debt of gratitude to many friends in the Ann Arbor area for offering to care for my children during the semesters I taught classes, the afternoons I absolutely needed to devote to research or writing, or the times they perceived that I simply craved a brief hiatus from the demands of being "Mommy." Most significantly, however, I must publicly acknowledge Karen and Curtis Cross of Ann Arbor and Elaine Saxton of Britton. I truly believe I could not have finished my degree without their help. I also want to collectively thank the congregation of Bethel AME Church in Ann Arbor, and the Ann Arbor Chapter of Jack and Jill of America, Inc., for serving to normalize (at least in part) the Calloway lifestyle and provide a loving "village" for my daughters.

Here at The Citadel, I am very appreciative of Jim Leonard, my department head, and Harry Carter, Vice President for Academic Affairs and Dean of the College, for granting me a course release in the first semester of my appointment to the English faculty and a curtailed department service load, in the interest of allowing me sufficient time to focus on getting this book published. My wonderful colleagues in the Department of English have made our wing of Capers Hall a lively, interesting, amusing, and remarkably comfortable place from which to work. I also have to express my appreciation to my students from the South Carolina Corps of Cadets for demonstrating an interest in my scholarly activity, professing admiration for my achievements to date, and promising to read this book once it is published. Working with them is a constant inspiration and makes me want to be the best professor I can possibly be. Special consideration goes to Bradley Ala, Justin Byczek, Mark Evans, Robert Killian, and the Delta '04 contingent for being constant reminders of why I love academia even on those inevitable days when teaching seems most unrewarding.

Finally, I acknowledge my family, without whom none of this could have come to fruition. My most heartfelt gratitude goes to my parents, both by birth and marriage, Lumon and Jacqueline Morrow, and Paul and Edith Calloway. Thank you for never doubting my capability and for always making me feel that I can meet and exceed any expectations of me. Thank you to Carla Morrow Sligh, Maya Morrow, Kwan Morrow, and Eric Calloway, my sisters and brothers, for allowing me to shed my austere intellectual persona from time to time and simply be the rather silly individual I have always been in their company.

To my amazing daughters, Jacqueline Ann, Micayla Denise, and Erica Joy, who have completely overrun my heart: you honestly overwhelm me with your uncommon intelligence, spirit, and beauty, and you motivate me to continually strive to make myself worthy of your devotion; I am so privileged and proud to be your mother. To my husband Denny, who has been there since the inception of the idea which evolved into this book: I know that whatever sacrifices I have made, you have made significantly more, and purely for my sake, which makes them all the more precious. I cannot begin to articulate the extent to which I recognize that I owe you infinitely more than I can ever repay.

Licia Morrow Calloway
Charleston, South Carolina
May 2001

Introduction

Representational Shifts and Homemade Family Values

In 1996, the writer Benilde Little had *Good Hair*, her first novel, published to a warm reception. According to the book jacket synopsis, "Little offers us a delicious, closely observed, eye-opening look at the world of upper-class Black Manhattan in a novel that is alternately humorous and touching, sexy and bold."[1] The narrative revolves around Alice Andrews of Newark, New Jersey, the middle-class daughter of a postal worker. Her mother, a housewife, has grand aspirations for Alice and her brother and endeavors to create a home atmosphere of privilege for her family. Alice excels in high school, attends Mount Holyoke, a selective women's college, on an academic scholarship, and becomes a reporter.

On an airline flight back to her home in New York from Atlanta, where she had been visiting a childhood friend, a black male gate agent upgrades Alice's seat assignment to first class as a gesture of racial solidarity, and she ends up sitting next to Jack Russworm, a third-generation doctor from an elite black Boston family. As a result of their unlikely encounter, Jack and Alice begin dating, but their relationship is constantly tested by the clash between their respective backgrounds. Jack is a prominent member of an informal national network of upper-class black socialites, and he incorrectly assumes Alice, due to her first-class passenger status, her Holyoke education, and her polished manner, is of the same social milieu. Though it takes considerable effort, Jack and Alice eventually work through all of their issues arising from her insecurities and his presumptions; they successfully bridge their class differences, and their story ends with conventional matrimony—figuratively speaking, a permanent first-class upgrade for the bride of Dr. Jack Russworm.

Good Hair is a notable example of the current trend in African-American culture to denounce the constant focus on images and narratives of inner-city turmoil and to encourage the promotion of alternative visions of black life which more accurately reflect the true variety and complexity of African-American experiences. The film version of Little's novel is currently in production. However, seventy years before the appearance of *Good Hair*, Little's literary precursors, Jessie Redmon Fauset and Nella Larsen, did not fare so well in their efforts to entextualize the secluded world of black privilege for American mass cultural consumption. The black intelligentsia of the 1920s warmly extolled their efforts, but white people felt the novels were impractical flights into overblown fancy. Later critics soundly excoriated the women for alleged elitism, frivolity, and sociopolitical indifference, while their spurned texts languished out of print.

Probing the other end of the socioeconomic class spectrum, Fannie Hurst's white woman's insight into the ideological conflict between a traditionally subservient black domestic and her discontented, rebellious daughter met with mixed reactions of outrage and appreciation in the black community, white popular approbation, and considerable critical notice. The novel, *Imitation of Life* (1933), was adapted for the silver screen the year after its publication, remade a quarter of a century after that, and retains its cultural currency to this day, although the thematic significance of Hurst's original narrative has been all but lost in the attention devoted to the two distorted film versions of the story.

Each of the chapters in this book explores various aspects of the issues of class formation and acculturation within the black community through fictional representations of maternity and domestic spaces. The authors in this study incorporate the effects on the family of living in the midst of a hostile social environment, and how women in particular respond to a repressive culture in their approaches to childbearing and childrearing. Where Fauset and Larsen concentrate mainly on the upwardly aspiring strata of blacks who felt the psychic dissonance caused by their ambitions and expectations for themselves coming into conflict with the limits and restrictions socially imposed upon them, Hurst centers the experience of a woman who submits without question to the existing system of racial oppression, accepting her obligatory role without protest.

Delilah Johnston of *Imitation of Life* is not such a far-fetched imaginative construct of Hurst's, as the similar portrayal by Leona Gray, in "Mammy Sue," and Dorothy West's reference to the "sterling loyalty" of black southerners to "what they quaintly called 'my white folks,'" would attest.[2] Hurst was responding to a stereotype extant in American culture at large and immediately recognizable to black and white Americans alike. My inclusion of her narrative is crucial to this discussion in that it explores the attempt to condition new generations into subservience and challenges the perpetuation of a permanent underclass through the vehicle of maternal acculturation.

Peola is depicted as white-skinned in order to heighten the drama of her sustained resistance to her mother's efforts to mold her into a replica of her own contentedly complicit servile dependence. Like the tragic mulattas of the turn of the century, Peola's race loyalty must depend upon motives extant to her inability to escape identification as a black woman. Delilah is not able to infuse her daughter with her own sense of social inferiority; she is extremely successful, however, at inculcating into Peola the understanding that race and class affiliations are indivisible—that whiteness is superior to blackness, and that, as her mother's pathetic delight in trying to make her a carbon copy of Jessie illustrated, resigning oneself to assume a black identity was in effect to exhibit a preference for the shadow over the substance. The error of Delilah's judgment in raising her child is shown in Peola's carefully considered and rationally presented repudiation of her racial philosophy.

Fauset and Larsen enlist alternative techniques to denounce maternal involvement in promoting white supremacist ideology, though they also rely upon the device of a single parent raising a girl who can pass for white. In Fauset's novels, the notion that domestic servants would dissuade their children from challenging prejudicial beliefs is hardly tolerated. In *Comedy: American Style*, Phebe Grant's mother produces a child who is proud to stand before her class and announce "I belong to the black or Negro race," even though she has to stay after school to show her disbelieving teacher her mother's picture and explain the circumstances of her illegitimate birth in order to prove it.[3] The difference is that Mrs. Grant has never taught her daughter to perceive blackness as a signifier of innate inferiority. Phebe is taught that injustice in various forms affects all people to varying degrees and that racism can be counteracted by making one's home and family a haven of love and acceptance. All of Phebe's friends are black, and she is exposed to other black families who share the same values and precepts she learns at home.

Larsen's Clare Kendry is the only one of her characters roughly comparable in social standing to Peola Johnston. Though, like Peola, she does elect to pass into the white world, her motivations are entirely different. Clare has no belief in the innate inferiority of black people and has never been taught by her father that her race would compel her to accept a position of deference to white people. In fact, Clare was raised in the midst of a community of middle-class black people, and she envied their accomplishments, their comparative wealth, their close-knit families, and their comfortable style of living. When her white great-aunts later try to bombard her with religious justifications for racial hierarchy, Clare is contemptuous of their doctrine. She passes because she wants to achieve, even surpass, the wealth and social status of her middle-class childhood intimates, who, she felt, pitied and looked down on her because of her relative indigence and lack of respectability. Because of her full understanding of the rules governing social interaction within the black elite, Clare knows that as the daughter of an alcoholic janitor killed in a bar brawl and a woman whom only death prevented from deserting her family shortly after the birth of her infant daughter, she would never have been accepted into the middle-class milieu nor considered a marriageable prospect. Her lack of "background" forces her to "become" a white woman in order to access the wealth and status she desires. Had Clare's mother lived and had Clare never been compelled to go live with her aunts, her life might have turned out differently—she might not have made the same choices.

All three novelists represent mothers as the conduits through which the transmission of culture, values, and self-concept is effected. The novels are very transparent in their internal indictments of "bad" mothering and their approbation of "good" mothering. Olivia Cary, for instance, is censured throughout *Comedy: American Style* by several different characters (and even the narrator) for her incapacity to provide the love, support, and unconditional acceptance her children need to develop into well-adjusted adults.

When Olivia tricks her golden-skinned son Oliver into pretending to be her Filipino butler so that the white women attending her club meeting will not suspect he is actually her son, the reader's predictable sense of outrage at her insensitivity is modeled by her older son Christopher's incensed response. It is intensified by young Oliver's pathetic excitement at the "game" he is playing with his mother, coupled with his affection-starved blindness to her true motives. In Larsen's *Quicksand*, Karen Nilssen's flawed mothering is signaled by Helga's painful reminiscences of her miserable childhood and her mother's failure to intervene to protect her. In *Passing*, Irene Redfield considers herself a dedicated and conscientious mother, but the text suggests that, though she rigidly adheres to the outward forms of nurturance, she deprives her children of the demonstrative affection they need from her; she remains curiously emotionally detached from the boys as well as from her husband. She is not personally invested in their relationships.

These novels are infused with an endorsed methodology of how to raise successful black children in an oppressive society. Larsen references the resilience implicit in the testimonies about the black mothers of the South. When Helga is overwhelmed by the exigencies of her maternal responsibilities, she goes to visit Sary Jones, a member of her husband's congregation, "who in all likelihood had toiled every day of her life since early childhood except on those days, totaling perhaps sixty, following the birth of her six children."[4] Helga reports feeling "humbled and oppressed" in her presence; her self-abasement beside the example of Sary Jones suggests that the comparative ease and indulgence of middle-class life in the urban metropolitan areas of the North curtail black women's abilities to manage a number of disparate tasks efficiently and simultaneously. Helga refers to herself as a "poor weak city-bred thing" and tries to mimic the stoic resolve of the women in her small Alabama town.[5] Mothers are to be strong and self-sacrificing, doing everything within their power to ensure that their children have all of their material needs fulfilled, are educated, spiritually grounded, and equipped to surpass their scale of living once they are on their own.

In the more upscale societies of the North, successful mothering is less strenuous but more complicated. Single mothers who must work to provide for their children, like Mrs. Grant in *Comedy: American Style*, and Susan Graves and Sallie Ellersley in *There Is Confusion*, are not only expected to furnish their material needs but to cultivate in them a mindset resistant to prejudicial attitudes, instill a sense of pride in their racial heritage, and ensure that their children are socializing with the "right" people. Mothers with husbands who share or assume completely the financial responsibility for the family are free to devote even more attention to conscientious childrearing.

There are several positive models of motherhood in the novels and a greater number of examples of what not to do. Mothers like Mrs. Davies in *Comedy: American Style* are glorified because of their warmth, approachability, and youthful spirits. Marise Davies's mother is set in opposition to the cold cruelty of Olivia Cary. The opening scene of the second part of the novel presents a young Teresa Cary coming home from school accompanied by two of her classmates, blond Phebe Grant and brown-skinned Marise Davies. Olivia intercepts them at the front door and invents a story about being concerned that Teresa would become overstimulated by too much company, so Phebe might remain, but Marise would have to go home and visit another time. Though she displays enough tact not to say it aloud, Olivia has no intention of ever allowing a child who shows color, as Marise does, into her home. Phebe refuses Mrs. Cary's invitation, declaring her preference to instead visit with Marise at the Davieses' home.

Olivia's strict policing of her threshold, which she defends by explaining to her daughter, "I don't like having colored people in the house if we can possibly avoid it," is contrasted by the playful sessions at Marise's house, loosely supervised by Mrs. Davies (34). The children reign over "the large old-fashioned sitting-room in the second story back" where "you could make as much noise, laughing, singing, romping as you pleased" (43). Marise and her guests express themselves creatively in a number of different forms—they write and tell each other stories, choreograph dances, perform original plays, and sing songs in their imaginary theater. Mrs. Davies, who operates a professional catering business with her husband, makes intermittent appearances to bring them sandwiches and desserts, smile brilliantly, and command them to "Have a good time, children. ... I want you all to be happy" (44). Teresa's idealized portrait of domesticity involves herself grown with four children who are just like her brother Oliver, "and she would be a mother like Mrs. Davies" (48). In opposition to the "inexplicable phenomenon" of Olivia Cary's maternal ambivalence towards her son Oliver, Mrs. Davies's affectionate fondness for all of the neighborhood children is extolled as a virtue (43).

In Fauset's *There Is Confusion*, Belle Bye, Peter's great-grandmother, provides another model of exemplary motherhood. She is a woman "who would have been an insurgent in any walk of life." Her husband, Joshua,

> was the genuine peasant type—the type, black or white, which believes in a superior class and yields blindly to its mandates. But Belle had seen too many changes even in her thirty-five years—she was far younger than Joshua—not to know that many things are possible if one just has courage.[6]

Belle supports her son, Isaiah, when he staunchly refuses to work in the Bye orchards after taking offense at an offhand comment made by young Meriwether Bye; Meriwether, the same man who in old age offers the Bye fortune to the son of Peter and Joanna, surmises that Isaiah would one day make him an excellent servant, just as Isaiah's father Joshua was a good servant to his own father, Aaron.

Isaiah inherits his mother's spirit and profits from her wisdom. She approves of his friendship with Meriwether Bye, realizing that her son's diction, vocabulary, manners, perception, and ambition could only benefit from his association with the scrupulously educated white youngster. Though she is delighted at Isaiah's refusal to work in the orchards, Belle also ensures that his optimism regarding what he might accomplish in his lifetime is tempered with realism, thereby safeguarding her son "from the initial mistake of aiming too high and of coming utterly to smash" (27). Belle's childrearing proficiency is aptly rewarded; after severing his connection to the white Byes, Isaiah founds a school, invests in real estate, secures profitable interests in local business establishments, and writes theological tracts for the African Methodist Episcopal Church. "No name and no figure in colored life in Philadelphia was ever better beloved and more revered than his" (28). In a

novel that stresses how the accomplishments of children reflect upon their parents, Isaiah's excellent standing reflects well upon Belle.

Fauset provides yet another example of good mothering in *The Chinaberry Tree*. When Laurentine Strange is devastated by her exclusion from the black society of her New Jersey town, Millie Ismay, a doctor's wife, reaches out and offers her friendship. Because she is nearly fifteen years older than her young charge, Mrs. Ismay operates as a sort of surrogate mother to Laurentine—she extends her patronage, prevails upon her husband to help her reclaim Laurentine from obscurity, virtually adopts Laurentine into their household, makes her a regular guest in their home, invites her on outings, speaks well of her to other elites, praises her clothing design talent, and, perhaps most importantly, instigates her courtship with the attractive and eligible Dr. Stephen Denleigh. Laurentine's real mother is powerless to do for her what Mrs. Ismay can. Though Aunt Sal loves her daughter dearly, Laurentine "was so sorry for her mother. She knew that her mother took upon herself the blame for everything which had gone awry in [Laurentine's] sorry, hateful, bitter, futile life."[7] While Sal Strange is rendered ineffectual by her feelings of remorse and her cognizance of her inability to advance her daughter's interests, Millie Ismay is perfectly positioned to advocate for Laurentine.

Even further, Laurentine connects with Mrs. Ismay in a way she has never been able to do with her own mother. The two women have long, interesting conversations in which Millie reveals her vast experience. "She knew life. ... She had known pleasure, and sorrow and disappointment and pain and fulfillment" (99). The maternal presence of Millie Ismay invigorates Laurentine and gives her hope for the future. At the Ismays' Laurentine is enveloped in the domestic harmony of the black elite household; she learns to drive, plays bridge, practices the piano, and even sings while she helps Mrs. Ismay wash the dishes after Sunday dinner. "'This,' Laurentine used to tell herself lying straight and relaxed in her dainty room, 'This is life, just as one would want it'" (100). The contrast between Laurentine's expressed contentment as the protégé of Millie Ismay and her prior loneliness and misery with little more than her guilt-ridden mother for company, demonstrates the critical nature of the proper motherly influence to orient the lives of young people.

The examples of Mrs. Davies, Belle Bye, and Millie Ismay provide a standard against which other black mothers in literature may then be measured. Like Mrs. Davies, a good mother loves her children unconditionally, welcomes their friends into her home, treats them with respect and kindness, and encourages their creative expression. Like Belle Bye, she imparts wisdom, instills pride and a spirit of self-sufficiency, and commends independent thought and the rejection of white patronage. Like Millie Ismay, she exhibits and fosters the acquisition of refinement, discernment, propriety, benevolence, and social generosity. Compared to this ideal, the failings exhibited by other literary mothers are magnified.

In Larsen's *Passing*, Irene Redfield's sons spend an inordinate amount of time isolated up in their playroom. Irene and her husband Brian seem to be the only couple in their social circle with children, and Irene does not approve of the boys' school classmates. Though Irene sends them to camp the summer she is visiting Chicago, she does not make entertaining their friends or promoting interaction with other children of co-equal social status a priority. Olivia Cary's constant pressure on her children to sublimate their racial heritage and drift across the color line confuses them and poisons their home environment. In *Imitation of Life*, Delilah Johnston's concentrated effort to repress her daughter's resistance to a white supremacist social order through counseling her to embrace her inferior status as a black woman is effective only in provoking her to challenge the legitimacy of the hierarchy by becoming white herself.

The literary models of excellence in motherhood illustrate that these women had other strategies available to them to raise their children successfully despite the hostile conditions in American society. In a culture bolstered by public institutions in many ways closed to African Americans, the home and the family provided the purest arena of support, of encouragement, of acceptance, and of love.

As late as 1942, black journalists were still making the type of exhortation black aristocrats were charged with snobbery for making at the turn of the century:

> If we fail to remember who we are, we should always remember where we are, and if the men and women of our race continue their vulgarity, profanity and indecency on the streets and in public places, if we do not cultivate a higher standard of culture, dignity and refinement, we will soon be pushed off the face of the earth.[8]

This ominous exhortation is a fair synopsis of the general sentiment invigorating the novels of Jessie Fauset. Fauset's focus on upwardly mobile blacks indicates her desire to model a standard of conduct which would facilitate a racial uplift agenda. In chapter 2, I will focus on her first novel, *There Is Confusion*, as a revolutionary narrative in its treatment of the black middle class as a culturally distinctive and insular community, and its celebration of an independent, progressive, black femininity. Whereas her novel may be interpreted as an endorsement of mainstream patriarchal values, I argue that

Fauset repudiates the uninterrogated acceptance of cultural hegemony, instead favoring an autonomous maternal model reflective of the African-American experience.

In chapter 3, I turn to a reading of Nella Larsen's novels that revisits the social issues that induced black intellectuals, professionals, and fair-skinned "voluntary Negroes" of the early twentieth century to limit their own reproduction. Most pointedly, *Quicksand* and *Passing* portray women contending with the notion that the hostile social climate in America makes procreation irresponsible, with black mothers paradoxically complicit in their own children's unmerited subjugation simply by giving birth to them.

In the final chapter, chapter 4, I will discuss representations of black maternity from a white perspective, contrasting Fannie Hurst's *Imitation of Life* with the two popular films based on her narrative. The black maternal images in all three formats grew out of the self-sacrificing mammy icon, a relic of the plantation tradition, which survived Reconstruction to become the eternally faithful household domestic. The conflict between this embodiment of black womanhood and the progressive vision of black modernity is then rooted in a cultural repudiation of the stereotypical black mammy.

Immediately following this introduction, chapter 1 lays the groundwork for the remainder of the discussion by explaining the historical contexts of maternity, socioeconomic class, and cultural heritage obtaining in the black community during the Harlem Renaissance. This book has been inspired by the work of such contemporary scholars as Ann duCille, Claudia Tate, Hazel Carby, Valerie Smith, Thadious Davis, Deborah McDowell, and Jacquelyn McLendon, who compel a consideration of the work of early twentieth-century black women writers in new and innovative ways. The fresh insights they bring to the significance and interpretive dynamic of these texts have provided a dialogic matrix into which I am able to situate my arguments about how figurations of maternity and the domestic realm are being employed in this literature to interrogate the compatibility of white middle-class didacticism and black cultural ostracization. As McLendon writes of Fauset and Larsen,

> In their literary and extraliterary writings both women pursued the theory that blacks were despised, not for their lack of education or money or manners, but simply because they were "colored"; light or dark, ignorant or intelligent, cultured or not, black people living amid hatred and bigotry shared a common problem.[9]

I am likewise convinced that these novels reveal a profound frustration with the flawed logic supposedly fueling prejudice and constitute challenges to the racist doctrine so relentlessly maligning the black collective. I hope that this book adequately reflects my conviction and makes a positive contribution to the creative body of scholarship formulating critical models of literary inquiry that work to dismantle conventional readings of resistant artists.

1 Conceiving Class and Culture
A Contextual Retrospective

Jessie Fauset, Nella Larsen, and Fannie Hurst all wrote novels that tested the limits of feminine domestic ambition within a class paradigm. Raising children provides the context for women's social engagement in their bodies of work. The premise of this study is that during the Harlem Renaissance women writers used representations of female characters as mothers in order to confront and work through issues of class divisions and acculturation in the black community. When women become mothers, whether by choice or compulsion, it in many ways necessitates an acceptance of a restrictive gender script determined by the cultural expectations obtaining in the dominant society; at the same time, for black women, becoming a mother symbolized the reappropriation of power because their "natural" maternal rights had historically been forcibly negated under the institution of slavery and within the racist cultural climate of the South. So, paradoxically, motherhood was simultaneously oppressive and liberating for African-American women, but how black women negotiated their maternal responsibilities depended not only on their shared racial identity but also on their social class positions and their particular cultural heritage.

Presuming this sociohistorical paradigm, in the literature considered here, imagining maternity is not simply about the narrative exploration of a privatized domestic relationship. Depicting motherhood extends beyond the individual household to become a way of dealing with the host of issues facing the black populace, ranging from how to come to terms with the legacy of slavery, to strategies for responding productively to discrimination and prejudice, to the possibility of fostering a collective racial consciousness which transcends the barriers of cultural differences determined largely by economic resources, level of education, and region of origin.

While Fauset, Larsen, and Hurst themselves remained childless, they provocatively used the experience of maternity as an imaginative mechanism by which to investigate the nexus of identities emerging from the layered coexistence of race, class, and gender affiliations created and experienced by black women in America. The differing ways in which the novelists engage the subjects of maternity and domesticity require different approaches to textual interpretation. Fauset's attention to working class privation, the striving attempts of black outsiders to position themselves to penetrate the ranks of the privileged class, and the hypocritical posturing of the entrenched elite, is most clearly understood through a materialist analysis of class dynamics and the adverse effects of social pressure on the individual. Larsen's interest in probing the interiority of the female psyche invites a psychoanalytical reading, and Hurst's status as an established white writer staging a black melodrama from the perspective of a self-proclaimed sympathetic spectator is best evaluated through a reading which interrogates her subject position as author, her motivation, and her familiarity with her subject matter.

Conceiving

Motherhood as a theoretical construct has recently begun to receive greater attention from white feminist critics determined to reclaim the prevailing discourse on maternity from popular cultural mythologies and the influence of Freudian analysis.[1] Marianne Hirsch registers concern that while feminists should be thinking and writing about maternity from a myriad of analytical perspectives,

> we are virtually prevented from doing so by a mythos of the nuclear family that is founded on maternal objectification and erasure. Jocasta, the silent and virtually absent mother in the narrative of Oedipus, serves as an emblem for the way in which the psychological story of subject-formation focuses on the child and leaves out the mother.[2]

However, as Hortense Spillers suggests when she inquires whether "the Freudian landscape" is "an applicable text (say nothing of appropriate) to social and historical situations that do not replicate moments of its own cultural origins and involvements," the silenced and marginalized figure of Jocasta may not be the model of maternity relevant to the African-American experience.[3] Gloria Wade-Gayles is emphatic about the contrast between the subject positions from which black and white women are able to conceptualize their embodiment of motherhood. Maternity must be enacted in a different way for black women; it retains a different social significance, and possesses a distinctive history, "Because Black women have not stood as fragile figurines on pedestals white feminists seek to dismantle."[4]

As Patricia Hill Collins argues, white feminist studies of motherhood have the luxury of exploring issues related to maternity that remain largely peripheral to the important aspects of mothering among black women and other American women of color. A full appreciation of the experiences of these marginalized mothers necessitates more than simply inserting their case studies into the present scholarship on motherhood, which presumes whiteness. Studies privileging race as a significant determinant of experiential variance would demand attention to an entirely different set of themes issuing from the study of motherhood.[5]

In 1892, Anna Julia Cooper recognized what W. E. B. Du Bois made explicit in his essay "On the Damnation of Women"—American rhetoric embraces motherhood as an ideal, in the abstract, but America demonstrates no reverence for the actual, embodied maternal presence, particularly when the maternal body is black. Cooper reports listening to a Northern orator

> who went into pious agonies at the thought of the future mothers of Americans having to stand all day at shop counters. ... But how many have ever given a thought to the pinched and down-trodden colored women bending over wash-tubs and ironing boards—with children to feed and house rent to pay, wood to buy, soap and starch to furnish—lugging home weekly great baskets of clothes for families who pay them for a month's laundrying barely enough to purchase a substantial pair of shoes![6]

Cooper evinced little faith that white people could be prompted to express the same consideration for black women as they displayed for white. A quarter of a century later, however, black women writers believed they could indeed elicit the sympathy of the white female community through the common affinity of maternal experience. Angelina Weld Grimké's play *Rachel*, first performed in 1916 and then published in 1920, dramatized the metamorphosis of a naive young girl harboring romantic dreams of someday becoming a mother, into an embittered young woman convinced that bringing a child into her racially polarized world would be nothing short of a tragedy. Forced out of the South by the lynchings of her father and brother, Rachel becomes even further disillusioned by the rampant prejudice, most pointedly against black children, she witnesses in the North. Her "natural" feminine desire to marry and raise a family is blunted by the racial intolerance leveled against her people and her own unwillingness to perpetuate the cycle of misery.[7]

Building upon the "Am I not a woman and a sister?" rhetoric used to galvanize white women's activism during the abolition movement, Grimké openly discloses her motives for her overt courtship of a white female audience. "Did they have a vulnerable point and if so what was it? I believed it to be motherhood. Certainly all the noblest, finest, most sacred things in their lives converge about this. If anything can make all women sisters underneath their skins, it is motherhood."[8] However, Grimké's conviction that the shared reverence for motherhood could bridge racial difference and bond women together comes under a certain amount of scrutiny in the work of her literary precursors and contemporaries.

It was a "common custom" where he was from, Frederick Douglass reports in his famous *Narrative* of 1845, to forcibly separate infant slave children from their mothers. He goes on to speculate that the rationale must have been "to hinder the development of the child's affection toward its mother, and to blunt and destroy the natural affection of the mother for the child. This is the inevitable result."[9] Douglass's account of his own experience and his more general statement about the coerced abandonment of children within the slave culture make a vital contribution to the recognition and documentation of a particularized history of maternity pertaining solely to Americans of African descent. Douglass's testimony constitutes a primary narrative of an assault on black motherhood that then becomes reiterated, reconfigured, and reacted against by subsequent texts contributing to the body of literature by and about African Americans.

In her 1861 narrative *Incidents in the Life of a Slave Girl*, Harriet Jacobs, writing under the pseudonym Linda Brent, makes the reappropriation of maternal identity the organizing principle of her emancipatory text. Claudia Tate persuasively argues that in contrast to Douglass's masculine story of physically overpowering his master in order to effect a psychic transcendence from brute to man, "Jacobs depicted freedom not simply as escape from the political condition of slavery but as the gaining of access to the social institutions of motherhood, family, and home."[10] Historically, the luxury of conventional domesticity had been denied black women under slavery, when they were mated and bred like livestock, and coerced or enticed into liaisons with white men against whom they had no legitimate avenue of recourse, even after Emancipation. Maternity then represents a tribute to the strength and endurance of the black foremothers who survived slavery and enabled the continuation of the race into contemporary life.

By contrast, the erasure of maternity speaks to a fundamental discomfort with the legacy of slavery. Present-day writers rather ironically heap praise upon "heroic" women "who refused to bear and keep children who might end up lynched and burned, their charred body parts passed around as souvenirs, their pictures snapped for postcards."[11] However, this celebration of so-called heroism seemingly disregards the fact that were it not for the women who bravely bore children despite such tragic possibilities, African Americans would have been rendered extinct generations ago. Maternal erasure—stemming from the transmission of a set of doctrinal beliefs destructive to modern black womanhood—is most clear in Zora Neale Hurston's *Their Eyes Were Watching God* (1937). Janie Mae Crawford's abandonment by her troubled young mother and her subjection to the antiquated dogma of her guilt-ridden grandmother constrain her to spend years battling a fundamentally distorted understanding of how to live as a woman that is then replicated in her own failure to become a mother.

As early as 1852, however, black leaders were extolling the virtues of the "good mother" as the most indispensable component in the effort to uplift the race. "Our females must be qualified, because they are to be the mothers of our children. As mothers are the first nurses and instructors of children; from them children consequently get their first impressions, which being always the most lasting should be the most correct."[12] In keeping with this didactic philosophy, Fauset, Larsen, and Hurst all invariably portrayed the maternal figure as the pivotal influence in the development of individual character. If the mother is not an overbearing personality in the text, then by virtue of her conspicuous absence she is, to paraphrase a theory formulated by Toni Morrison, a very glaring presence.[13] The gendered identity of motherhood, as delineated by these writers, is tightly enmeshed with regionalized class identities, and both are shaped by the pervasive impact of racial agitation in America. As Patricia Hill Collins notes, control over the representation of black maternity remains a source of contention between the races, and black women themselves are divided in their attitudes. There are those who "view motherhood as a truly burdensome condition that stifles their creativity, exploits their labor, and makes them partners in their own oppression. Others see motherhood as providing a base for self-actualization, status in the Black community, and a catalyst for social activism."[14] These two polarized sets of perceptions accurately represent the feelings toward maternity exhibited by the female characters in the novels Fauset, Larsen, and Hurst wrote during the Harlem Renaissance. Some women, including Joanna Marshall of Fauset's *There Is Confusion* (1924), discover motherhood to be the definitive experience of their lives, replacing chaos and lack of purpose with order and serenity. However, there are also women like Irene Redfield of Larsen's *Passing* (1929), who hinges so much of her identity upon her maternal function that she completely loses touch with herself as an individual. At the other extreme, Helga Crane of Larsen's *Quicksand* (1928) epitomizes the sentiment of the woman who experiences motherhood as an insurmountable obstacle to self-realization, while Delilah Johnston of Hurst's *Imitation of Life* indulges herself in hypermaternal excess as a way of deferentially embracing Christian martyrdom. Black women's maternity, however, was more than just a private household matter. In addition to the personal implications they felt, their motherhood exacted much broader consequences for the race collectively.

Kevin Kelley Gaines points to the Rhinelander case of the mid-1920s, a highly publicized divorce sought by a young white aristocrat from the mulatto chambermaid he had married in alleged ignorance of her black ancestry, as "a lightning-rod for concerns within the black middle class over racial identity and the imperative to ensure its own reproduction."[15] Certainly, the issues raised by the potentially genocidal abdication of black women from their implicit responsibility to bear children for the race emphasized the relevance of the performance of motherhood to class and uplift concerns. Class concerns became important as the recognition of declining birth rates within the middle class came into conflict with the realization that the maintenance of a viable middle class was dependent on its continued expansion, where accretion by procreation was inherently the most reliable, and for many, the most desirable, process.[16] Uplift, meaning the effort to raise the masses of black people to the standards of conduct and lifestyle already embraced by the middle class/elites, could be a successful enterprise only to the extent that socioeconomically privileged black people were able to lead by example. Finally, anxiety over fair-skinned black women marrying outside of the race and abandoning the genetic pool provoked the linking of maternity with concerns about passing and the retention of a racial collective identity despite the absence of perceptible signs of affiliation with black people as a people.

Exacerbating the apprehension over which type of black women would be producing the next generation for the race was the fact that at the cultural moment in which these novels were written, the necessary and absolute trade-off between having a career and having children was a very real phenomenon, for African-American as well as white women. The middle-class college-educated women who pursued professional success, though they did often marry, married later in life than did the general population and were largely ambivalent about motherhood. American women as a whole, however, were being held accountable for the future demographic outlook of the nation. The poor, the uneducated, and the immigrants were reproducing in far greater numbers than the middle and upper classes. Native white Americans harbored a widespread concern about the "endangered" white race due to disproportionate population growth. As Shari Thurer reports, "President Theodore Roosevelt went around the country exhorting white native-born Americans to have more children in order to preserve the national character."[17] Before 1920 the theory of "race suicide" had been popularized by Madison Grant, author of *The Passing of the Great Race* (1916), who inspired a movement to promote parenthood among high-status white people and birth control among "undesirable" others.

When the 1920s ushered in Margaret Sanger and the era of democratized birth control, the possibility of sex divorced from procreation became conceivable for women outside of the privileged upper classes, who had been provided exclusive access to medically reliable contraceptive measures for decades. Women began to view childlessness as a marker of independence and refinement, reflecting choice rather than barrenness, and the black elite produced as few descendants as the white. Historian Darlene Clark Hine speculates that in an effort to conform to the accepted model of African-American prosperity, many "urban black middle-class aspirants" sought contraception in order to escape the "social stigma of having many children."[18] At the same time, many of the women at the forefront of the political, social, and cultural advancement of the race opted never to have children at all.[19] In the literature, too, a recurring theme is that children rob women of their energy and self-directed ambition—to fully realize oneself as an individual, one must be childless. Conversely, the troubled relationships between mothers and their children in these novels can almost always be traced back to maternal immaturity—when women become mothers before they are secure or fulfilled in their own identities.

Motherhood is a complex representational phenomenon in these works of literature; maternity is figured as both a social responsibility and demonstration of race pride. The recuperation of maternal autonomy provides a forum for addressing many of the contemporary issues plaguing the black community. The representation of motherhood becomes a mechanism by which to interrogate class consciousness and class mobility, to explore the issues surrounding self-determination and individuation, to investigate the workings of collective racial uplift and moral responsibility. Practicing maternity is represented as a tangible investment in the future of the race and an act of direct participation in molding that future.

As a rejoinder to the expression of optimism in the possibilities for an improved outlook for the race in times to come, other novels record the attitudes provoked by the dismal prospects for black children in America. Helga Crane's nearly forty-eight-hour childbirth ordeal near the conclusion of Nella Larsen's *Quicksand* (1928) pointedly illustrates this anti-idealism:

> It seemed, for some reason, not to go off just right. And when, after that long frightfulness, the fourth little dab of amber humanity which Helga had contributed to a despised race was held before her for maternal approval, she failed entirely to respond properly to this sop of consolation for the suffering and horror through which she had passed. There was from her no pleased, proud smile, no loving, possessive gesture. ... Instead she deliberately closed her eyes, mutely shutting out the sickly infant. ...[20]

This vision of childbirth deviates from the simultaneous elation and relief a new mother might feel in a romanticized portrait of maternal adoration; Larsen contrasts Helga's impassive response to her newborn infant with the "pleased, proud smile" and "loving, possessive gesture" she should have displayed. Unwanted pregnancy and postpartum depression have no place in a "proper" domestic environment. The baby dies within a week, and the novel closes as Helga, having barely recovered from the devastating experience of giving birth to that fourth child, learns that she is carrying her fifth.

Helga's plight portrays maternity as a project in self-effacement—each additional child drains more of her will, energy, and spirit; bringing more lives into the world is essentially killing her. Her interminable pregnancies manifest her inability to escape the marriage and life which have become loathsome to her, for Helga is not really in danger of imminent death. Instead, she faces a perhaps worse fate: perpetual misery, from which death would be a welcome reprieve.

As Larsen imagines it, pregnancy becomes a symbol of female entrapment. The domestic realm is figured as an inescapable site with impregnation used as the masculine weapon of control and confinement. Men are figured as aggressive sexual predators seeking more than immediate gratification; they want fertile wombs in which to deposit their seed.[21] Dorothy West's *The Living Is Easy* (1948) replicates this vision of masculine desire. Cleo Judson's abstinence after the birth of the only child she wants, West pointedly discloses, is practiced in spite of her healthy sexual appetite. Her repression of her own passion, then, becomes meaningful because her celibacy is not a result of frigidity or distaste, but is an expression of personal autonomy from a prescribed domestic script. Still, she is vulnerable, as was Helga, to men who want her not only for *their* gratuitous physical pleasure, but for *her* procreative utility.

An admirer of Cleo's, mistakenly assuming it is her husband's dedication to his business which accounts for their having only one child, fantasizes about fulfilling her needs himself. Interestingly though, her desirability to him is conflated with her reproductive potential. When Cleo plans a party she knows her husband will be unable to attend, she explains to her assembled company that Mr. Judson would be spending the evening with his newly-arrived shipment of produce. Her announcement provokes Cleo's impassioned guest into presumptuous speculation: "No wonder Bart Judson had given her only one dark daughter, Mr. Davies thought jealously. In that magnificent body were golden sons."[22]

Many of the novels confront these issues of the marital and maternal aspirations of women, and the masculine drive to mate and procreate. They then actively proceed to interrogate which gender is truly in command of family planning. This battle of the sexes continues in the depiction of childrearing, where the refugees of flawed parenting wander all over the pages of the fiction, and mothers are the typical aggressors. While these maternal characters struggle to raise their African-American children within a repressive culture, most are misguided, as was Vera Manning's mother when she pressured her pale daughter to give up Harley, her brown-skinned fiancé, in *There Is Confusion*; Delilah Johnston, whose cheerful acceptance of her servility to white people incites her pale-skinned daughter's abhorrence of her own black identity; and Olivia Cary, whose perverse obsession with whiteness drove her olive-skinned son to suicide in *Comedy: American Style*.

Olivia Blanchard Cary, anti-heroine of *Comedy: American Style* (1933), Jessie Fauset's fourth novel, becomes a mother for purely selfish reasons. She is confident that her husband's light skin will guarantee her pale children to serve as incontrovertible evidence of her "white" womanhood. When her third child, ironically named Oliver, for herself, inherits the golden brown complexion of her dead father, Olivia is stunned and incensed; her driving obsession with collectively transcending the social stigma of blackness is inhibited by her younger son's presence in the family. Once he discovers the source of her resentful indifference toward him, Oliver commits suicide, believing it is the one thing he can do for his mother to make her happy. The virulence of American color prejudice and the psychological damage it does to black people as individuals are made culpable for perverting the most sacred bond between mother and child. Oliver is the visible manifestation of what Olivia hates about herself: her black racial identity. Self-loathing completely unfits Olivia for motherhood, in accordance with an argument made by Gloria Wade-Gayles:

Because women are biologically capable of bearing children, we assume that they are, by definition, capable of nurturing children, but there is no gene for parental nurturing. Women bring to the role of mother their individual strengths and weaknesses as persons, and what they feel about themselves as persons influences their performance as mothers.[23]

Mothers flawed by the oppressive social conditions in America receive little assistance from their partners—fathers are often portrayed as ineffectual or inept, if they are involved in raising their children at all. Arguably, it is a critique of the developing social mores of the new black middle class that frequently the very professionalization that establishes their children's privileged class standing simultaneously subverts men's involvement as fathers. Their parental authority is undermined both by their wives, who maintain that their childrearing inexperience renders them totally incompetent, and their own feelings of inadequacy to the task. The alienating climate of disempowerment in the domestic sphere discourages men from intervening in their wives's (mis)management of the children's lives, even when their inaction is detrimental or even disastrous to their children's welfare. In the case from *Comedy: American Style*, for instance, Christopher Cary does nothing to prevent his wife Olivia from systematically destroying their son's life. The tenet of separate spheres gets firmly pushed to its logical conclusion, exploring the consequences of matriarchal tyranny unchecked by passive fathers, and denouncing the advocacy of blind adherence to the white middle-class model of the well-managed American family dynamic.

Children represent the future, and progress towards true racial equality. To effect this progress, the literature presents two competing social ideologies. One involves the deliberate whitening of the race through selective pairing based upon skin color, or what the novelist Charles Chesnutt once termed "the upward process of absorption" into Anglo-American culture by the exclusive intermarriage of light-skinned black people. The other depends upon the race pride inherent in either a program of socially conscious political agitation to win mainstream social acceptance or the hope of a gradual erosion of prejudice through the methodical infiltration of black people into various social institutions.[24] The multiple strategies employed to prepare children to either assimilate into or participate in the dominant culture can be interpreted as broader political statements about how a mass racial reconciliation could best be achieved in American society. The textual rejection of maternity, then, might be read as a guarded cynicism regarding this possibility.

In Zora Neale Hurston's *Their Eyes Were Watching God*, Janie's childlessness is not only necessary to effect her independence and mobility in her journey toward self-discovery, but also manifests the impotence of her succession of husbands; as the second-generation product of rape, Janie has inherited a legacy of susceptibility to male domination. Her successful resistance to victimization is demonstrated by her triumphant solitary return to her house in Eatonville and the recounting of her story to her friend Phoeby, but, more significantly, also by her breaking of the cycle of abuse by not having a daughter of her own—in this way, Janie constitutes an imaginative precursor to the character of Ursa in Gayl Jones's *Corregidora* (1975).

Pushing Hurston's theme even further, Nella Larsen's novels explore the viewpoint raised in Angelina Weld Grimké's *Rachel*—that black motherhood should be avoided on principle. Larsen's images of flawed black mothers and her consistent representation of America as an inherently cold and hostile environment to black people, find a parallel in Fannie Hurst's *Imitation of Life*. The tragedy of Delilah and Peola Johnston is rooted in Delilah's repeated efforts to raise her daughter to respect white supremacy and gratefully accept her position of subservience.

In other works, maternity is promoted as the only reasonable path to the establishment of a flourishing black community which could successfully withstand, and from which individuals could successfully combat, racial antagonism. One of the strongest advocates of maternity found in these novels, Virginia Murray, comes from Jessie Fauset's most critically appreciated novel, *Plum Bun* (1929). During a church service she attends with her parents and older sister, Virginia is distracted from the sermon by a reverie upon churchgoing as a family. She dismisses the notion of measuring well-being as a function of the accumulation of material goods; "this unity was the core of happiness, all other satisfactions must radiate from this one"(22). Fauset belabors Virginia's point in order to emphasize her location of meaningful satisfaction with life in close-knit family relationships and solid Christian values, which are meant to represent a universal set of standards superseding the influence of middle-class white America. Virginia means to emulate every aspect of her family life, except in one respect: "she would pray very hard every day for five children, two boys and two girls and then a last little one,—it was hard for her to decide whether this should be a boy or a girl,—which should stay small for a long, long time" (22). To Virginia Murray, happiness apart from maternity is absolutely inconceivable.

Class

The history of class relations in the black community remains an underexplored phenomenon, though recently scholars have begun to give the subject more serious consideration.[25] My understanding of the intricacies of class relations during the Harlem Renaissance era, especially in terms of clarifying the terms deployed and their significance during the 1920s, is shaped by *Black Metropolis: A Study of Negro Life in a Northern City* (1945) by St. Clair Drake and Horace R. Cayton, and E. Franklin Frazier's contemporaneous work on the black class structure and the characteristics defining class position. Bart Landry's more recent, more technical *The New Black Middle Class* (1987) has helped to clarify my sense of the relationship between the existence of the so-called aristocrats of color, who descended primarily from distinguished antebellum free mulatto families, and the development of the upwardly mobile group of black people who gained access to a lifestyle commensurate with that of the white American middle class.[26]

Landry's position takes issue with the application of the term "class" in reference to the system of stratified social relations which obtained prior to the Great Migration of 1915–1920. Using principles of categorization established by Marxist and Weberian theory, Landry cogently argues that the black aristocrats or elites who maintained social precedence in the black community prior to 1915 should be considered a status group rather than an economic class. Class, he contends, is strictly a function of how an individual is positioned with relation to the means of production of goods in a capitalistic society. Those who own the major manufacturing and financial enterprises and employ workers constitute the upper class, while those workers who depend upon the members of the upper class for wages belong to the working class. The middle class, then, would be comprised of those educated professionals who operate outside of this wage labor system, such as doctors, lawyers, or teachers, as well as "white-collar workers" within the system—managers and office workers who are not themselves engaged in manual labor.[27] The black elite in existence from the antebellum period through Reconstruction up through the first decade or so of the twentieth century did not qualify as a middle or upper class in terms of this general structure. What Landry terms "the old elite" drew its members from an incongruous cross section of occupations and income levels, where standards for inclusion were based upon traceable, distinguished ancestry, movement within exclusive social circles, refinement, and gentility.[28]

According to Landry, the year 1915 marks the endpoint of a transitional era by which time this original "old elite" had been completely displaced from the pinnacle of black society throughout the nation by "the new elite," the rising black middle class. The coalescence of this black middle class, however, was in large part dependent upon the resources of the "status group" which preceded it. Many entrants into the middle class were the sons of the status elite who had been educated into professions with money earned by fathers who were caterers, railroad porters, hostlers, barbers, or domestic servants to wealthy white people. Those who were not born into the elite group often married elite women in order to secure their own status within the upper echelon of black society. Even further, Landry argues, in contrast to the black aristocrats who depended primarily upon white patronage for the prosperity they enjoyed, the black middle class was able to establish itself principally as a consequence of its ability to serve the black community.

> The poverty, disillusionment, and misery blacks suffered in the industrial North has often been documented. But another, brighter side of that picture is usually overlooked. These burgeoning black urban communities provided an opportunity for the emergence of a black middle class of teachers, doctors, dentists, undertakers, realtors, insurance agents, ministers, newspaper editors, and small businessmen who attempted to meet the needs of a black community that whites were often unwilling to serve.[29]

The black middle class professions Landry enumerates are solidly represented by the characters peopling the urban landscapes enlivened by Jessie Redmon Fauset, Nella Larsen, and Dorothy West. The account he provides of the genesis of this class also contains a persuasive rationale for why we should value the attention these authors paid to the "brighter side of that picture." Pervasive critical discomfort with the so-called middle-class bias inherent in their novels might be assuaged by the recollection that their depictions are among the few extant close descriptions of early black middle-class home life. Sociologist Andrew Billingsley noted in 1968 that due to the dearth of scholarly attention given to black families, "we must look largely to Negro writers ... for intimate glimpses of Negro family life."[30] Fauset, Larsen, and West proved to be remarkably astute cultural observers, encoding the transition in the black community from aristocratic status group to middle-class upward mobility in perfect accordance with retrospective analyses of the phenomenon.

The Marshall family in Jessie Fauset's *There Is Confusion* (1924) is sired by Joel Marshall, a successful New York caterer to wealthy white clients; he sends his sons to Harvard and discourages them from becoming involved in the service-oriented business that made their expensive educations possible.

Instead, his elder son becomes a Harlem real estate agent, and his younger son leads a racial uplift organization. Similarly, Nella Larsen presents us with Irene Westover Redfield in *Passing* (1929), a college-bred doctor's wife who returns to her college-bred father's home in Chicago for a visit and re-enters a whirlwind of upscale social activities, including teas, card and dinner parties, and resort weekends. Then, in *The Living Is Easy* (1948), Dorothy West focuses on Cleo Judson, a Southern-born social climber who marries a produce wholesaler for his money but cultivates friendships among the impoverished, yet genteel, faded aristocracy in order to maneuver her way into upper-crust Boston black society. These types of women may have been drawn from the comparatively small percentage of black people of the early twentieth century who did not suffer the privations of the working or itinerant poor, but such individuals did in fact exist, and their history is certainly worth preserving.

According to Drake and Cayton, the characters enumerated above would most assuredly have been counted within the upper class, with the possible exception of Cleo Judson, who because of her lack of cultural capital might be more appropriately classified as an upper-middle-class woman aspiring to secure a position in the upper class. While their appraisal is roughly akin to Landry's broader analysis regarding precisely what constituted the preeminent social cluster in the black community, Drake and Cayton emphasize relative status and the significance of public perception in the post-World War I era. They divide the community into three basic classes: lower, middle, and upper. The lower class is the largest, comprised largely of recent migrants from the South with low incomes, low-status occupations, and "low" standards of living. The middle class, though it has the most variety, differs from the lower class less in terms of economic well-being than in terms of values, goals, and manner of living; it is a "'model' that emphasizes a type of disciplined public behavior which will distinguish a segment of the population from the 'crude' and 'unpolished' masses."[31] The middle class ranges from the lower middle, still struggling to effect a complete dissociation from the lower class, to the upper middle, perpetually attempting to elevate their status into the upper class.

The upper class would then be defined largely by way of a cultural barometer that rewards those who successfully accumulate the critical markers of achievement. Drake and Cayton provide a comprehensive description of "Bronzeville's" (a pseudonym for Chicago) black upper class:

> [P]hysicians and their wives, along with the majority of the dentists, lawyers, and the more prominent businessmen, social workers, schoolteachers, and

public administrators, make up the core of Bronzeville's upper class. With family incomes ranging from $3,000 to $50,000 a year, their prestige is based not primarily on income ... but rather on education and professional status, and upon a definite way of life.[32]

This list of upper-class occupations bears a striking similarity to Landry's middle-class litany of "teachers, doctors, dentists, undertakers, realtors, insurance agents, ministers, newspaper editors, and small businessmen." In fact, according to statistics reported in *Black Metropolis*, Landry's so-called middle-class "insurance officials" earned the highest median annual income among college-educated black men in the North during this era, at $4,250—a figure $1,500 higher than the average doctor. Clearly, it seems the distinction between Landry's middle class and the upper class delineated by Drake and Cayton is largely a semantic one. Regardless of their label, these people shared the "definite way of life" exemplified in *Black Metropolis* by a doctor who lived in an

> exclusive residential area ... where a small group of well-to-do Negroes were beginning to establish homes. His children had been sent to college and graduate school; the family owned two automobiles, took an annual vacation, and had traveled abroad. ... His wife and children were schoolteachers.[33]

Drake and Cayton readily acknowledge that the appellation "upper class" means something very different within the circumscribed black community than it does to the larger American population. As opposed to the "wealthy leisure class" description characterizing upper-class white people, "Bronzeville's upper class is a well-trained but only moderately well-to-do group who have more leisure than the rank and file, but who nevertheless must work for a living."[34] In this context, what *Black Metropolis* presents as the black upper class essentially corresponds in its lifestyle and level of prosperity to the white middle class. Furthermore, the members of the black upper class share the basic values, family form, and social agenda associated with the "middle class" in America generally, which serves to further confuse the terminology used within the scholarship on class relations in the black community.

Some scholars, like Landry, choose to prioritize the class aspect, and so emphasize the coequal status of this group of black people with middle-class white people; the "black" then becomes a modifier to convey the understanding that this is the black segment of what is commonly known as the middle-class population. This formulation would certainly allege the nonexistence of a black upper class, considering there were no black people even close to approximating the status of extremely wealthy white people. However, those who prefer to designate this faction of black people an upper class prioritize race, using the rationale that if black people as an insular group are divided into classes, then the most prosperous of them would logically comprise the "upper class," relative to the status of the black people beneath them. E. Franklin Frazier spoke of "the so-called upper class" as a "sector of the new middle class" which "sets the patterns of behavior and aspirations of the new middle class."[35] As Landry would assert decades later, Frazier argued that it was not income differential, but lifestyle and social connections that formed the basis of the distinctions between black people: "To this extent the middle class group of which I wrote [in 1925] may be regarded as a caste in the Negro community."[36] By employing the term "caste," as distinct from "class," Frazier means to describe a hereditary social ranking linked to status indicators unrelated to material wealth. Frazier also prefigures Landry in his identification of the impact of mass Northern migration on the development of this middle class. He identified three major developments which fostered the collective upward mobility of the black community and enabled greater prosperity: "access to standard American education" for black children, "occupational differentiation" which stemmed from "the entrance of the Negro into industrial employment and into occupations that had been closed to him in the South," as well as "the new needs of the Negro communities which were served by Negroes," and "access to political power which helped [the Negro] to improve his economic as well as his social position."[37] Frazier rejects the term "upper class" on the grounds that he believes its use participates in a media-driven pathology of self-aggrandizement arising from a deep-rooted collective insecurity regarding the comparative standing of black people as a race to white America. Frazier reviles the black society pages that publish articles and photographs of black pretenders to true wealth featuring their barely affordable houses, cars, and social entertainments. White Americans, he declares, "are only beginning to learn of the gaudy carnival in which middle class Negroes find an escape from their inferior status in American life."[38] Frazier insists that black people "can achieve personal dignity and peace within themselves only through acceptance of their racial identification and their real position in American economic life."[39] In many ways, this statement echoes the sentiment pervading the novels by Fauset, Larsen, and Hurst. However, while all three novelists advocate black "acceptance of their racial identification" in the sense of developing sincere pride in and commitment to the race, passive resignation to a second-class social rank is universally anathematized. Each writer explores various forms of resistance to racial hierarchy, though all rely upon the repudiation of "lower-class" behavioral models and servile demeanors. They avoid the semantic dissension inherent in using the "upper, middle, lower" classification system by employing alternative terms to describe the relative status of the characters in their novels.

Jessie Fauset uses phrases like "the better class of colored people," "colored society," and "colored ladies"; black people of lesser station speak of "them real hinckty culled folks." Nella Larsen is more subtle, occasionally deploying such referents as "Negro society," "Negro circles," and "people of consequence," but preferring to describe personal attributes, such as religious affiliation, education, taste, or habits, to signal social status. Dorothy West refers to "the nicer colored people," "these self-styled better Negroes," "the genteel poor," and the "Old Colored Families." However, perhaps in keeping with her narrative premise that white people do not generally recognize differentiation within the black community, Fannie Hurst does not appear to register any cognizance of social stratification among black people in *Imitation of Life*.

While there is no overt reference to a system of class distinction in the black community in Hurst's novel, there is an allusion to an element of black society transcending the realm of domestics and laborers. After Peola is caught passing for white at the local public school, Delilah prevails upon Bea to have her daughter sent to Washington, D.C., for private tutelage "in the home of Miss Abbie Deacon, daughter of a colored professor of mathematics at Howard University and herself a teacher in the public schools."[40] That Delilah is only able to make the new arrangements for Peola's education through "a colored school teacher … [she] used to work for," implying a cohort of black people prosperous enough to hire domestic help, and that Peola is being exposed to an exclusive arena of black civilization she never knew existed, are subject to no narrative comment. Apparently, the experience also makes little impression upon Peola; she promptly refuses the opportunity to enroll at Howard and evinces no inclination to attempt to integrate herself into elite black society.

Despite the critical resistance to the textual exploits of the members of this early black upper/middle class, their treatment in fiction is an indispensable contribution to African-American social and cultural history as well as the literary tradition. The invisibility of black intellectuals and professionals in a text like *Imitation of Life*, in which Bea Pullman perceives the entire black community of Atlantic City, New Jersey, as nothing more than a pool of potential domestic laborers ("[i]n a town with nine thousand colored population, reliable houseworkers were nevertheless difficult to obtain"), is a problematic misrepresentation in its own right.[41] Furthermore, Fauset and

Larsen especially were persistent and pointed critics of the pretension and elitism pervading the black upper class, and they were heavily invested in the promotion of a black American aesthetic which drew upon the cultural formations of the rural South as well as the urban North.

Sensitivity to regional dissimilarity between black people surfaces in different forms in the novels, though the South is universally represented as an environment in desperate need of reform, and its black inhabitants as a population in desperate need of regeneration. Dorothy West provides an assessment of the stereotypes Northern white people formed about Southern black people, based upon the images proliferated by the media. In *The Living Is Easy*, fifteen-year-old Cleo Jericho is sent North to Springfield, Illinois, with Miss Peterson, an elderly white lady who travels to the Jerichos' backwoods neighborhood seeking a more temperate climate to relieve a terminal ailment. The concerned dowager entreats Cleo's parents to deliver the beautiful young girl out of the "amoral atmosphere of the South."[42] Anticipating Miss Peterson's impending death after five years of the gradual deterioration of her condition, her suddenly solicitous relatives make arrangements for Cleo to take up residence in Boston with a Miss Boorum, a friend of Miss Peterson's. Miss Boorum welcomes the addition to her household:

> From what Miss Boorum had read of southern colored people they were devoted to what they quaintly called "my white folks," and quite disdainful of their own kind, often referring to them as "niggers." They liked to think of themselves as an integral part of the family, and preferred to die in its bosom rather than any place else. It was to be hoped that Cleo would show the same sterling loyalty.[43]

This romanticized vision of black servility and fidelity is denounced through Cleo's contempt for black people who appear to fuel the racialist convictions. The stark distinction Cleo, who herself worked in service before her marriage to Bart Judson, draws between herself and the domestic servants she encounters becomes clear through the speech she pretends to address to her daughter Judy, but really means for a maid who makes the mistake of presuming to be familiar with her: "'Always remember,' said Cleo loudly and sweetly to Judy, 'that good manners put you in the parlor and poor manners keep you in the kitchen.'"[44] During the early twentieth-century timeframe encompassed by *The Living Is Easy*, as well as the works of Fauset, Larsen, and Hurst, many married black women were compelled to find employment as domestics, abandoning their own homes to care for the households of wealthier people. The upscale characters peopling Larsen's novels all have black female servants, though Larsen never delves into the personal lives of the hired help.

Fauset's *There Is Confusion* briefly considers the private concerns of Essie, "a fixture in the service of the Marshalls" who has a teenaged daughter, Myrtle. Myrtle firmly resolves to finish high school despite the taunts of her white classmates who insist upon the futility of her efforts since the diploma will afford her no advantage when it comes to finding work (223). Essie's untutored diction and Myrtle's plight stand in vivid contrast to Joanna and the definite prospects laid out before her: at this point in the narrative, though Joanna has abandoned all hope of reconciling with her former fiancé Peter Bye, she is confident of locating a position as music director at one of the black schools for which she has performed during her several tours throughout the South.

Though the resolution of Myrtle's conflict is immaterial to the concerns of the novel, the invocation of her character demonstrates Fauset's consciousness of the difficulty involved in transcending class stratification. However, Joel Marshall's translation of his experience in domestic service into a lucrative catering enterprise does reinforce Fauset's conviction that it could indeed be accomplished. Rather, Essie's preoccupation with Myrtle's problems and the distracted response she receives from Joanna when she confides in her ("Yes, yes, I know. White people are hard to get along with. Better times coming, I hope, Essie" [224]), illustrate the difficulty faced by female household servants whose lives are so consumed by the needs of their employers, they have little time to devote to the needs of their own families. Historically, domestic work was forced upon them because their husbands did not earn enough to support their families alone, and there were few alternatives open to black women in search of employment, especially after World War I. As historian Paula Giddings notes,

> The tenuous foothold that Black women had carved out in industry—and thus in all aspects of social and economic progress—began to erode when the war ended in 1918. With the demobilization of more than 4 million soldiers, with immigrants beginning to look to America again, with the slowdown of industry, competition and Negrophobia were again on the march.[45]

"Competition and Negrophobia" were responsible for postwar black women being pushed out of the jobs they had finally acquired as a result of upwardly mobile white women securing better ones.[46] Fauset accurately reflects this dismal occupational outlook for black women within the fictive worlds of her novels. Black women were barred from office, retail, and factory work; the characters who are able to obtain such jobs are compelled to pass for white to do so. In *There Is Confusion*, Vera Manning is an office clerk, while in

Comedy: American Style, Phebe Grant is a shopgirl, and Janet Blanchard is assistant forewoman at a Massachusetts mill. The dearth of opportunities available to black women to advance their own economic prospects made them largely dependent upon marriage and motherhood to access a comfortable lifestyle and elevated class standing.

Culture

Identifying a legitimate, embraceable black culture was a strong motivational force for the artists of the Harlem Renaissance. While the ultimate failure of the movement was attributed to the general discomfort middle-class black people had with creating cultural distance between themselves and the mainstream American public, Toni Morrison pushes contemporary critics to do precisely that when she articulates the need for "the development of a theory of literature that truly accommodates Afro-American literature: one that is based on its culture, its history, and the artistic strategies the works employ to negotiate the world it inhabits."[47] In response to Morrison's challenge, like Claudia Tate, I read the texts I consider in this book "against the cultural history of the epoch of their production" in an effort to "recover much of the cultural meaning, values, expectations, and rituals of African Americans of that era, which are symbolically embedded" in them.[48] Fauset, Larsen, and Hurst were writing at a moment when there was considerable anxiety over the representational accuracy of African Americans in literature. The proliferation of texts written during the Harlem Renaissance incited a long-running literary debate over which population was a true and authentic representation of African-American culture—the urban masses, or the rural "folk."

If the contemporary analysis contended that the coalescence of an urban black middle-class depended primarily upon a wholesale assimilation of white middle class values, it inevitably follows that the domestic material of Fauset and Larsen must have been involved in a project of cultural mimesis.[49] However, is the sensational, exotic, or folk literature of the period arguably more culturally "authentic" simply because the celebration of African-American cultural difference is couched within a wholesale rejection of "white" values? The argument over regional integrity displaced what was perhaps the more pressing concern over intraracial class hierarchy, and whether or not the so-called "colored aristocracy" (many of the writers either belonged to or aspired to become a part of it) was a legitimate model for all black people to follow to achieve success in the American public arena. The artists of the Harlem Renaissance were not particularly fond of these cliquish aristocrats and continued a full-fledged assault, via literature, which had begun in the black press many years earlier.[50] Even those authors who were descended from aristocratic families registered a measure of contempt for the lifestyle.

Jean Toomer, whose book *Cane* (1923) is the earliest prose publication critics have associated with the Renaissance, vehemently repudiated any association with a race-conscious literary movement. He even claimed that his famous maternal grandfather, Reconstruction governor of Louisiana P. B. S. Pinchback, had invented his black ancestry only to facilitate his rise to political prominence. In any event, Toomer regarded his upbringing among the "colored aristocracy" in Washington, D.C., as culturally bankrupt. Only after a sojourn South to Sparta, Georgia, did he feel inspired to record: "There, for the first time I really saw the Negro, not as pseudo-urbanized and vulgarized, a semi-Americanized product, but the Negro peasant, strong with the tang of fields and soil."[51]

Langston Hughes's great-uncle was John Mercer Langston, a lawyer who held successive important appointments in the federal government during Reconstruction and was considered a leader of black society at the nation's capital. After a protracted visit to his family in Washington, D.C., however, Hughes emerged convinced that "the folk culture of the black masses was infinitely preferable and richer than the superficial culture of the city's aristocrats of color."[52]

Unlike their male peers within the Renaissance circle, Fauset and Larsen did not have the luxury of rejecting the black upper class from the position of privileged insider. Fauset was one of thirteen children reared in the household of a poor African Methodist Episcopal minister located in the vicinity of Philadelphia, Pennsylvania. Cultural historian Steven Watson succinctly captures the distinction between Fauset and the elite:

> Her family was indeed an old one—the family Bible recorded ancestors in the United States in the 1700s—and her father was a revered minister. But she carried that less-pure strain of aristocracy in which the aspiration for respectability thrives. She was born near Philadelphia rather than in the city itself, she was the only black student in Philadelphia public schools where she was snubbed for her racial identity, and her family appreciated haut-bourgeois values but didn't possess the funds to sustain such a lifestyle.[53]

Fauset's degree from Cornell University, close association with W. E. B. Du Bois, and position on the editorial staff of *Crisis* magazine translated into a spot on the fringe of New York's elite, but many of her younger Renaissance contemporaries considered her manner an affectation. Neither were they particularly enthused about Nella Larsen. Larsen's perpetual evasiveness regarding her family background was symptomatic of her self-consciousness about her lack of pedigree in a social order where ancestral origins were so crucial to acceptance. The daughter of a racially ambiguous, working-class Chicago couple, she was estranged from her family because her complexion made her own African ancestry unmistakable. Her difficult marriage to Dr. Elmer Imes, a man from a prominent black elite family who earned his Ph.D. in physics from the University of Michigan, only served to intensify her social insecurities. Throughout her life she was driven intensively by her desire to achieve success despite her exclusion from the elite of both races.[54]

The very existence of the colored aristocracy was a leading source of divisiveness within the black community. The notion of an aristocracy either lurked in the background or loomed in the forefront of every major issue faced by the black population in its metamorphosis from slave to citizen status—from the publicly waged protracted debate between Booker T. Washington and W. E. B. Du Bois over industrial versus classical education, to which style of religious worship black people should embrace, to how to contend with Jim Crow segregation. Relations between the aristocrats and the masses were strained, at best. As one historian of the black elite notes, though privileged black people sought to uplift the rest of their racial community, they shrank from any personal association with them. "[W]hile aristocrats of color sought to reform the conduct of the masses, they also held that gentility required one to place social distance between oneself and those considered vulgar and crude."[55] Critics of Jessie Fauset and Nella Larsen contend that the novelists replicate this attitude of deliberate reserve toward the black masses. They have faulted the writers for completely ignoring the oppressive social conditions to which the majority of black people were being subjected, even though their novels codify how prejudice and discrimination infiltrate and infect the lives of even those black people fortunate enough to elude poverty and dissipation. The novelists' investment in the self-contained world of black social relations promotes the objectives of the black modernist aesthetic by asserting the existence of an autonomous black culture.

Ann Douglas suggests that the evolution of American modernism constituted a post-World War I national identity reassessment. "Newly fascinated with their own cultural resources, the American moderns repudiated the long ascendant English and European traditions and their genteel American custodians as emblems of cultural cowardice."[56] At the same time, Douglas goes on to argue, "black America, in an inevitable corollary movement, was recovering its own heritage from the dominant white culture."[57] Interestingly, the wartime-inspired patriotism which provoked white artists to sever the creative umbilical cord connecting them to the Old World was likely not the development which triggered black artists to do likewise, isolating their own cultural origins to prevent them from becoming subsumed by the larger culture. Rather, the disillusionment arising from black participation in the war effort and the hostile postwar social climate were the culmination of the declared provocations for black people to stake out their own cultural terrain.

The black war experience proved to be painfully enlightening to those African Americans who believed that fighting for a common cause overseas would finally eradicate the breach between the races at home. Instead, the years during and immediately following the Great War witnessed an unprecedented rash of racially motivated violence; the 2.3 million black men who enlisted in the United States Army between 1917 and 1918 returned home from service to "the Red Summer of 1919," marked by lynchings and race riots in numerous major cities surely instigated by the discrepancy between freshly revitalized black aspirations to assume equal citizenship status and white determination to maintain the prewar status quo.[58]

As black people grew more discouraged about the possibilities of obtaining political victories without a complete rehabilitation of the attitudes the white masses held towards them, race leaders aggressively began to advocate other avenues by which to effect this improvement of the black public image. One of the principal avenues was literature. As the *Ithaca* [NY] *Journal News* reported on the eve of the Renaissance, "The Great War made all things new, even the traditional relation between whites and blacks in this country. The colored man of romance and sentiment is dying off. In his place is coming one who is not content to be picturesque and exploited."[59]

The immediate impact of the war was in fact preceded by a number of retrogressive public policy changes at the federal level. Kevin Kelley Gaines points to a series of political setbacks black people suffered under the highly anticipated Woodrow Wilson administration which led W. E. B. Du Bois and other race leaders to counsel a redirection of group energies from efforts toward political empowerment to a large-scale reformation of the public image of black people, to be achieved principally through the fine arts.

> Almost immediately, Wilson's administration put to rest whatever optimism existed among blacks. As a portent of things to come, just before

his inauguration, the House passed a law making racial intermarriage a felony in the District of Columbia. In 1913, Wilson established segregation in federal office buildings. Throughout his administration, he effectively condoned outbreaks of racial violence with federal nonintervention. ... Then in 1915 he warmly endorsed the film epic *Birth of a Nation*, based on Thomas Dixon's anti-Reconstruction novel *The Clansman*.[60]

Wilson's policies were especially demoralizing to members of the black elite, who could not help but feel as if the measures were being directed primarily at themselves. Black people who held political office or civil service appointments were the most obvious targets of enforced segregation in federal buildings. Elites had so carefully labored to maintain the distinction between themselves and the black masses, but their efforts profited them nothing in the esteem of the white public from whom they desired acceptance and preferential treatment.

The approval of D. W. Griffith's *Birth of a Nation*, however, which refigured the history of the American South as essentially a white man's struggle to conquer the twin black threats of insatiable temptresses and demented rapists, thereby restoring the safety and sanctity of the white nuclear home, drew the battle line for racial equality in terms of public images.[61] The film, which pioneered a number of innovative cinematic techniques that surely accounted in part for its massive appeal, represented the Reconstruction South as the site of an honorable battle waged by white men against the black menace seeking to destroy their families.

As *The Half-Century Magazine*, a Chicago-based black bi-monthly publication, reported in 1922, "The novel had lost but little of its popularity when the photoplay ... appeared to revive any prejudice that might be dormant and to plant seeds of hatred in new soil."[62] A national majority accustomed to perceiving black people by way of the most negative stereotypes imaginable would surely not disapprove of governmental indifference with respect to the demands of black people for full and equal participation in American society, especially when those stereotypes receive the hearty sanction of the president of the United States—the president to whom a delegation from the NAACP led by prominent Harlemite James Weldon Johnson appealed in 1917 with the words: "We realize that your high position and the tremendous moral influence which you wield in the world will give a word from you greater force than could come from any other source."[63] According to Johnson's logic, President Wilson's endorsement of Griffith's film was a tacit encouragement of white supremacy.

The 1925 rerelease of *Birth of a Nation* prompted an outraged protest from black leaders and intellectuals who legitimately feared a revival of negative sentiment against African Americans with the exposure of a new generation of white Americans to the picture. The film's reappearance in New York must have been counted a rather uncordial reception for the cohort of "New Negro" intellectuals committed to rehabilitating the public perception of African Americans. Griffith's movie does not contain a single depiction of black family life. Instead, with the notable exception of the mammy figure, black people are seen only as agents of destruction to white families—pillaging and burning their homes as undisciplined soldiers in the Union army, brazenly seducing their husbands into adulterous encounters, driving their virginal sisters to virtuous suicide with relentless sexual pursuit. In an attempt to put to rest the painful images of deranged rapist, shameless seductress, and obsequious mammy, black artists were called upon to produce correctives to such slander.

Because they did aspire to artistic excellence, these novelists were somewhat ambivalent about their work being situated as merely part of an arsenal of weapons in the political battle to secure civil parity for African Americans. Despite their discomfort with the prospect of their writing being dismissed as propaganda rather than being received as literature, they were cognizant that protracted inaction "would allow whites to continue their practice of considering all blacks as an undifferentiated mass and of judging the entire race by its worst elements."[64]

Fauset, Larsen, and Walter White, a member of the black elite from Atlanta who later became the leader of the NAACP, jointly decided to attempt novels after sharing their mutual dissatisfaction with the representation of black people in *Birthright* (1922), a novel by white author T. S. Stribling. Stribling had endeavored to chronicle the fate of a Northern-educated black man of mixed blood who returns to his Southern hometown. His protagonist finds, like John Jones in W. E. B. Du Bois's "Of the Coming of John" (1903), that the social terrain of the South is extremely difficult for an educated black man to negotiate.[65] While they sympathized with the basic premise of the narrative, the triumvirate of fledgling novelists were galvanized to action by what they felt to be Stribling's unsuccessful effort to render authentic black characters; as Fauset later testified, they thought: "Here is an audience waiting to hear the truth about us. Let we who are better qualified to present that truth than any white writer, try to do so."[66]

What qualified them, according to Fauset's declaration, was not necessarily greater talent, but the natural affinity of their racial identity. In a society where the color line was demarcated very starkly, they believed that realistic

African-American characters could be created only by writers who had lived the black experience. Their conviction prefigured the articulated objectives of the first literary contest sponsored by *Opportunity* magazine:

> [T]o locate and orient Negro writers of ability; to stimulate and encourage interest in the serious development of a body of literature about Negro life ... to encourage the reading of [this] literature ... not merely because they are Negro authors but because what they write is literature and because the literature is interesting. ... [67]

The Urban League's *Opportunity* magazine inaugurated its contests chiefly to nurture black achievement in literature and to increase the representation of black America in the development of the national culture. In this way, the Urban League was perhaps principally responsible for sustaining the momentum of the Harlem Renaissance, which ultimately floundered, according to E. Franklin Frazier, because the burgeoning, tunnel-visioned middle-class black community "rejected it. ... Instead of being interested in gaining a new conception of themselves, the new middle class was hoping to escape from themselves."[68] Frazier's harsh assessment of middle-class priorities finds a parallel in Nella Larsen's *Quicksand*, in which Helga Crane accuses her friend Anne Grey of "proclaiming loudly the undiluted good of all things Negro," but imitating the tastes and preferences of refined white people.[69] In *Domestic Allegories of Political Desire*, Claudia Tate's study of black women novelists like Pauline Hopkins and Frances Harper, who dominated the black literary scene around the turn of the century, she argues that they borrowed the sentimental conventions of the domestic novels popularized by white women writers because the form, traditionally the tool of the socially disempowered, was particularly useful for encoding the social ambitions of an oppressed population.[70] Tate bases her analysis on the claim that while slave narratives had been designed to appeal to white sympathies, the domestic novels of the 1890s were primarily targeted at upwardly mobile black people. "The story of ideal family formation was especially well suited to this first audience because its formulaic plot line encoded bourgeois constructions of the successful individual, community, and society to which that audience subscribed."[71]

Thirty years later, during the Harlem Renaissance, black women writers such as Fauset, Larsen, Hurston, and Dorothy West, presupposed a mixed audience. Among the literate public they expected to reach were not only the progressive black people for whom their predecessors had written, but also white readers—both those whose perceptions of black people had been shaped by comedic minstrel figures and white supremacist propaganda alleging black depravity, and sympathetic white people who were nevertheless unfamiliar with the interior lives of African Americans and their true attitudes toward their restricted social environment. The difference in target readership meant a different orientation toward the subject matter. These writers were not interested in "encoding bourgeois constructions" of success as were their turn-of-the-century predecessors but in dramatizing precisely where those constructions came into conflict with black historical circumstances and the material reality of black modern experience. They wanted to illustrate the damage to the black psyche caused by adopting white middle-class ideological standards, values, and outward forms of living without accounting for the fundamental cultural incongruity between the races.

Perhaps the conviction shared by Fauset and the Urban League that the white reading public was primarily interested in discerning the "truth" about the black population in their midst was naive. Twenty years after the demise of the Harlem Renaissance, a skeptical Ralph Ellison insisted, in fact, that representational accuracy remained in the eye of the beholder:

> Too often what is presented as the American Negro ... emerges an oversimplified clown, a beast or an angel. Seldom is he drawn as that sensitively focused process of opposites, of good and evil, of instinct and intellect, of passion and spirituality, which great literary art has projected as the image of man.[72]

Although Ellison organizes his argument around the generic male subject, his essential point is equally applicable to the depictions of women—white people did not seem to be open to the possibility of a black character on the literary stage who rose above the uncomplicated plane of flat two-dimensionality. However, regardless of the reception of her fiction, Fauset was determined to prove that when the "colored American ... is not being pressed too hard by the Furies of Prejudice, Ignorance, and Economic Injustice," s/he "is not so vastly different from any other American, just distinctive."[73] To this end, she and her contemporaries engaged characterizations which relieved them of the obligation to rehash the effects of the untenable social circumstances that contributed to the stereotypical perception of black people as criminal, immoral, and ignorant. The writers reverse this dynamic by foregrounding the importance of stable family groups through which the characters in their novels negotiate their participation in larger social formations.

The attention paid by the novelists to the operations of family relationships is a site for investigating what historian Earl Lewis contends must be a critical shift in scholarly focus from defining the form of the black family to assessing the particular responsibilities and interactions of family members.

Lewis insists that too much time and energy have been invested in debating the structural integrity of the black family, when the more relevant and useful line of inquiry concerns the process by which black people adopted the predominant mainstream familial arrangement, and subsequently adapted it to their own needs by reshaping the various functions of the individual roles.[74] Pursuing these questions would lead to a better understanding of the "particular requirements for Negro families" Andrew Billingsley identified as emerging from the following trio of conditions:

a) the peculiar historical development,

b) the caste-like qualities in the American stratification system which relegates all Negroes to inferior status, and

c) the social class and economic systems which keep most Negroes in the lower social classes.[75]

Black families did indeed respond in specialized and culturally specific ways to the demands of becoming involved in American public life, especially considering that "For the Negro family, socialization is doubly challenging, for the family must teach its young members not only how to be human, but also how to be black in a white society."[76] I contend that this acculturation process begins with the essential figure in the family structure: the mother.

2 Revising the Victorian Maternal Ideal in Jessie Fauset's *There Is Confusion*

Critics have thoroughly investigated the fanfare surrounding the 1924 appearance of Jessie Redmon Fauset's first novel, *There Is Confusion*. Although the publication of *Cane,* Jean Toomer's genre-resistant, textual hybrid of poetry and prose vignettes, had preceded it in 1923, Fauset's publishing house, Boni & Liveright, launched an aggressive advertising campaign to promote her novel as the first to emerge out of the literary efflorescence in Harlem.[1] Charles S. Johnson, editor of the Urban League's *Opportunity* magazine, organized an elegant dinner reception at Manhattan's Civic Club (the only quality establishment in the city that would accommodate patrons of color) to applaud Fauset's achievement. Approximately one hundred literary New Yorkers, "the cream of publishers, magazine editors, and distinguished white writers along with a full roster of the most promising young black writers," turned out to pay tribute to Jessie Fauset and her novel.[2]

The account appearing in the May 1924 issue of *Opportunity* suggests that the dinner was planned as a formal presentation of up-and-coming black writers rather than a celebration of Fauset's accomplishment. Still, it does acknowledge that the publication of her novel afforded the definitive catalyst for the event. The article, bearing the headline "The Debut of the Younger School of Negro Writers," dubbed the gathering an open

> meeting of the Writer's Guild, an informal group whose membership includes Countee Cullen, Eric Walrond, Langston Hughes, Jessie Fauset, ... and a few others. The occasion was a "coming out party," at the Civic Club on March 21—a date selected around the appearance of the novel "There Is Confusion" by Jessie Fauset.[3]

So while recognizing the publication of Fauset's first novel was not formally avowed to be the purpose of the evening's affair, the deliberate timing of the "coming-out party" to coincide with the initial distribution of *There Is Confusion* firmly established Fauset's book as the premier text launching the literary invasion by the modern generation of black writers.

Especially considering it was her first novel, *There Is Confusion* was unquestionably an ambitious undertaking. Fauset attempts to cover a great deal of narrative ground in her nearly 300 pages of text. Her stated intentions were to combat the distorted images of black people then circulating in popular literature by white writers, and to present an accurate depiction of the daily lives of many African Americans.[4] In this way, the novel represents a key transitional work in the development of African-American literature. *There Is Confusion* links the earlier tradition dominated by such trailblazing authors as Pauline Hopkins, Frances E. W. Harper, and Charles W. Chesnutt, with the new direction of black fiction—works characterized increasingly by city settings, progressive character types, and plots activated by conflicts other than hostile confrontations with white supremacy.

At a cultural moment when literary audiences demonstrated their absolute fascination with books featuring black characters by buying them as quickly as white writers could get them written, published, and released, Fauset's urban drama sought to draw the attention of the reading public away from white fictive fantasy and speculation about black life, to black people themselves as the authors of and authorities on their own modern experience. Fauset's visionary manuscript became the inaugural treatise of the new generation of black novelists. She thereby paved the way not only for the reception of her own later work, *Plum Bun* (1929), *The Chinaberry Tree* (1931), and *Comedy: American Style* (1933), but also the work of her gifted contemporaries Nella Larsen, Walter White, Langston Hughes, Zora Neale Hurston, and Dorothy West, among others.[5]

Aside from her focus on the modern, urban black experience, many other important features signal *There Is Confusion* as a revolutionary work of fiction in the history of African-American literature. Howard University English professor Montgomery Gregory, a contemporary reviewer of Fauset, wrote in the June 1924 issue of *Opportunity* that the novel was as important to the progression of black American culture as the celebrated volume of poetry penned by the African slave Phillis Wheatley in 1773; both publications, Gregory contends, have "significance far beyond their intrinsic merit."[6] Like Wheatley's book of verse, he argues, Fauset's text "is also a 'first' book, being the first recognized novel written by a Negro woman and, in fact, the first treatment in fiction of the educated strata of Negro urban life." Though

Chesnutt's "Blue Veins" of Groveland, Ohio, should rightfully claim this particular distinction of being the first fictionalized circle of learned, cosmopolitan black people, Gregory perhaps discounted their narratives because Chesnutt rarely depicted them in a favorable light. The review then shifts to a consideration of the white male critical response to the text:

> Is it strange that several well known critics express surprise that a standard novel should be written by a woman of the black race or that the cultured group of that race described in the novel actually exists? ... Here lies the great value of this novel, in interpreting the better elements of our life to those who know us only as domestic servants, "uncles," or criminals.[7]

Gregory praises the narrative for its practical function as a sociological case study of the interior lives of the black bourgeoisie. The political benefit of acquainting masses of white people with progressive black people, he contends, is of paramount importance in changing attitudes polluted by derogatory stereotypes and improving race relations. Fauset's text clearly made a significant impact upon the white critics Gregory claims were universally oblivious to the class of black intellectuals and professionals she focused on in *There Is Confusion*.

Impressed as "these gentlemen" were by Fauset's choice of subject matter, they were concerned about her narrative focus standardizing the topical parameters for the modern black novel. Representative gentleman Horace Liveright, whose firm published Fauset's book, delivered an address at the Civic Club "coming-out" dinner in which he made a point of formally and emphatically cautioning the assembly of young black writers "against the danger of reflecting in one's writings the 'inferiority complex' which is so insistently and frequently apparent in an overbalanced emphasis on 'impossibly good' fiction types."[8]

Through his diagnosis of the representation of a sizable cast of admirable black characters as the manifestation of a racial "inferiority complex," Liveright reveals a number of his own personal imaginative deficiencies: his inability to conceive of the legitimacy of the culture Fauset describes outside of its fictional trappings, his myopic assumptions about what fortuitous combination of fine qualities would constitute an "impossibly good" individual within a black context, his failure to comprehend the range of functions positive characterizations of black people in literature had performed historically for both the black and white reading publics, as well as his more mercenary anxieties about black-authored literature perhaps not materializing as the exotic novelty which would make it so potently marketable.[9]

Liveright's remarks were perhaps not intended to be taken as a veiled critique of Fauset's novel, but it is probable that they were exactly that. Subsequent critics have faulted her for disproportionately concentrating her attention on middle-class black people and ignoring the plight and the fictive possibilities of a story centered on the experience of the black folk or the urban culture of the black masses. Gregory makes a crucial point, however, when he argues that white America had become accustomed to accepting a finite set of unflattering images as representative of the limits of black subjectivity and that Fauset introduced an invaluable literary corrective to those racialist assumptions by presenting well-developed models of blackness which transcended the circumscribed space of moral, intellectual, and cultural inferiority America had reserved for its black citizens. Unquestionably, countless stories inspired by the lives of the black masses were there to be told, but it should not be counted a deficiency of Fauset's that she did not opt to tell them. Her alternative narrative focus does not reflect a belief that no noble or worthwhile characters existed outside the purview of the middle class. Rather, it reflects her conviction that definitive racial progress entailed a significant elevation of the collective standards for personal values, educational achievements, cultural development, and occupational goals in the black community.

The Endorsement of Black Patriarchal Authority

Paternity functions within the family dynamic in Fauset's novels in a variety of ways; how she depicts men participating in the private sphere of their home lives can be understood as contributing to a prescriptive strategy for constructing the ideal household environment. In *There Is Confusion*, the most comprehensive influence at work in the development of Joanna Marshall's character is her remarkable closeness to her father, Joel. Joanna's identification with her father leads her to pursue a "masculine" dream of fame and success rather than a "feminine" dream of romantic love and domestic harmony; as a child Joanna registers her disdain for the household chores she and her siblings are required to perform. "Joanna ... made up her mind early that as a woman she would never do this kind of work. Not that she despised it, she simply considered it labor lost for a person who like herself might be spending her time in more beautiful and more graceful activities" (17). Fittingly, Joanna becomes a celebrated vocalist whose performances seem to be most inspired when she appears before a humble gathering of her own race in some tiny rural church. In such a venue, the narrator confides, Joanna develops an instantaneous, wordless rapport with her auditors that gently soothes, reassures, and encourages them: "I am no better than you. You are no worse than I. Whatever I am, you, in your children, may be. Whatever you are, I in my father have been" (131). The synchronicity between father and daughter to which Joanna alludes here is a key ingredient in understanding the dynamics involved in several of the novel's relationships. Joel proudly recognizes in his daughter a singular opportunity to revitalize his own abandoned pursuit of "greatness." She is the virtual reincarnation of himself as he sat on his mother's lap as a child and innocently queried, "Mammy, I'll be a great man some day, won't I? Mammy, you're going to help me to be great?" (1). Joel's "Mammy," unfortunately, is ill equipped to help him, and in fact ends up draining the painstakingly accumulated savings he had put aside for his education with the expenses of a lingering illness. Joanna's parroting of his own youthful entreaty enables Joel to reenact his mother's role in his life, erasing her legacy of impotence with his own ability to make a significant and beneficial contribution to the outcome of his daughter's life.

Joanna even seems to consider herself a sort of extension of her father; from the opening sentence of the novel, Fauset impresses upon her readers that "Joanna's first consciousness of the close understanding which existed between herself and her father dated back to a time when she was very young" (9). The sympathy between them is reinforced repeatedly throughout the narrative, notably so in the scene where Joanna is imagined to reassure her rustic black audience, "Whatever you are, I in my father have been." Certainly, it makes perfect sense for Joanna to express her sense of solidarity with less fortunate black people by tracing her ancestry through Joel, who was born a slave and the son of slaves in the South. Even so, this speech in particular begs the question of why Joanna so consistently and thoroughly privileges her father's over her mother's influence in her development.

Their driving ambition to achieve "greatness" links Joel and his youngest daughter psychically from Joanna's infancy, and Fauset uses their special connection metaphorically to draw attention to the practical necessity of economic prosperity in order to lay the groundwork for social and political influence. Whereas Joel's mother had been powerless to assist him in his bid for great achievement, his entrepreneurial success enables him to support Joanna. However, while Joel provides the financial backing for Joanna's bid for "greatness," he makes no effort to direct her ambition. He encourages her to develop her natural talents but never admits that he would have preferred his daughter to succeed in another avenue until after she expresses her own disenchantment with her chosen profession. Fauset thus presents a striking contrast to the Dorothy West short story "An Unimportant Man" (1928), in which the protagonist Zebediah Jenkins finally comes to understand the necessity of sending his rebellious young daughter Essie to college only after he receives notification that he will have to repeat his attempt to pass the Massachusetts state bar exam a fourth time because there was a suspicion of fraud among some of the examinees.

Zeb Jenkins is nearly forty and works as second cook in a white-owned restaurant. Becoming a lawyer would have liberated his family from social obscurity and the inferior status conferred by a dependence on menial labor for subsistence. His repeated failures alert him to the legitimacy of his wife's and his mother's insistence upon the impracticability of his daughter's dream of eschewing academics in favor of becoming a dancer, or "something that's beautiful."[10] While the prospect of dancing professionally is an impossible dream for young Essie Jenkins, financial security enables Joanna Marshall to afford the luxury of following whatever inclination she so desires. Joanna can rest assured that regardless of whether she succeeds or fails at her chosen pursuit, her father will take care of her until she eventually marries a man who shares her privileged class status.

The impoverished Maggie Ellersley constitutes a perfect foil to the characterization of Joanna. Maggie grew up without her father; her mother may proudly designate herself "a widow who considered herself fortunate to be one," but Maggie feels the adverse effects of her father's absence (57). As an early adolescent she discovers that men constitute "one avenue of escape" from tenement life, and her determination to find a man to "rescue" her from poverty and oblivion proves to be the source of all of her problems throughout the novel. She searches for a husband to perform not a romantic but a paternal function and is therefore willing to accept a marriage of convenience in order to meet her material needs.

After Maggie's romantic fixation on Philip Marshall is thwarted by Joanna, his little sister, Maggie marries Henderson Neal, one of her mother's boarders, on the rebound; twenty years her senior, Neal is old enough to be her father, and though being married to him "was not what she wanted," Maggie believes it will bring her "security, a home for herself and her mother, freedom from all the little nagging worries that beset the woman who fights her own way through the world" (90). Maggie's dreams of respectability are dashed quite suddenly, however, when she learns that her newlywed husband is a professional gambler, disdained and ostracized by polite society. It takes her peremptory divorce from Neal, a protracted, awkward, and dispassionate engagement to the poor but well-connected Peter Bye, and an overseas mission to provide support services for black soldiers during World War I, to finally teach Maggie the importance of love independent of mercenary considerations—what Joanna calls "a pattern to guide us out of the confusion"—and she is rewarded by being reunited with Philip, now a wounded veteran (283). She finally convinces Philip of her sincerity in expressing her devotion to him when she desperately sheds "the last tatters of her old obsession, that oldest desire of all for sheer decency," and vows to become his mistress if he refuses to wed her honestly (268). When Maggie is finally able to appreciate love for its own sake and renounce her effort to use a man as a substitute for her absent father, she is enabled to find happiness. Only Vera Manning, the last of the triad of women who, Joanna once complains to her sister Sylvia, have had their lives "all broken up" by their botched encounters with love, is not as fortunate as Maggie. Though she comes to repent of her forfeited engagement to her childhood sweetheart Harley Alexander, their relationship unfortunately proves to be irreparable.

The structure of the Manning household could be described as a matriarchal dictatorship. Vera's mother is a watered-down version of Olivia Blanchard Cary, the obsessive-compulsive mother whose singular aversion to her olive-skinned son drives him to suicide in *Comedy: American Style*. Mrs. Manning alienates Vera's fiancé by telling Harley that she did not want her daughter to marry a dark man, since if they "should have children they'd be brown and would have to be humiliated like all other colored children" (199). Like Olivia's husband Dr. Christopher Cary, Mr. Manning is unwilling or unable to contradict his wife; Vera admits to Joanna, "Father always follows mother's lead" (199). Though he is elsewhere described as "a remarkably successful business man," Mr. Manning does not translate any of his public prestige into the private sphere, in which he permits his wife to preside uncontested.

At the opposite end of the spectrum of domestic organization, Fauset crafts an idyllic final scene in which Joanna affirms her satisfaction with Peter after he refuses the elderly white Meriwether Bye (his great-grandfather Joshua's youngest half-brother, and therefore Peter's great-great-uncle) who, bereft of direct descendents after his namesake grandson Meriwether dies in combat during the Great War, wants to make the newest little Meriwether Bye, Peter and Joanna's son, his heir, despite his dark skin. The elderly Meriwether cannot bring himself to consent to Peter's condition that the blood relationship between the black and white Bye families be publicly acknowledged in order for his son to accept the bequest. When his uncle fails the test, as Peter was certain he would, Peter flatly refuses the offer of the entire Bye fortune.

Joanna is present but remains silent throughout the exchange between Peter and his uncle. The scene is oddly like the formal observation a supervisor might make of a newly trained employee or even like a young boy tentatively demonstrating his painstakingly rehearsed social skills for his mother. At one point during the interview, after Peter has recounted his personal history for his uncle, he seems to solicit Joanna's approval of his performance.

> He smiled gratefully at Joanna, who smiled back at him with gratitude of another sort. He had uttered no word of complaint nor of the difficulties attendant on being a colored man in America. She was very proud of him. He was so charming, so handsome, growing daily in independence. (294)

Peter even makes the decision to reject the inheritance for their son without discussing it with his wife, although her astonished, though wordless, reaction to the elderly man's proposition had certainly communicated her disapproval rather clearly. Thadious Davis would read this scene as further corroboration of her argument that Joanna's conversion to the model homemaker constitutes a sustained repression of her own character in order to allow her husband to emerge as her voice and ideological representative:

> She embraces an ideal external to the novel proper, but she underscores its conclusion: that the African-American woman must subordinate gender issues and personal ambitions to the advancement of the race through the male's attainment of parity—notwithstanding the fact that she is his equal. (xxi)

Joanna has indeed lost her will to continue battling the formidable combination of racism and sexism that restricts her career possibilities, but this happens even before she reconciles with Peter. She has indeed come to the conclusion that racism is a more virulent obstacle than sexism, as Davis contends. When she is invited to join a selective club for high achievers, she comes into contact with many young white women who have distinguished themselves in their chosen fields, and "For a while she was puzzled, a little ashamed when she realized that so many of these women had outstripped her so early." After much thought, she finally has her revelation: "These women had not been compelled to endure her long, heartrending struggle against color" (234–35). In any event, Joanna's acceptance of an auxiliary role in the "male's attainment of parity" is due to a commitment more personal than collective in scope. She is committed to the transformation of her husband into the strong, self-sufficient man she knows he can be. Allowing him to refuse his uncle's offer with no interference on her part is a successful test for Joanna as well as for Peter. Peter conquers his instinct to take the easy way out—accepting the money unconditionally—and Joanna suppresses her instinct to take control of the situation—speaking her mind before Peter has had an opportunity to express his opinion. The novel does not advocate the submissive housewife, but it looks with equal disfavor upon the "Father always follows mother's lead" disempowerment represented by the Mannings. Consequently, the narrative as a whole affirms a confidence and optimism in the autonomy of the black nuclear family and the enduring potency of paternal leadership tempered by maternal influence.

Confronting the Bourgeois Sensibility

Far from being "impossibly good" types, Fauset's characters were not so distantly removed from the reasonable expectations of black people who wanted to improve their status and lifestyles. *There Is Confusion*'s Joanna Marshall is the daughter of a former slave, and her love interest, Peter Bye, is the descendant of a venerable old Philadelphia family fallen into decline. In *Plum Bun*, Angela and Virginia Murray are the daughters of a couple who met while both were in the domestic service of a white actress. Set in the small town of Red Brook, New Jersey, *The Chinaberry Tree* features Laurentine Strange, the offspring of a long-standing extramarital affair between her mother, a Mississippi-born former housemaid, and the town's leading white citizen. Yet another less-than-stellar pedigree is that of *Comedy: American Style*'s Olivia Cary, the daughter of a hotel chambermaid who marries a middle-class medical student. The origins of these and many other characters in Fauset's four novels illustrate that within the black community social class barriers are highly permeable and that one can elevate one's class status in any number of ways irrespective of the socioeconomic classification one inherits at birth.

Characters like *Comedy: American Style*'s Alicia Barrett, Teresa Cary's classmate at the upscale white boarding school she attends at her mother's insistence, are not the type routinely featured in Fauset's novels. Alicia is a legitimate member of the black elite; she is from Chicago, where her father is a judge, and her mother had been a renowned musician. Teresa instinctively recognizes Alicia as "a girl of family, breeding and tradition."[11] The Barretts own a vacation home at Idlewild, a fashionable black resort,[12] and though they are not avowed to be rich, Alicia and her brother Alex are equipped with all of the accoutrements of a privileged upbringing: extensive musical training, preparatory and finishing school educations, travel throughout Europe, expensive white colleges. Alicia's presence is necessary to introduce Teresa to the self-contained world of black society; Alicia's inclusion in the narrative also dramatizes the contrast between the promising future Teresa might have accessed had she been able to take advantage of her opportunity to assume a place within that society and the consequences of the choices she did make under the influence of her color-obsessed mother.

Unlike Alicia Barrett, the typical Fauset heroine is rarely college educated and is not born into a family with a long history of distinction. The Fauset-crafted family usually derives its livelihood from either a skills-based, service-oriented business or from domestic labor, and children are reared by parents who model a successful work ethic, promote a system of wholesome moral values, and provide a loving and supportive home environment. All of these elements combine to position children to be high achievers and surpass the standard of living their parents were able to provide. Fauset endorses the belief that all parents can equip their children to secure a greater range and quality of options to increase their chances of achieving future comfort and happiness.

In *There Is Confusion,* the Marshall family squarely fits the profile of the group that sociologists St. Clair Drake and Horace R. Cayton designated Chicago's black upper class. After analyzing a representative sample of thirty-one individuals universally affirmed by their peers as members of the elite social set, Drake and Cayton identified characteristics such as:

> extreme emphasis on maintaining "a good home," with fine furniture, linen, glassware, china, and silver much in evidence. ... [T]he majority kept at least a part-time maid, and a few had more than one servant, even during the Depression. ... The majority owned automobiles. ... All were interested in real estate. ...
>
> These upper-class people took "respectability" for granted. They were concerned with "refinement," "culture," and graceful living as a class-ideal ... [T]hey all talked like ardent Race Men and Race Women.[13]

The Marshalls live in precisely such a home environment. Those who seek out their society "esteemed rightly the correctness of the old-fashioned walnut furniture, the heavy curtains, the kidney table in the parlor, the massive silver service and good linen" (51). The Marshalls also retain domestic help and have a car; their oldest son forms a real estate partnership, while their younger son becomes a race leader. When Joanna Marshall defends her older sister's claim to preeminence, she appeals to "respectability," "refinement," and "culture": "Sylvia's my sister, thank you. She's Joel Marshall's daughter. She has background, she knows good music and pictures and worth while [*sic*] people" (78). Joel and his wife embrace the "ordered and disciplined family life" attributed to the upper-class modality and have high expectations for their children.[14] However, the novel firmly rejects the concept of class-based exclusivity.

Social class position, contrary to the widely disseminated assumption of Fauset's pronounced middle-class bias, is actually a quite slippery concept in the author's fictive world. The brief racial affinity speech Joanna is imagined to deliver from the backwoods stage ("I am no better than you. You are no worse than I.") reinforces the anti-aristocratic message Fauset attempts to convey through several different avenues in the text of *Confusion*: Class identity within the black community is a fluid concept rooted in the common heritage of chattel slavery. Consequently, to base an intraracial system of distinction upon how far an individual has advanced beyond the condition of enslavement simply perpetuates the same objectionable form of oppression perpetrated by the white establishment. Fauset avoids endorsing the pompous practice of chronicling generations of free ancestry by making the head of the Marshall family, a family most assuredly included in "the better class of colored people," a man who was born into slavery (49). It is interesting, though, that Joanna's utopian sentiment of equality within the race, echoing Peter's democratic simile that "the queen has children, in agony ... just like the poorest charwoman," makes cross-class identification dependent upon the natural process of biological reproduction (94).

The members of her audience can match Joanna's success not through formal education, nor specialized training, nor relocating to another part of the country, nor converting to a particular religion, nor reforming their moral values, nor refining their taste and conduct, nor even a stroke of capricious luck; instead, the novel privileges advancement by what might be characterized as generational evolution: "Whatever I am, you, in your children, may be." Joanna's mental declaration is paralleled by the black Bye family motto inscribed by Peter's grandfather Isaiah in the Bye family Bible: "By *his* fruits shall ye know *me*" (29).[15] The deeds and accomplishments of children reflect back upon their parents.

This message is not intended to condone the practice of burdening one's children with one's own unfulfilled ambitions but to encourage parents to do everything in their power to assist their children to utilize their individual talents and achieve the dreams they envision for themselves. Certainly, what parents want for their children and what their children want for themselves do not usually coincide. Fauset mobilizes Joel Marshall to enact the endorsed parental response to this common dilemma when he endeavors to help

Joanna to achieve national recognition as an entertainer, despite his wish that she had been inclined to pursue another vocation, because "Joel Marshall believed in using the gifts nearest at hand" (19).

Joel had applied this philosophy to his own life when he drew upon the culinary skill he had acquired as a kitchen domestic for a wealthy white Virginia family to establish his phenomenally successful catering business in New York City.

Catering is not the profession Joel envisions for himself as a boy when he dreams of one day being "great." Although he is born a slave, the Emancipation Proclamation upgrades his condition early in life, and he nurtures a fantasy of overcoming his humble beginnings to achieve the eminence of such historical figures as Abraham Lincoln or Napoleon Bonaparte. Though an unfavorable conspiracy of circumstances compels him to abandon that dream, catering still makes Joel Marshall not only wealthy enough to become "one of the first ten colored men in Harlem to possess an automobile," but also to be easily able to educate his two sons at Harvard, provide a home for his daughter Sylvia and her family, and finance the expensive singing and dancing lessons Joanna needs in preparation for her stage career (109).

While his catering business does provide economic wealth, it is not the occupation Joel wanted for himself and certainly not a business he expects or desires to pass on to his children. When Maggie Ellersley approaches him with the proposition that she become an apprentice of a sort to his operation because she and her mother could use the extra income, Joel's first inclination is to offer to lend her some money; he "had no desire to see either her or any of his children become caterers," but, like other "colored men of old Joel's type," he was "obsessed with the idea of a progressing younger generation" (68). Even so, working for Joel Marshall is in actuality quite a step up from Maggie's meager origins in a shabby three-room tenement. She and her mother occupy the dark, damp back rooms fed by airshafts, while the more commodious front room, the only one with windows, they rent out to itinerant roomers—mostly railroad men, like her father had been before he died when Maggie was eight.

Maggie's self-actuated drive, ambition, and initiative are consistently represented as admirable traits. The Marshall children are born into their class position, but Maggie creates her own chances for upward mobility. When she is just fourteen, Maggie devises a plan to take herself and her mother from the tenement to a house in the vicinity of the Marshalls' neighborhood. After Maggie patiently nurses one of her mother's boarders, a divinity student by the name of John Howe, through a bout with typhoid fever, he is eager to do something for the Ellersleys to show his appreciation. Maggie already has a detailed proposal in mind: she convinces Howe to continue on as their roomer during the year he has already planned to stay out of school and regain his strength, paying as much of his rent as possible up front, and to write to his acquaintances and persuade them to board with the Ellersleys as well. With the advance rent, which Maggie has reasoned would provide railroad workers with the security of always having a place to stay regardless of the amount of cash they have at any given moment, Maggie and her mother can afford the formidable start-up costs of leasing and furnishing a large house in a respectable black neighborhood. Thus, Maggie achieves her objective of escaping the "Tenderloin" and moving to a part of the city where she can come into contact with "decent people."

When Maggie starts school in her new neighborhood, she is placed in the same eighth-grade class as young Sylvia Marshall. The gregarious Sylvia offers to show the new student around on her first day, and thereafter Maggie becomes her constant companion. Maggie is both fascinated and overwhelmed by the Marshalls' way of life. Her first overnight visit exceeds her wildest expectations as she witnesses a world where daughters brush their hair and dust themselves with talcum powder after their nightly baths, sons wear perfectly polished footwear, mothers with headaches are served breakfast in bed on silver trays, and fathers have fully stocked humidors in their dens: "Maggie looked, listened, stored in her memory" (66). Fauset is careful not to depict Maggie as some sort of pathetic street waif completely alien to the habits of cultivated society. She uses Maggie's humble beginnings to highlight the superficial differences between people based upon class distinctions. Maggie may not be able to afford the lifestyle the Marshalls enjoy—a lifestyle the Marshall children take for granted—but she can weave herself relatively seamlessly into their milieu. As Sylvia's boyfriend Brian reprimands Joanna when she expresses disdain for Maggie's intention to train under the rising "hair culturist," Madame Harkness, "Maggie's as good as any of us. Why look here, she graduated from high school with Sylvia. You can't look down on her" (78). Still, Joanna persists in her effort to distance the family from Maggie, and, most pointedly, discourage Maggie from considering herself a viable love-interest of Philip's. She writes a letter informing Maggie of the Marshall family's "official" disapproval of her as a prospective member of their clan: "You can see that a girl of your lowly aims would only be a hindrance to him. Philip Marshall cannot marry a hair-dresser!" (86–87). However, the narrative voice expresses a gentle condemnation of Joanna's attitude by alluding to Maggie's similarity to Joel, a man who built his modest fortune on the strength of culinary skill acquired as a former slave turned domestic servant.

When Joanna complains of Maggie's lack of "ambition," the narrator points out that Joanna is "forgetting to measure the depth of the abyss of poverty and wretchedness from which Maggie had sprung" (79). As remarkable as Joel's pull-yourself-up-by-your-own-bootstraps story is, Maggie, who is burdened by the added disadvantage of her gender, orchestrates an escape from the miserable existence promised to her by her tenement upbringing through a reliance on her own initiative and ingenuity. Along with the intractable Joanna, Fauset's readers learn that classes are not static, fixed entities, but that the socioeconomic boundaries between groups of people are highly penetrable, imaginary obstacles. Maggie's story is intended to caution the black community, and especially the black privileged minority, from blindly imitating the custom of white America in policing constructed class barriers and practicing elitism. Considering the common heritage of all black Americans in the "peculiar institution," regardless of the timing of or reason for manumission, it is unjustifiable to fault individuals seeking to improve themselves for being too few generations removed from poverty.

Revisiting the Tragic Mulatto

As many scholars have observed, mixed racial ancestry had a very definite impact on class status and social standing in the black community. Willard Gatewood points out that not "all mulattoes belonged to the upper class. Color alone, without proper family credentials, education, or evidences of good breeding and respectability" was insufficient to merit "a passport to the upper stratum of black society."[16] However, as Kevin Kelley Gaines notes, miscegenation produced "African Americans with access to wealth, education, and power, and many of the race's leaders during Reconstruction had emerged from the social advantages that accrued to whiteness."[17] Whereas Fauset's novels certainly encode these historical observations of the collusion of color and class and how they operate to structure social relations in the black community, she displays resistance to the invariably fair-skinned heroine and the reification of color discrimination within the race.

In a radical and daring departure from established literary convention, Fauset takes great pains not to replicate the "fair mulatta" heroine type widely popularized through Harriet Beecher Stowe's *Uncle Tom's Cabin*, and made standard by Hopkins, Harper, Chesnutt, and other turn-of-the-century African-American novelists.[18] As critic Claudia Tate contends, "Without a doubt the ideology of Western beauty had conditioned readers—black and white alike—to expect fair heroines and to bestow sympathy on the basis of the purity of character, aligned to the purity of Caucasoid comeliness."[19] Fauset's first novel boldly resists this audience expectation; the reader is reminded insistently throughout the text of *There Is Confusion* that the principal character, Joanna Marshall, is brown-skinned and scorns the use of artificial methods to straighten her hair. Fauset then divests the traditional pale heroine of her supposedly intrinsic quasi-perfection by encumbering the representative lighter-skinned women in the novel with quintessentially anti-heroic baggage: they are women whose suitors are less than ardent, who get mired in the shameful business of obsessive social climbing, who possess such unenviable qualities as questionable judgment, superficial values, skin color prejudice, working-class poverty, retrogressive domestic servility, and a plebeian work ethic. By contrast, the undeniably brown Joanna is the beneficiary of beauty which requires no cosmetic enhancement, above-average intelligence, artistic talent, healthy ambition, good breeding, solid family values, and natural refinement, all in addition to the requisite unimpeachable virtue. In this way, Fauset both expands the boundaries of acceptable, sympathetic black female characters and reverses the image of the black feminine ideal by severing the "natural" link between desirable attributes and near-white skin tones.

Like her mentor W. E. B. Du Bois, who mused, "Now can there be any question but that as colors bronze, mahogany, coffee and gold are far lovelier than pink, gray, and marble?" Fauset emerged as a strong advocate for the appreciation of the spectrum of skin hues visible in the black community.[20] In her effort to configure a set of culturally autonomous maternal standards, Fauset first and foremost labored to promote and validate images of black femininity which defied the Eurocentric formula for what is aesthetically pleasing. Laurentine Strange of *The Chinaberry Tree* is "a beautiful deep gold" mulatta, while the "maidenly prettiness" of her cousin Melissa Paul shines through "her clear light brown skin, her carefully treated reddish hair, her surprising green eyes, her thin supple figure" (16, 26, 93). Angela Murray of *Plum Bun*, with her "creamy complexion and her soft cloudy, chestnut hair," can pass for white effortlessly, but her type of beauty "pales" in comparison to that of her darker little sister, Virginia, who is distinguished by "the rose and gold of her smooth skin. Her eyes were bright and dancing. Her hair, black, alive and curling, ended in a thick velvety straightness like cut plush" (14, 164). The visible contrast between Angela and Virginia complicates the issue of racial identity and its connection to appearance. The Murray sisters share an identical genetic ancestry, even though they look as if they belong to different races. For social entitlement to be based solely upon the arbitrary distribution of melanin content and hair texture, Fauset demonstrates, is fundamentally unsound.

In the other of Fauset's novels that deals substantively with the phenomenon of passing, *Comedy: American Style*, she similarly uses a woman capable of being taken for white to remark upon the beauty of the browner women of the race. When the exclusive prep school Teresa Cary is attending as a "white" female alerts the student body that a black girl, Alicia Barrett, has been accepted for the following term, it causes quite an uproar on the small campus. In an effort to relieve their apprehensions about having a "colored" classmate, Teresa informs the other girls, "Why, when I was in the graded schools, the prettiest and the most popular girl there was a dark, brown girl; not black, you know, but brown, like—like a young chestnut. Her skin was just as thin. You could see the red under it."[21] Teresa is describing her childhood playmate Marise Davies, who later becomes a critically acclaimed dancer on Broadway, as does *Confusion*'s Joanna Marshall.

The characterization of Joanna as a "rosy brown vision" with "thick crinkling hair" challenges the claim that Fauset devoted her literary talents to the fetishization of Anglo-Saxon facial features, pale skins, and silky tresses (131). Furthermore, it debunks the corollary allegation that she depicted such characteristics as the inevitable genetic property of the black privileged classes. Fauset's effort to fashion admirable darker-skinned black heroines continues a legacy of increasingly resistant portrayals of black femininity by her most significant literary predecessors. Literary critic Hazel Carby has pointed out how, irrespective of the hue of their skins, early black female characters unilaterally become excluded from the "cult of true womanhood" which provided the model criteria governing feminine behavior in the nineteenth century:

> Measured against the sentimental heroines of domestic novels, the black woman repeatedly failed the test of true womanhood because she survived her institutionalized rape, whereas the true heroine would rather die than be sexually abused. Comparison between these figurations of black versus white womanhood also encouraged readers to conclude that the slave woman must be less sensitive and spiritually inferior.[22]

Since surviving degradation was perceived as suspect, rather than a remarkable display of resilience under extremely adverse circumstances, turn-of-the-century black authors set out to reform the literary image of black women who conceive children with white men.

Marie, the mother of Iola Leroy in Frances E. W. Harper's 1892 novel of the same name, is actually the lawfully wedded wife of the father of her children; although she had been his slave, Marie was as fair as any white woman, and her three children never suspected their African ancestry. In Pauline Hopkins's *Contending Forces* (1900), Sappho Clark, born Mabelle Beaubean, is abducted and raped at fourteen by her own uncle, her father's white half-brother. Her uncle deposits her in a brothel, where her father eventually finds her and brings her home. When Mr. Beaubean threatens legal action against his rich, well-connected brother, mob violence is the response. With the exception of the pregnant Mabelle, who is rescued by a family friend and conveyed to the safety of a convent, the entire Beaubean family is brutally murdered. To protect herself, and effectually perform a figurative suicide upon her true identity, Mabelle adopts the name Sappho Clark. Sappho's shame about her past, her illegitimate son, and the sordid circumstances of his conception, are each interrogated through a variety of avenues in the novel, and Sappho's journey to reclaim her child is a moment of epiphany that exonerates her of any culpability in her ordeal, celebrates her strength to overcome her victimization, and demonstrates that love supersedes the violation of conventional morality. As Hazel Carby argues, in order to fit herself for marriage, Sappho Clark had to achieve a reconciliation with her child in order to come to terms with what she had endured as Mabelle Beaubean. "'Mother-love' was present in the text as a process of purification, a spiritual revival that could purge the circumstances of birth and that prepared Sappho for the future."[23] Sappho, along with Hopkins's audience, learns that maternal devotion transcends the socially dictated demands of the "true woman" ideal regarding feminine delicacy.

Charles Chesnutt engages the same issue of the black woman's difficulty in conforming to social convention in his novel *The Marrow of Tradition* (1901). Towards the end of the narrative Chesnutt engineers the discovery of the certificate documenting the legal marriage of Samuel Merkell, a white man, to Julia Brown, his former housemaid. The marriage, which is Julia's firm precondition for continuing to reside in the Merkell home after the death of her former mistress, proves the legitimacy of their daughter, Janet. Janet has long been repudiated by her white half-sister Olivia Merkell Carteret, who is married to their town's most virulent white supremacist, but it is Olivia who finds the marriage certificate long after both her father and his black second wife are dead. The marriage has been kept secret from even the reader; Chesnutt exploits the "traditional" assumption that Julia is Sam Merkell's willing concubine not only by revealing that they had been married but by ensuring that Julia's virtue is unquestioned. Accompanying his will, Merkell leaves a letter addressed to his lawyer which explains in detail why the marriage had never been openly acknowledged: "It was her own proposition that nothing be said of this marriage. If any shame should fall on her, it would fall lightly, for it would be undeserved."[24] Chesnutt's wry plot twist remarks not only upon this particular relationship, for he does not present Julia as an anomalous black woman. Instead, he seems to suggest that moral condemnation is rarely, if ever, justified because we can never be certain we have all of the pertinent information necessary to make an accurate judgment. Chesnutt's larger message notwithstanding, Julia's bold dismissal of the weight of public opinion is meant to be indicative of true virtue, which does not demand social recognition but remains a private covenant between an individual and God.

While Sarah "Aunt Sal" Strange cannot produce a concealed document certifying her legitimate marriage to Colonel Francis Halloway in *The Chinaberry Tree*, Fauset is revisiting Chesnutt's script when she defends the unconventional relationship between Laurentine Strange's parents. Fauset defiantly opts to validate the love they shared not through the socially sanctioned vehicle of marriage, but through various signs of intimacy demonstrating the depth and mutuality of their emotion. Halloway gives Sarah the house where he visits her every day, and when he is on the brink of death he sends his white wife to bring her to his bedside so that he can say goodbye. In his will he makes a provision for Sarah to receive a fixed percentage of the profits from his commercial holdings, not anticipating that his vindictive (and perhaps understandably so) wife would sabotage his business in order to minimize the income of her dead husband's mistress. He even has a chinaberry tree delivered from Sarah's native Alabama planted on the grounds of her house. The tree serves as an everlasting reminder of the strength, vitality, and permanence of their love.[25] Sarah fondly recalls that she had always addressed Halloway as "Frank," attesting to a familiarity that would have been unthinkable had their relationship been akin to the forced submission that proliferated under slavery. Still, literary critic Cheryl Wall laments the fact that the novel does not concentrate more on the Frank and Sal storyline:

> Fauset minimizes the most compelling narrative in the novel. Far more dramatic than the lifeless romance between protagonist Laurentine Strange and Dr. Denleigh or the courtship of the doomed young lovers, Melissa and Malory, is the love story involving the wealthy white Colonel Halloway and the black servant woman, Sal.[26]

Their unsanctioned romance is indeed provocative, but Fauset wants her subject to be the more contemporary issue of how the "unorthodox" sexual choices made by women in the generation immediately following Emancipation impact the status and reputation of their children. Like Chesnutt's Julia Brown before her, Aunt Sal Strange is completely impervious to the disapproving public opinion of her in the town of Red Brook, New Jersey. With Frank she had experienced "a special kind of happiness which many other people would have mistaken for suffering, pain, and disgrace. 'But it suited me,' she thought, smiling impenitently within her wayward heart" (168). Sal's memories are kept largely contained and unarticulated for a reason she herself identifies—she remains silent on the subject for her daughter's sake; she knows that Laurentine is uncomfortable with and shamed by her mother's public notoriety as the late Colonel Halloway's mistress. Laurentine's social position is reminiscent of that of Alice Johnson, whom the famous black surgeon Daniel Hale Williams chose to marry despite the vociferous objections of several mothers of eligible young women in Washington, DC, the "capital of the colored aristocracy" in the late 1800s. Dr. Williams's courtship of Alice incurred the disapproval of the society matrons whose daughters had been overlooked, and who were consequently

> only too ready to cast aspersions on the background of his most frequent companion, the daughter of an inter-racial union, sans wedlock. Irregular relationships of that nature were unacceptable in Washington's colored society. It was too reminiscent of the days of slavery and spoke too directly to the origins that many sought to forget by ultra conservatism and propriety.[27]

Laurentine, of course, also shares quite a bit in common with the outraged mothers of Washington's proper young ladies. Driven by her self-conscious discomfort with her own parentage, Laurentine adopts an "ultraconservative" demeanor and prays obsessively, "Oh God, you know all I want is a chance to show them how decent I am" (36). In *The Chinaberry Tree*, Fauset is less concerned with the probability that real love relationships flourished between black women and white men than with how the modern black community can accommodate the legacy of such "irregular" unions.

Even the scant attention Fauset gives her justification of the love affair between Halloway and Sal is more than we know of the circumstances surrounding the conception of Joshua Bye, son of the Quaker Aaron Bye and his manumitted slave, Judy. The revelation that Joshua had been in reality Aaron Bye's firstborn son comes at the conclusion of *There Is Confusion*, and the only indication we have that the pregnancy may have issued from a consensual relationship is that Judy remained with Aaron Bye and his white family even after she had been freed and proudly assumed his surname as her own. However, her determination to continue living with the Byes could have also been an expression of her refusal to disappear quietly and consequently enable Aaron Bye to abandon his responsibility to their child. Perhaps she wanted her presence with Joshua to serve as a constant reminder to Aaron Bye of his transgression and moral obligation to care for his black family. Judy might possibly have stayed with her former owners because she wanted her son to know his father, even if he were ignorant of their true relationship, and she understood the difficulties she would have encountered trying to provide for herself and her son without the financial support of Aaron Bye. As Fauset illustrates, there are clear and compelling reasons why the "true woman" ideal, derived from a Victorian sensibility and championed by white middle-class America, would have been a largely unattainable goal for black women before the modern era.

Fauset's novels are more concerned, however, with the modern issue of light-skin privilege. Jacquelyn McLendon argues that in *Comedy: American Style*, Olivia Blanchard's negrophobic attitudes issue from her mother passing along her "class/color bias."[28] I am less sure that Janet Blanchard has such a bias; I submit that though Janet disparages "ordinary colored people," she speaks equally contemptuously of "ordinary white people," and she recognizes that the mill town population she brings her daughter to live among are precisely that class of people.

For Janet, passing for white to secure a job at the mill is a matter of practicality, not social aspiration. As the widow of an aspiring doctor who was an acknowledged member of the black elite, the former chambermaid had been thrust into a level of black society to which she had previously been only a spectator, but Lee's death severs her only connection to that exclusive circle. Because she is suddenly rendered a single mother with little formal education and few job skills, she opts for the relative dignity and anonymity of mill work as opposed to returning to domestic labor. Fauset makes it abundantly clear that Janet views her tenure at the mill as a temporary fix and that her ultimate goal is to earn readmission to the black middle class on her own merits. While she is working she begins taking academic courses through Harvard's extension program, and she makes no pretense of trying to assimilate socially into the white working class.

If Fauset holds Janet at all culpable for her daughter's warped mentality, she faults her for her oblivion to the further damage done to Olivia's psyche by exposing her exclusively to white people during her crucial formative years. However, by emphasizing Janet's propensity for the study of psychology, Fauset seems to want to suggest that Olivia's basic character was intact upon birth and that the Blanchards were powerless to change it. Though this interpretation contradicts McLendon's reading of Janet's and Lee's disinterest in their daughter, the scene in which Olivia at four years of age demonstrates her complete indifference to her parents is preceded by an account of their wholehearted devotion to her prior to the incident.

The day trip Lee and Janet take to the beach with another young couple marks the first time they have left little Olivia in the care of a babysitter. Fauset remarks that "All through the lovely drowsy hours the parents had worried" about Olivia's welfare (7). When they return to pick her up, the other couple's children eagerly rush to greet their parents, but Olivia remains preoccupied with her solitary play. Distressed by their daughter's apparent lack of attachment to them, Lee comments to his wife, "it appears to me that your child isn't so fond of us." Janet's reply is a sober "I'm just wondering, Lee, how she can be the child of either one of us. Do you know she's never hung around us or clung to us the way that little Porter boy clung to his mother tonight" (8).

The history of Olivia's emotional remoteness is included to absolve Janet of any personal culpability in the outcome of her daughter's development. To argue that Fauset uses Janet to counteract the supposition that "all women are naturally suited to be mothers" overlooks the fact that Janet remarries and subsequently has twin children (ironically, her mother's second union is the source of Olivia's desire to marry and procreate herself) who grow up to become perfectly well-adjusted, happy young elites.[29] The twins' psychic distance from their older sister is figured most significantly in the novel when they actively maneuver to assist their niece Teresa in outwitting her mother Olivia in order to continue her romance with her "chestnut brown" boyfriend Henry Bates.

The assumption that "Olivia completely accepts her mother's and the dominant body's belief in the inferiority of the 'black' body," duplicates Olivia's error in receiving that belief as Janet's mindset.[30] Janet is attracted to the world of black privilege—the class of refined intellectuals and professionals not absolutely restricted to pale-skinned black people, and Janet does not discriminate on the basis of skin color. Her first marriage, to brown-skinned Lee Blanchard, was not an opportunistic venture, but the expression of pure emotion. Perhaps the more compelling issue raised by the intersection of color and class concerns would involve the black male fetishization of white skin that would motivate a man like Lee Blanchard to defy social conventions and marry outside of his middle class milieu to "rescue" a woman like Janet from poverty and debasement.[31]

The linking of class and color comes under fire most pointedly in *There Is Confusion*, when Fauset inverts the presumption of all positive character attributes being inherited from the white genetic pool. When Peter Bye learns that his great-great-grandfather was the eminent Aaron Bye, he turns to his wife, the former Joanna Marshall, and declares, "See, dear, there is the source of all I used to be. My ingratitude, my inability to adopt responsibility, my very irresoluteness come from that strain of white Bye blood" (297). Peter locates all of the undesirable traits Joanna condemns in him throughout the narrative in his white ancestry. His "ingratitude," Peter reasons, comes from his white forefather, who never adequately demonstrated his appreciation of the black Byes who built his agricultural fortune. Peter's great-grandfather Joshua, a "born agriculturist" with "an uncanny knowledge of planting, of grafting, of fertilizing," dedicates his life to the careful maintenance of the Bye family peach orchards, but instead of his birthright—a share of the family property—he receives only a pittance of compensation for his labor (24). Peter sees his "inability to adopt responsibility" modeled by Aaron Bye's refusal to publicly admit his paternity of Joshua.

On his deathbed, Aaron Bye confesses his secret to his oldest legitimate son, imploring him to rectify the injustice perpetrated by his silence and include Joshua among the heirs to the Bye estate. However, Aaron's son Elmer is appalled by the revelation and privately resolves to disregard his father's final request and tell no one of Joshua's true connection to the Bye family. Then, after all of Elmer's sons are killed in the Civil War, he becomes convinced that "the loss of his sons was a curse upon him because he had failed to obey [his] father's wishes," and he divulges the family secret to his last living brother—the Meriwether Bye who comes to visit Peter and Joanna in their home (296).

The elderly Meriwether's lack of conviction about what to do with the information with which he has been entrusted epitomizes the "irresoluteness" Peter traces back to his white Bye heritage. When Peter asks his great-uncle Meriwether if the offer to designate his son the Bye heir entails an acknowledgment of kinship, the old man becomes flustered: "Surely it would not be necessary—think of my father. What good would it do the boy to know that Aaron Bye's blood flowed in his veins?" (297). Clearly, Meriwether Bye is more concerned about protecting a dead man's reputation than he is about affirming the truth.

Peter's assessment of the elements of his character he owes to his white progenitor constitutes a derisive rebuttal to those members of the mixed-blood black elite who exhibited such pompous pride in their "distinguished" white ancestry. Peter's refusal to accept the inheritance the last surviving white Bye offers his son is both a bold expression of autonomy from white patriarchy and a proud endorsement of the nobility of African character traits. Fauset's version of the tragic mulatto phenomenon ascribes the tragedy not to the injustice of a white-skinned victim of the "one-drop rule" being treated with all of the indignity of other black people, but to the degenerative infusion of white heredity into the black American population.

Celebrating Motherhood and Domesticity

The race leader Anna Julia Cooper was emphatic in her statements about the importance of good mothering: "Woman, mother,—your responsibility is one that might make angels tremble and fear to take hold! To trifle with it, to ignore or misuse it, is to treat lightly the most sacred and solemn trust ever confided by God to human kind."[32] In addition to her impassioned injunctions to women to honor themselves through maternity and to perform the duties of motherhood as an act of spiritual obedience, Cooper rhetorically fashioned mothers into the bedrock of the country as a whole. "The atmosphere of homes is no rarer and purer and sweeter than are the mothers in those homes. A race is but a total of families. The nation is the aggregate of its homes."[33]

Fauset builds upon the sentiments Cooper articulated in her fictional representations of maternity and home life. Perhaps Fauset's most definitive and notable contribution to the African-American literary tradition was the provocative way she made the primacy of the black family, meaning both blood relatives and the extended racial collective, central to her literature; becoming alienated from the family is consistently a source of discord, and seeking reconciliation with the family is invariably key to the achievement of closure in her novels. It is totally unthinkable for a Fauset novel to have a resolution like the one Charles Chesnutt provided for his story "Her Virginia Mammy."

Chesnutt's tale ends when a black mother who has miraculously discovered the daughter from whom she had become separated years earlier in the aftermath of a steamboat explosion, pretends to be the girl's long-lost slave "mammy" in order to safeguard her "white" daughter's impending marriage to a blue-blooded white man. Within Fauset's imaginative universe, where the most necessary prerequisite of true happiness is the faithful preservation of harmonious family relationships, a good mother never disowns her children, and the fabrication of ancestral lineage would never be used in order to manipulate a happy ending. Fauset's conclusions always hinge upon the proper restoration of blood ties and the concomitant process of coming to terms with the truth of one's heritage—an exercise in self-discovery in which mothers play a central role.

Fauset's mothers comprise a fascinating array of character types. Whether revered or reviled, respected or rejected, the mothers she fashions in her novels demonstrate the profound ambivalence she felt for the culturally beloved icon of American maternity. As a woman who never knew her own natural mother (Annie Seamon Fauset died shortly following Jessie's birth), was raised by her father and an understandably preoccupied stepmother (Bella Huff Fauset, a widow, brought three children from her previous marriage into the household, and then proceeded to have three more with Jessie's father), postponed marriage until she was well into middle age (she was forty-seven years old when she wed insurance agent Herbert Harris in 1929), and never gave birth to a child of her own, Fauset may possibly have felt herself ill-equipped to render a fully developed treatment of the maternal figure. Because she so emphatically located her authority to represent black people in fiction squarely within her own black identity and sweepingly dismissed the efforts of white writers to depict black characters as sorely unconvincing, she may have been self-consciously reluctant to claim that same "natural" authority to represent motherhood—a social identity she herself never assumed.

In Fauset's four novels, mothers seldom occupy center stage and often operate in one of two equally troubling modes: they either exert a detrimental influence on their offspring or have a curiously minimized impact on their children's lives. The representational choices Fauset makes in crafting her mothers, though, are excellent signifiers of how she configures the reproduction of class consciousness and the transmission of cultural ideals as well as the cultivation of character traits and personal values.

Historian James Oliver Horton contends that black cultural expectations of maternity began to take shape during the antebellum period when influential black newspapers such as the *Colored American Magazine* and *Freedom's Journal* admonished their readers to conform to the gender conventions of the dominant society. Throughout the era in which Fauset was writing, women were still expected to assume full domestic responsibility for the care of their families. For black people, conformity to such strictures was not only suggested for ease of social interaction between the races but was counseled as a political imperative. Demonstrating to the general populace their worthiness as American citizens required "that each black person ... become a living refutation of the racial stereotypes held by white society."[34] Moral rectitude, personal cleanliness, sobriety, intelligence, industriousness, honesty, and proper etiquette were all held at a premium in the larger struggle for political rights—rights black people were essentially encouraged to earn *ex gratia* rather than demand as an inalienable consequence of free birth. Black people occupied such a precarious position in the American social order that they could ill afford to lead an upheaval of the nation's cultural protocol, as Horton usefully points out:

> During the nineteenth century, as now, black liberation was often defined in terms of the ability of black women and men to become full participants in American life. Ironically, this not only meant the acquisition of citizenship rights, almost all of which were applied only to men, but also entailed an obligation to live out the gender ideals of American patriarchal society. There were surely greater potential advantages in this brand of liberation for black men than for black women.[35]

On account of their sex, women's lives were tightly circumscribed and subject to intense scrutiny. Many women who sought the unorthodox path of a professional career were compelled to either defer or forfeit entirely becoming wives and mothers. As North Carolinian-turned-Harlemite Bessie Delany's mother advised her before she began dental school at Columbia University in 1919, "You must decide whether you want to get married someday, or have a career. Don't go putting all that time and effort into your education and career if you think you want to get married."[36] Delany, who was nearly a decade younger than Fauset, herself remarked that people in the early twentieth century generally did not consider the possibility of a woman maintaining a career while raising a family. "It didn't occur to anyone that you could be married and have a career. … [W]hy would I want to give up my freedom and independence to take care of some man?"[37] Delany also suggests that the driving motivation for marriage was often the desire for children, and childbearing was expected as a social responsibility of the married woman. President Theodore Roosevelt made maternity an act of sincere patriotism when he proclaimed that "The woman who flinches from childbirth stands on a par with the soldier who drops his rifle and runs in battle."[38] The salience of the military analogy is clear, considering this statement was made by the Commander-in-Chief of the United States armed forces, a man who distinguished himself in the Spanish-American War. In a very concrete way, the availability of able-bodied men to serve in the military depended upon the willingness of women to become mothers and supply new baby boys to replenish the soldiers lost in action. In metaphorical terms, the president is suggesting that foregoing one's reproductive capability is an act of cowardice, a neglect of patriotic duty. However, Roosevelt's pronouncement also carries overtones of an allusion to a race war between native-born white people and the minority and ethnic immigrant populations whose birth rates were outstripping those of white natives; since the fertility of black people and immigrants was unquestioned, it is likely that Roosevelt was speaking directly to Anglo-American women—implicating the "race suicide" fear of a threat posed by ethnic and nonwhite people to surpass native white people in numbers, strip them of their majority status, and overthrow their claim to power.[39]

The ominous presage of a massive conflict between the races prefigured the Red Summer of 1919, when the tension arising from the large-scale return of black troops to American soil, and the discontent raised by the inconsistency between black people fighting for "democracy" overseas and returning to undemocratic discrimination at home, erupted into lynchings and race riots in several major cities across the nation.[40] A particularly vicious riot actually preceded the Red Summer; on July 2, 1917, in East St. Louis, Illinois, "four hundred thousand dollars' worth of property was destroyed, nearly six thousand Negroes driven from their homes, and hundreds murdered, a number of them burned alive in houses set afire over their heads."[41] In a Congressional hearing conferred to investigate the incident, the most graphic condemnation of the mob violence was reserved for the atrocities committed against mothers and their children. Congressman William August Rodenberg from Illinois testified that

> In one case, for instance, a little ten-year-old boy, whose mother had been shot down, was running around sobbing and looking for his mother, and some members of the mob shot the boy, and before life had passed from his body they picked the little fellow up and threw him into the flames.
>
> Another colored woman with a little two-year-old baby in her arms was trying to protect the child, and they shot her and also shot the child, and threw them in the flames.[42]

The documentation of this assault upon black motherhood reifies the sentiment Nella Larsen encodes in her novel *Quicksand*. The heroine of the text, Helga Crane, determines to remain childless to avoid "add[ing] any more unwanted, tortured Negroes to America."[43] Jessie Fauset resists the endorsement of a passive submission to this fatalistic philosophy while still maintaining the legitimacy of female choice in childbearing.

During the 1920s, the prevailing "cult of domesticity" had discarded the Victorianist relic of sexually reticent ladies focused on the newest scientific advances in child care, in favor of promoting the ideal of the sensual married woman with no more than two or three children. Simultaneously, "the continual barrage of propaganda launched by sexologists, doctors, and educators in favour of efficient sexuality, motherhood, and childrearing, begun in the 1900s ... had successfully implanted the notion that a woman who did not reproduce was somehow incomplete."[44] In such a maternity-obsessed social climate, Fauset's critique of the Victorian version of motherhood—the selfless, patient, morally pure nurturer to whom the black middle class clung as the panacea for all of the race's woes—was a pointedly feminist endeavor in the sense that it sought to provoke social reform to improve the quality of women's independent lives and make the same sorts of options available to them that were commonly available to men.

As Ann duCille argues in a defense of black writers maligned by "ahistorical" critiques, Fauset's efforts should not be underestimated by modern standards.[45] Considering the history of prominent black people to advocate the wholesale adoption of patriarchal values, for Fauset to have produced narrative alternatives to that script is of landmark significance in the movement to uproot the tenets of patriarchy and Victorianism as the standards for black American home life. Fauset counteracted the Victorian maternal ideal by crafting fictional mothers who deviated from that ideal, and contrasting the actual practice of motherhood in her novels with the perceptions and expectations held by her younger female characters.

By attributing the design of the flattering costumes Joanna wears onstage to her older sister Sylvia, a happily married woman with two small children, Fauset offers us a female character whose creative artistry flourishes unchecked by the drudgery of housekeeping and the duties of mothering, though certainly on a smaller scale than if she were able to devote her full attention to a career in fashion. While admiring Joanna modeling one of the dresses she has made for her, Sylvia jokingly muses, "If Brian just wouldn't treat me right we'd run away to Paris, Jan, and set up a dressmaking establishment. You should be my manikin" (225). The immense potential of her own talent is underscored here as Sylvia figuratively reverses the dynamic of her professional connection to her sister and relegates Joanna to the supporting role in a venture in which she herself is the featured artist. Total immersion in her craft is not what Sylvia really wants, however, regardless of her flippant comments to that effect. Her complete satisfaction in her life with her husband and children, coupled with her ability to channel her creative energy into an outlet that is both manageable and worthwhile, is consistently held up as the model upon which her female peers should pattern their conduct in order to bring fulfillment to all aspects of their own lives.

Joanna evidently recognizes her sister as a positive role model; to reassure Peter of her full commitment to him and the family they intend to build together after she accepts his second marriage proposal, she sobs, "Oh, Peter, you won't ever say again that I'm different from Sylvia" (285). Even so, the comparative ease of Sylvia's life is attributed not as much to her particular temperament, though her identification with her mother is certainly significant, as to the lack of externally imposed obstacles to thwart her romance with her childhood sweetheart Brian Spencer. Conversely, after the years of struggle it takes to sort out her relationship with Peter, Joanna is well equipped to philosophize, "Why, nothing in the world is so hard to face as this problem of being colored in America. ... Oh, it takes courage to fight against it, Peter, to keep it from choking us, submerging us. But now that we have love, Peter, we have a pattern to guide us out of the confusion" (283). Joanna's experiences and observations over the course of the narrative have taught her that Sylvia's chosen alternative of true love, the domesticated romantic connection leading to the natural consequence of marriage and family, is the refuge harboring black Americans from the hardships they will most assuredly encounter, regardless of their relative class status, in the outside world.

For reasons that become clear as we witness Joanna's sustained resistance to the prevailing gender conventions, Fauset wants to minimize Mrs. Marshall's role in Joanna's upbringing. From the outset of the novel, Mrs. Marshall's presence seems to be necessary primarily to help provide an easily identifiable foil for Joanna's characterization; Sylvia is as complete a replica of her mother as Joanna is of her father. Joanna, the fourth and last Marshall child, is the baby Joel is finally permitted to name after himself. Unfortunately, we are not able to determine if Sylvia was named for her mother, because Mrs. Marshall is never referenced by her given name. In fact, much of what the reader can discern about Mrs. Marshall is picked up in bits and pieces over the course of the novel; in contrast to the textual attention devoted to Joel's early life, there is no cohesive narrative of his wife's personal history.

The text reveals that Mrs. Marshall is from Philadelphia, a city with a long history of a free and distinguished black populace, and that she had been a schoolteacher before she married Joel, which indicates that she was well educated. Joel, of course, had little formal education since he was forced to abandon his hopes of attending seminary and becoming a minister when his own mother needed to be nursed through her illness for ten years. So when he met the future Mrs. Marshall, "her precision of language and exactitude in small matters made Joel think again of the education and subsequent greatness which were to have been his. His wife was kind and sweet, but fundamentally unambitious," thereby setting the stage for Joel's affinity with his youngest daughter, who inherits his disdain for mediocrity (13).

Revising the Victorian Maternal Ideal

It is somewhat difficult, however, to determine exactly how Fauset wants her audience to respond to the "kind and sweet, but fundamentally unambitious" Mrs. Marshall. As Ann duCille has noted, "Fauset frequently seems neither to love nor even like many of the men and women she creates."[46] Mrs. Marshall is one of these characters toward whom Fauset displays pronounced ambivalence. On the rare occasion that Joanna credits her mother with having contributed something to her character, the maternal bequest is quickly censured by the narrator. When Joanna discovers that Sylvia's best friend, Maggie, the working class girl from the tenement district, has set her romantic sights on their brother Philip, a single-minded race man who founds a national organization (much like the NAACP) to work towards "the suppression of lynching and peonage, the restoration of the ballot, equal schools, and a share in civic rights," she promptly dashes off a scathing letter to Maggie which effectively and immediately sabotages the incipient union (130). In that letter, Joanna clearly implies that she would not be the only family member opposed to their wedding, should it materialize: "I've often heard my mother say that only people of like position should marry each other, and I hardly think that would be true in the case of you and Philip" (86). When the narrative voice condemns these as "childish cruel words," one might be generous enough to interpret the reprimand as directed solely at Joanna for having repeated her mother's platitude in an effort to alienate, humiliate, and discourage Maggie, but it is surely no accident that Joanna's father is not implicated in the aspect of her personality which tends toward elitism and meanness, and her mother most pointedly is (87).

However, Mrs. Marshall's character is not consistently maligned. Fauset is careful to include details to facilitate an understanding of what might otherwise be interpreted as Mrs. Marshall's particular failings. For instance, although the Victorianist maternal tradition dictates that the mother oversee the early education of her children, and Mrs. Marshall is even a former schoolteacher, it is Joel, we are informed, who teaches Joanna to read. In defense of Mrs. Marshall, then, the text suggests that the difficulties of raising her three older children would have made Joanna's mother more than willing to allow her husband to assume substantial responsibility for their youngest.

Fauset is careful to avoid unrealistically glossing over the genuine effort required to rear small children. Instead, the narrator points out that while Joanna provided a welcome reprieve, since from infancy she was quite content spending considerable amounts of time observing her father work in his home office, "Mrs. Marshall had fretted somewhat over the time and strength expended in caring for the other little Marshalls" (13). The experience of motherhood, though certainly welcomed, is a bit unnerving even for

Mrs. Marshall, who enjoys the decided advantages of having married into financial security. The portrayal of Mrs. Marshall conforms perfectly to the description of the women of her era in *Aristocrats of Color*, historian Willard Gatewood's study of black elites from Reconstruction through the early decades of the twentieth century. "Even though many upper-class women had servants to assist with housekeeping, they spent much of their time and energy in managing their households and on child-rearing and home-related activities."[47] Mrs. Marshall employs the dependable Essie, described as "a fixture in the service of the Marshalls" and encourages her children to have their friends over on the weekends: "Friday and Saturday nights were being regularly set apart for the children's amusement and for the reception and entertainment of the various young people who dropped in" (223, 49).

Mrs. Marshall is clearly not the type of mother who reminds her children of her sacrifices for them, however. While she confides to her daughters that dressing for church each Sunday morning in one of the many beautiful outfits their father had purchased for her had always caused her to reflect upon how fortunate she was to have married him, it is the narrator who interjects the deromanticized version of the typical Sunday routine, one in which Mrs. Marshall is singly responsible for outfitting her four children in their Sunday best and ensuring "they did not break the thousand inhibitions which made the day sacred," while playing the gracious hostess to their inevitable assortment of guests (72). This omniscient intrusion elicits a brief moment of compassion for Mrs. Marshall, the overtaxed and underappreciated wife and mother, but the moment is quickly lost when we turn to the more pressing concerns of the other characters in the novel. Mrs. Marshall then fades quietly again into the background, as is probably befitting a woman who can be described only through her relationships to other people: she is the wife of the eminent Joel Marshall, the devoted mother of Alexander, Philip, Sylvia, and Joanna.

It is Mrs. Marshall who, because she is suffering from the acute pangs of empty-nest syndrome, implores Sylvia and her newlywed husband Brian to take up residence in the Marshall family home after their marriage. Though Philip and Joanna still live with their parents, they are constantly on the road fulfilling the obligations of their demanding careers. Contriving to keep as much of the family as possible under a single roof might have been a device intended to simplify the plot, but by attributing the plan to Mrs. Marshall, Fauset draws attention to what is either her inability or unwillingness to conceive an identity for herself apart from her usefulness to her husband and children.[48] The turn-of-the-century middle-class homemaker is depicted as idle and insular, wary and distrustful of the world looming outside of the haven of her carefully maintained domicile.

Mrs. Marshall cannot comprehend unconventional morality. When she meets Peter's aunt Susan at a church function, the other woman introduces herself as "*Miss* Graves," but speaks of "her boy," leaving Mrs. Marshall genuinely "puzzled," as if she is truly unaware that unmarried women could indeed bear children or at least disconcerted that she would be approached by such a woman in a religious setting (51). Of course, she is placated when she learns that Susan Graves is the maiden sister of Peter's late mother, but Fauset's point about Mrs. Marshall's delicate sensibilities is clearly made. Her delicacy is complemented by her reclusiveness. Unlike Sallie Ellersley, Maggie's working-class single mother, Mrs. Marshall is not credited with having any sustained interests outside of her home.

Mrs. Ellersley, along with her cousin and constant companion Mis' Jinny Sparrow, establishes a routine for herself which completely absorbs the spare time she has left over after fulfilling her duties as proprietor of a thriving, reputable rooming house. When Maggie begs off an open invitation to go out socializing with the women, Mrs. Ellersley protests to her daughter that she and Jinny have "done our share of stayin' in the house in our time"; the narrator elaborates further, explaining that Maggie's mother is now involved in "a life which included much attention to churches, strawberry festivals, lodge meetings, bits of gossip, funerals, visits to ladies similarly faded and wizened, and a sort of shrewd indiscriminate charity," (206). By contrast, Mrs. Marshall's greatest flurry of activity in the novel surrounds the announcement of Sylvia's engagement during a Christmas season, and the attendant planning of the appropriate parties and luncheons. Even so, this action is not given the significance of being described firsthand within the narrative but is mentioned only in passing when Joanna explains to Peter, now a first-year college student in Philadelphia, why she will be so busy while he is back in New York for the Christmas holidays. Mrs. Marshall's character is repeatedly overshadowed in order to highlight the accomplishments of her children. Even in her own well-appointed home Mrs. Marshall is displaced by the discriminating Sylvia, who, with the gift of impeccable taste ostensibly inherited from her mother, completely refurnishes the house.

By neglecting to name or fully develop Mrs. Marshall as a distinct individual, Fauset is able to use her as a generic point of departure from which to figure a variety of models of the modern ideal wife and mother. Mrs. Marshall exemplifies the ideal promulgated by the race leaders of the black middle class as the means by which to improve the social standing of the race and mollify the persistent problems, rooted in the disintegration of the family unit, inhibiting the rate of racial advancement. Mrs. Marshall also exposes the limitations and fallacies inherent in the ideal. She displays the long-term effects of being compelled to abandon a career and concentrate all of her mental and physical energy on the upkeep of her home and the preparation of her children for independence at the moment she agrees to become a wife. Lillian E. Johnson, a charter member of the Detroit Study Club, founded in 1898, reflected forty years later upon the mental lethargy accompanying prolonged involvement in homemaking:

> Our women were not in industry and professions as these of later days, with their clubs and many activities, but moved in a very limited sphere, so no matter how bright a scholar they might have been before graduating from High School or college before marrying and settling down ... they were apt to become so dull by the cobwebs collecting in their brain ... being so engrossed in the care and comfort of their families, as there were few good lectures and meetings of an educational nature. Hence a literary club of this sort ... was an oasis in the weekly routine of duties, eagerly looked forward to by its members.[49]

Joanna exhibits a similar attitude toward the effect of marriage and motherhood on the quality of a woman's life when she remarks that "for a woman love usually means a household of children, the getting of a thousand meals, picking up laundry, no time to herself for meditation, or reading ..." (95). Joanna may base her conclusion on her observations of her own mother, but Mrs. Marshall's fate is not necessarily portrayed as tragic, since she is ideally suited to the role she accepts. The tragedy is that the rigid cultural expectations dissuade many potentially good mothers from having children because they feel they must choose between maternity and their intellectual, professional, artistic, or other worthwhile aspirations. Joanna's revolt from a life like her mother's concretizes this conflict, which concludes with the understanding that maternity must be reconceptualized in a culturally sensitive paradigm in order to avoid the pitfall of alienating progressive women who find the responsibility too constricting. As the younger women in the novel do mature, marry, and have children, it is instructive to compare their experiences with the precedent set by the example of Mrs. Marshall.

Sylvia is an updated version of her beloved mother; she shares Mrs. Marshall's naiveté and essentially rose-colored view of life—Joanna once chastises her, "Oh, Sylvia, you and Brian have had such a simple, easy, jog-trot time of it, you don't know what it means to have your life all broken up like Maggie's and mine have been, and poor Vera Manning's" (289). Sylvia does marry Brian Spencer, her childhood sweetheart, as soon as he completes his Harvard education and settles into the real estate business with Alexander, the eldest Marshall brother. However, Sylvia's life deviates in significant ways from Mrs. Marshall's rather narrow domestic focus. To complement her mother's traits, Sylvia adds her independent interests of fashion design and interior decoration, as well as greater freedom from the minutiae of managing her children—the extended family network liberates Sylvia from the "constant oversight" which constrained her mother. Sylvia retains a reliable motherhood support system even after her parents and sister move out, Peter discovers, when a mutual friend informs him that while Joanna and the elder Marshalls vacated the 135th Street family home to give Sylvia, Brian, and their children their own space, "The kids are always over at Joanna's, though" (278).

Finding Narrative Closure

The ultimate resolution of *There Is Confusion* has generated substantial critical discomfort deriving from what seems to be Fauset's conservative resort to a conventional narrative closing stratagem: she consigns her spirited protagonist to the restricted domain of the home once Joanna enters into matrimony and motherhood. In an effort to lend perspective to the potential for utility in the means by which Fauset opted to resolve her plot, critic Mary F. Sisney names Fauset, along with Nella Larsen, as the pair of writers constituting the "first black novelists of manners."[50] However, by classifying Fauset's work within the genre of novels of manners, Sisney becomes locked into a reading of the characters as performing a traditional whiteness—a point emphasized by her identification of passing as a primary plot activator in novels of manners. In an effort to align Fauset with white women authors who depicted heroines transcending supposedly inflexible class barriers in order to secure a rich, successful husband and the respectable social position he could guarantee, Sisney focuses on the literary representation of color line passing as the catalyst for action in Fauset's novels. Passing, however, is not one of Fauset's primary concerns. She is much more interested in making a claim for the satisfaction and happiness to be derived from black middle-class life.

Passing is decisively rejected in the Vera Manning subplot of *There Is Confusion* as an endeavor of complete self-indulgence and self-fragmentation when ostensibly practiced for one's own convenience. Vera avows that she begins passing in order to "get away from everybody and everything I'd ever known," following her break-up with Harley Alexander but pronounces it an empty lifestyle, except that she no longer has to worry about being victimized by racism (198). Laurentine Strange, the heroine of *The Chinaberry Tree*, though it is remarked she is virtually identical to her white half-sisters, never once considers pretending to be white for temporary convenience or living as a white woman. Even in the novels where passing is more of a central concern—*Plum Bun* and *Comedy: American Style*—the practice is neither endorsed nor permitted to succeed as a strategy to secure social advancement.

The Fauset plot, then, is principally activated not by passing but by the same stimuli operating in the classic literary comedy: protracted reconciliations of interpersonal relationships problematized by a series of miscommunications and misunderstandings. Even so, a good marriage is never the sum of a Fauset woman's ambition; if she misguidedly harbors such romanticized notions, she is soundly cured of them by the end of the novel. Effectively reversing standard renditions of gendered perspectives, Fauset depicts antiquated domestic fantasies of complete marital fulfillment, typically the domain of the female, as principally articulated by men. A scene from *There Is Confusion* illustrates how Joanna and Peter's engagement has become threatened by the change in his attitude regarding marital expectations. After they finish a lunch she prepares for him at her house, Joanna solicits Peter's help in clearing the table, but he is reluctant. "He lounged in his chair. 'Oh, come, Joanna, I'm used to being waited on, not doing the waiting'" (151). When she incredulously presses him to account for his unanticipated refusal, "He spoke from a contented reminiscence. 'When I have dinner at Maggie Neal's, she's not everlastingly asking me to do this and do that. "Sit still, Peter," she says, "this isn't a man's work"'" (152). Only after Peter has become engaged to Maggie does he realize that the bare prospect of a life with a woman who will wait upon him hand and foot is empty in comparison to a life with Joanna, the woman he genuinely loves and respects.

When Joanna and Peter finally establish their own family, Fauset begins to engage in what some critics have interpreted as unconvincing textual maneuvering in order to bring closure to the novel. The success-driven Joanna submits herself to become first Peter Bye's wife, then baby boy Meriwether's mother, and she finds that she "surprised herself by the pleasure which came to her out of what she had always considered the ordinary things of life. Realizing how nearly she had lost the essentials in grasping after the trimmings of existence, she experienced a deep, almost holy joy in the routine of the day" (290). Thadious Davis has protested that "Despite her rationale, Joanna's reversal comes too completely and too abruptly" (xxi). Critical consensus tends to support Davis's contention that there is insufficient motivation for Joanna's change of heart; Cheryl Wall suggests that "Joanna quickly grows disillusioned with her success" in order "[t]o meet the demands of the marriage plot."[51]

While the modern female sensibility may bristle at the feisty Joanna's perceived retreat into convention and find her "sudden" conversion improbable, her decision to marry Peter is not completely unforeseeable; Joanna's eventual discontent with her career is repeatedly foreshadowed over the course of the narrative. She implies early on in their courtship that the pursuit of celebrity is a way to occupy her time while Peter is away at school. Without her career she could easily have fallen victim to the "lack of interest and purpose on the part of girls which brought about hasty marriages which terminated in—no, not poverty—mediocrity" (146). Here, Joanna clearly suggests that she expects her singing and dancing to act as only a temporary preoccupation designed to prevent her from rushing into a premature wedding to an unestablished fiancé. When Peter begins to flounder and lose focus, thinking he might drift into playing the piano professionally instead of finishing his surgical training, Joanna breaks off her engagement with Peter as a stratagem designed to push him into resuming his medical studies. When Peter sends her a letter suggesting they get married immediately and he could travel with her as her musical accompanist, Joanna precipitously dispatches a disgusted refusal: "I don't want and won't have a husband who is just an ordinary strumming accompanist, playing one, two, three, one, two, three. Sometimes, Peter, I think you must be crazy" (145). Unfortunately, Joanna's plot backfires, and Peter becomes engaged to Maggie, who demands virtually nothing of him.

When she finally finds out about Peter's new marital plans, Joanna is completely devastated. Losing Peter alters her outlook on life: "What did a knowledge of singing, dancing, or any of the arts amount to without people, without parents, brothers, sisters, lovers to share one's failures, one's triumphs?" (177). Joanna reevaluates her priorities and decides that sustaining closeness with the people most important to her must take precedence over professional ambitions. Even so, Joanna does not experience an absolute metamorphosis when she marries Peter. While superficially she does appear to eagerly assume her supporting role, Joanna retains power within her household by projecting her drive for preeminence onto her husband, surreptitiously manipulating and molding Peter into the man she needs and wants him to be: "In a thousand little ways she deferred to him, and showed him that as a matter of course he was the arbiter of her own and her child's destiny, the fons et origo of authority" (292). Joanna perceives her covert cultivation of Peter into the ideal husband and father as part of the practice of competent and responsible mothering. She must perform the maternal function of inculcating the proper values into Peter because his own mother, Alice

Graves, had died in childbirth, leaving him without her guiding influence. Peter's father, one of the novel's four Meriwethers, gradually squanders away the considerable wealth his father Isaiah had amassed, and rears his son to adopt the credo: "The world owes me a living." As a further detriment to combating Peter's lack of responsibility, Miss Susan Graves, Alice's older sister, takes in Peter when he is just twelve, after the death of his father. Aunt Susan is well-meaning but unexacting, afraid of making Peter feel as if he is indebted to her in exchange for his place in her home. So, unlike the conscientious Marshall boys, who get jobs during the summer to help finance their college expenses, Peter is never expected or encouraged to work to support himself, and he never learns the value of diligent labor. Peter's aversion to effort and discipline is what makes him so comfortable with Maggie, who expects so little of him.

Fauset's critique and broad revision of traditional gender roles within marriage rehearse the institution within the context of the narrative, rather than making the achievement of the wedding the climactic moment in the novels. This presents a departure from the classic novel of manners, which neglects to address the potential pitfalls of adjusting from the rituals of courtship to the permanence of a marriage. Characters in Fauset novels usually endure long engagements, many times to the "wrong" people, and some even survive bad marriages in order to clarify their own expectations from a prospective partner. Relationships are invariably learning experiences, as becomes clear in the case of Dr. Stephen Denleigh, Laurentine Strange's eventual suitor, who comes to their relationship as a survivor of a bad marriage to a selfish woman:

> Her father, mother, brothers had indulged her from birth. She didn't know what self-denial, or self-control meant. I wasn't much better. And when she found she couldn't get her own way with me, she went to some one from whom she thought she could ... and from him to another and then to another. I hated her for betraying me ... she hated the man whose severity and lack of understanding forced her into that betrayal.[52]

Interestingly enough, what precipitated the ultimate failure of Denleigh's first marriage was the same deceiving lure that enticed Peter away from Joanna: the illusory performance of a perfect domesticity. Denleigh wryly remembers "the tempting welcome given to young fellows, homesick and lonely and on their uppers! The Sunday night suppers, the pleasant mother, the hospitable father, the ravishing girl..." (156–57). Denleigh's wistful recollection doubles as Fauset's embedded criticism of the superficiality of many black "society" marriages, as "pleasant" and "hospitable" parents get into the business of ensnaring promising young men to wed their daughters. The supposed refuge of marriage is shown to be superfluous for Laurentine, however. Having endured one disastrous courtship with a man whose concern for his public image made a marriage proposal to her impossible, when Laurentine becomes the eminently respectable Dr. Denleigh's publicly acknowledged fiancée in spite of her scandalous family history, she declares he has by that gesture alone empowered her to find happiness on her own. "You restored me; you made me respect myself. You made me alive to my own inner resources. No matter what fate may spring on me, Stephen, I can never be that wretched, diffident, submissive girl again" (204). Laurentine's dismissal of marriage as the primary goal of her existence, the defining feature of her hope for inclusion in an exclusive social circle, is only emphasized by the ongoing debate throughout the novel regarding the nature of the extramarital romance between Laurentine's parents, the Southern-born black housemaid, Sarah "Aunt Sal" Strange, and the lordly young scion of her wealthy white employers, Colonel Francis Halloway. The final word on the subject puts the circulating speculations to rest. When Aunt Sal is finally certain that her daughter and her niece have found love as she had once experienced it, "suddenly she felt free to think of her dead lover,—with ease and gratefulness and the complete acceptance which had always made their lack of conformity of absolutely no moment" (340). Her private reminiscence of the deep mutual love she and "Frank" had shared exonerates Aunt Sal of being stigmatized as a social pariah and eliminates any lingering suspicions of her having simply been an easy target of Halloway's tawdry lust.

The restitution of Aunt Sal's character in *The Chinaberry Tree* is more convincing than the final resolution of *There Is Confusion*, which, despite the liberal foreshadowing of Joanna's conversion throughout the novel, still retains the feel of an appended revision. The humbling of the proud, ambitious Joanna Marshall does seem disconcertingly sudden, and Fauset appears to acknowledge as much in her choice of imagery—she describes her heroine's former obsession as a fully removable external mechanism. The narrator alleges that Joanna "had always had these possibilities of domesticity. Her desire for greatness had been a sort of superimposed structure which, having been taken off, left her her true self" (291). Throughout the closing chapters of the novel, there appears to be an almost self-conscious embarrassment perceptible in Fauset's belabored effort to justify the change in her protagonist. Critic Nina Miller has suggested that "the tang of masochism" pervading Joanna's renunciation of her former attitudes and priorities "raises the spectre of Fauset's own discomfort with the marital 'happiness' she has bestowed upon her heroine."[53] Miller reads the working-class Maggie's marriage to the dying Philip and the promise of her entrepreneurial prosperity and personal tranquility in widowhood as a "companion fantasy" compensating for the imposed retreat from public engagement characterizing Joanna's position within the middle-class family.

In a similar fashion, the pedigreed, refined Joanna produces a son for Peter while Maggie remains childless, and consequently not tied to the Marshall clan by blood. Miller concludes that "Within the new regime of eugenic family values, ... Maggie must finally be peripheral to the racial future."[54] The globally based eugenics movement, which stressed selective reproduction among the more desirable elements of society in order to improve the genetic quality of the human race, generally considered black people as a racial collective among the populations to be contained. Fauset may be invoking the concern within the African-American community that the more prosperous, better-educated, and higher-status black people were sustaining a much lower birth rate than other segments of the race. It is much more likely, however, that she would have been a supporter of the euthenicist position, outlined in Ben Lindsay's *The Revolt of Modern Youth*, another Boni and Liveright title published in 1925, the year following *There Is Confusion*. The euthenicists promoted the improvement of the public environment, rather than restricting births among the "less fit" as the preferred strategy for social elevation.[55]

Beth McCoy pushes her interpretation of the novel beyond Miller to argue that Fauset's forced, provokingly artificial resolution of *There Is Confusion* is a deliberate construct which has been misunderstood because it has been taken too literally; McCoy contends that Fauset's "saccharine and ironic conclusion martyrs Joanna" to the demands of an oppressive patriarchy in which she is finally supplanted by her husband in her father's estimation: "Joel was as proud of Peter as he had been of Joanna" (290). McCoy marks the moment in which Joanna solicits her father's opinion of the version of "greatness" she had achieved, and he, "his voice half glad, half sorry, told her that he, too, had hoped for something different," as the event which catalyzes her retreat into traditional domesticity and her vicarious pursuit of success and significance through her husband (236).

> *There Is Confusion* thus articulates a need for self-constructed black female identity where neither a pastiche of dominant culture's metanarratives nor a naive faith in the transcendence of "art" or "individual" will do. Under the weight of "universal" ideologies denying the agency of race, gender, and sexuality, women like Joanna are doomed to collapse; they must sink by

default into marriage, the only plausible literary and/or sociohistorical closure remaining.⁵⁶

This interpretation of Joanna's reversion makes the household she forms with Peter a satiric parody rather than an optimistic picture of the ideal nuclear family unit, and Joanna's clandestine machinations to outfit Peter for his succession to her inherited yearning for "greatness" appear more pathetically parasitic than subversively powerful. It is important to note, however, that Fauset lays the blame for Joanna's ineffectualness not to her heroine's lack of ability, talent, or determination but to society's unwillingness to permit her to occupy the position of distinction she seeks. Instead, Joanna shares her brand of fame not with Sojourner Truth, Harriet Tubman, or Phillis Wheatley, the women she idolizes from her youth, but with a "dark colored girl wearing Russian boots and a hat with three feathers sticking up straight, Indian fashion. ... Lenox Avenue stared, pointed, laughed and enjoyed itself" (274). Joanna sees herself through the eyes of the white crowd on the street as nothing more than an exotic novelty who will fade from the public memory as quickly as the anonymous spectacle with the feathers in her hat.

Fauset is also making a comment upon the potential of the performing arts to make a lasting impact on American race relations. Early in the novel Joanna dreams of her future as a sort of ambassador between the races, showcasing the considerable artistic capabilities of African Americans. She declares to her future brother-in-law Brian Spencer, "I want to show us to the world" (76). She is further inspired to pursue what she perceives as her calling at a concert she and Brian attend later that evening, where Joanna marvels at the capacity of music to dissipate racial antagonism. "Did you see that white woman next to me edge away when I sat down? But when she heard me humming after it was over, she leaned over and asked me if I knew the words" (77). The aversion the white woman feels for Joanna, like a naturalized reflex, is overcome by her recognition of Joanna as a person of culture, one who comprehends the universal high-brow language of the fine arts.

When Joanna is selected to portray "America" in an off-Broadway production called *The Dance of the Nations*, however, the problem of color resurfaces. The white producers of the show are concerned about personifying America with a black woman; they are wary of how the public would react to such a subversive political statement about the representative American identity. As a potential manager explains to Joanna earlier in the novel, "America doesn't want to see a colored dancer in the role of a *première danseuse*. ... She wants you to be absurd, grotesque" (148). Sylvia solves the dilemma by suggesting that Joanna perform the dance while wearing a mask. The scene in which Joanna takes the stage and ingratiates herself to a white audience by concealing her blackness invokes the history of the minstrel tradition that proliferated in New York City from the early decades of the nineteenth century. Historian Robert Toll names New York as "the birthplace of the minstrel show."[57] Fittingly, then, Fauset uses Joanna's experience to invert the legend of famed "Ethiopian Delineator" Thomas D. Rice, who learned to "jump Jim Crow" by watching an old, crippled black man singing and dancing, and subsequently innovated a stage act which "created a public sensation and took him on a triumphant tour of major entertainment centers."[58]

Joanna learns the "Barn" dancing game she performs for her *Dance of the Nations* audition from observing black children frolicking in the New York City streets. By elevating the street dance to the realm of legitimate art, Joanna reconfigures the common practice of white people exploiting the raw materials of indigenous black folk expression by perverting and then marketing them to white audiences enraptured by the primitivistic interpretations. Fauset uses the scenario to advocate the beauty and intrinsic merit of black culture and to encourage black people to take pride in and draw on the elements of their heritage in making viable contributions to the American arts. Instead of perceiving blackness as a symbol of shame and degradation, Fauset proposes an alternative vision of blackness as a source of authenticity, innocence, and purity of form. However, when one of the spectators at Joanna's debut as the featured dancer leads an encore, demanding that she unmask herself, the audience is shocked at the unexpected revelation of her blackness:

> There was a moment's silence, a moment's tenseness. Then Joanna smiled and spoke. "I hardly need to tell you that there is no one in the audience more American than I am. My great-grandfather fought in the Revolution, my uncle fought in the Civil War, and my brother is 'over there' now." (232)

Still, Fauset is careful to remain within the realm of plausibility: "Perhaps it would not have succeeded anywhere else but in New York, and perhaps not even there but in Greenwich Village, but the tightly packed audience took up the applause again and Joanna was a star" (232). Joanna establishes her claim to Americanness in terms of demonstrative patriotism—a patriotism evidenced by a consistent record of participation in military action in defense of the nation. Her optimism regarding her ability to use her dancing as a means of reconditioning white America to recognize the merits of its black citizens is at its highest following the enthusiastic reception of this speech from the audience at the District Line Theater.

Unfortunately, all of Joanna's illusions about the power of the fine arts to conciliate the rift between the races are shattered by the end of the novel when she laments her inability to turn her talent "to the advantage of her people" (274). The scope of Joanna's influence is too narrow, too fleeting, and too inconsequential, as she discovers when the momentary recognition she receives on Lenox Avenue is abruptly displaced and supplanted by the exhibitionistic appearance of the black girl in the Indian-feather hat. Not only is high-brow art insufficient, but its effect is negated by the more common scenarios of African Americans in less flattering postures. As McCoy points out, however, Fauset's task in *There Is Confusion* is only to identify the dilemma facing the black woman who seeks to reconcile professional ambition with the biological imperative to reproduce. It is in her later novels that she works through possible solutions. But love and happy marriages are the objects of derision and contempt in the novels written by Fauset's contemporary, Nella Larsen. As the next chapter will argue, Larsen's narratives continuously challenge domestic harmony and question the wisdom of motherhood for black American women.

3 Elite Rejection of Maternity in Nella Larsen's *Quicksand* and *Passing*

Jessie Fauset may have been optimistic about the potential of the well-managed nuclear family to prevail as the most certain strategy for black people to gain an unmitigated welcome into the bastions of American public respectability, but Nella Larsen was decidedly and emphatically skeptical. Instead of showcasing positive images of the modern, fashionable black woman expertly functioning as wife and mother within her upwardly mobile family, Larsen's novels persistently dramatize the complications to motherhood generated by what W. E. B. Du Bois called "the problem of the color line"—in so scathing a fashion that one would be hard-pressed to read her intent as anything other than to firmly denounce any woman's desire to bring more black children into the racially hostile social climate of 1920s America.[1]

Larsen's pair of published novels, *Quicksand* (1928) and *Passing* (1929), are deft explorations of the overabundance of contradictions inherent in the black experience of middle-class life, including the failure of prestige within the black community to carry over into the wider society; the perplexing inability of an elevated lifestyle, refined manners, and impressive achievements to overcome racial discrimination, objectification, and phobic hatred; and the replication of color prejudice and skin color hierarchy within an intraracial context. For black elites, many of the social benefits that should reasonably have been attached to their class status were effectively negated by their racial identity. Larsen frames many of the contradictions she exposes between class and racial entitlements within the context of maternity.

Motherhood is the ideal vehicle for Larsen to use to explore the tensions of black middle-class culture because it affects the personal autonomy of the women she centers in her narratives; it forms the definitive trope of the domesticity through which women traditionally established a legitimate and respectable social identity, and it constitutes the pivotal point of conflict between romanticized fantasies of home-centered bliss and rational assessments of the social conditions to which one's child would assuredly be subjected. Larsen's characters have very complicated responses to the prospect and experience of motherhood: they are emotionally conflicted about whether they should have children and how best to raise them, at least in part due to the troubled, superficial, or nonexistent relationships they have experienced with their own mothers. *Quicksand* explores the impact an emotionally distant white mother has upon her biracial daughter, while *Passing* features heroines whose dominant parental influences are their fathers.

In *Quicksand*, Helga Crane's inability to find her niche in the world is firmly rooted in her unresolved, unresolvable conflict with her Danish mother, Karen Nilssen. Though Karen Nilssen has died of an undisclosed cause seven years before the novel even opens, she maintains a disturbing presence throughout the novel. Helga's obsessive thoughts of her mother resurface during her frequent instances of psychological distress, nagging dissatisfaction, sensory paralysis, and/or preemptive flight from her surroundings. Helga romantically envisions her white immigrant mother as a "fair Scandinavian girl in love with life, with love, with passion, dreaming, and risking all in one blind surrender" to Helga's black father, the "gay suave scoundrel" who abandons his young daughter and her mother for reasons Helga seems not at all concerned with making an effort to unearth.[2] While she often expresses regret over the impact her parents' separation had upon her childhood, Helga never articulates a desire to locate her biological father nor contact her paternal relatives.

In an interview with Dr. Robert Anderson, the principal of Naxos, the Southern black school where she teaches at the beginning of the novel, Helga dismisses her father as "a gambler who deserted my mother" (55).[3] She also admits that she herself is unsure whether her parents ever lawfully married, perhaps insinuating that her father is not the sort of man she would even care to know in the event the opportunity were to present itself.[4] She consistently characterizes her mother as having been victimized and degraded by her father. According to Helga, her mother was "gently bred, fresh from an older, more polished civilization, flung into poverty, sordidness, and dissipation" (56). Helga conceives her mother's eventual marriage to a bigoted white man as a "grievous necessity": her father's fault for having deserted his young family, and her own fault, since "even unloved little Negro girls must be somehow provided for" (56). Helga methodically rationalizes her mother's emotional ambivalence toward her. She fully absolves Karen Nilssen of responsibility for subjecting her to the "jealous, malicious hatred" and "savage unkindness" of her cruel stepfather and his children from a previous marriage and for failing to protect, nurture, and demonstrate affection for her. Instead of blaming her mother, she scapegoats her own dark skin.

For nine difficult years, from the impressionable age of six until her mother's death when she is fifteen, Helga is thrust into an antagonistic, contemptuous, unceasingly white social milieu. Without the support of her mother as an ally, she develops a system of defense mechanisms that effectually function to undercut her ability to see herself as a worthwhile individual. She recalls her "childish self-effacement" and the nine years in her stepfamily "passing in one long, changeless stretch of aching misery of soul" (56, 57). Then, after his sister's death, Helga's maternal uncle Peter mercifully sends his niece down to Nashville to a black boarding school, where in adolescence she finally "discovered that because one was dark one was not necessarily loathsome, and could, therefore, consider oneself without repulsion" (57).

Unfortunately, contact with the privileged black students of Devon does not rid Helga of her inferiority complex but reinforces it. She is painfully conscious of the distinction between herself and her schoolmates, with their close-knit families, their exclusive social circles, their similar backgrounds, and their distinguished ancestral bloodlines. Helga conceptualizes blackness as an assault upon white "purity" and associates it exclusively with "poverty, sordidness, and dissipation." Consequently, she comes to terms with her mother's emotional withdrawal from her by simultaneously externalizing it through the identification of the primary cause as a feature of her physiognomy rather than a flaw of her personality, and internalizing it through the recognition of herself as the visual sign of offending blackness and the repository of the "inferior" strain of African blood.

Neither Irene Redfield nor Clare Kendry of *Passing* have such thoroughly flawed relationships with their mothers. As Martha J. Cutter has noted in her discussion of the different figurations of passing in the two novels, in many ways *Quicksand* "stands in direct contrast" to *Passing*.[5] So, conversely to Helga Crane, Irene and Clare identify primarily with their fathers, which introduces a different set of maternal issues. Irene's mother is alive throughout her youth, but she is mentioned briefly only a few times in the narrative; she dies before the primary action of the novel takes place. While Mrs. Westover is not overtly criticized or maligned, her impact upon Irene is clearly unequal to that of her husband.

Irene's father is depicted as a paragon of virtue: he is loyal, thoughtful, and scrupulously discreet. When one of Irene's brothers asks him how Clare's father, Bob Kendry, managed to descend down the socioeconomic ladder from being in college with many of the well-situated men in their circle to winding up an alcoholic janitor, Mr. Westover firmly replies, "That's something that doesn't concern you" (183). Irene's father remains friends with Kendry despite the difference in their relative class status and exerts himself to investigate what has happened to Clare when she abruptly stops coming around to visit the Westover family a few years after her father's untimely death. Even Clare herself demonstrates respect for Mr. Westover's discretion. When she expresses regret that her white aunts might have informed Irene's father of their suspicion that Clare had run away from their home to "live in sin," which would have diminished his opinion of her, Irene assures her, "I'm not sure that they did. ... He didn't say so, anyway." Then Clare promptly replies, "He wouldn't, 'Rene dear. Not your father" (190).

Clare Kendry likely envies Irene her polished, socially respected father, as well as the material possessions she so readily admits to having coveted.[6] It is highly improbable that Irene was ever compelled to defend her father from the taunts of her schoolmates, a feat Clare "savagely" accomplishes when a group of boys "had hooted her parent and sung a derisive rhyme, of their own composing, which pointed out certain eccentricities in his gait," likely arising from his drunkenness (173). Bob Kendry, the illegitimate son of an unscrupulous white man and an anonymous black woman, raises his daughter all alone. Clare's mother is mentioned only twice in the novel, once when a group of young people are discussing the potentially scandalous implications of their sightings of Clare among wealthy white people after she has left the South Side to live with her maiden aunts: "Poor girl, I suppose it's true enough, but what can you expect? Look at her father. And her mother, they say, would have run away if she hadn't died" (182). The other reference comes when Irene is scrutinizing Clare's face for some feature even remotely betraying her African heritage, and finally fastens upon her arresting "Negro eyes": "Yes, Clare Kendry's loveliness was absolute, beyond challenge, thanks to those eyes which her grandmother and later her mother and father had given her" (191). Other than those fascinating eyes, however, Clare's mother is not credited with having given her anything.

The absence of a maternal influence perhaps accounts for certain elements of Clare's personality. Most pointedly, once both of her parents are dead, Clare, like Helga Crane, has no "people," no natural connection to the black community and nothing to hinder her from straying across the color line to pursue her fortune as a white woman. Clare is self-serving and manipulative, qualities she boldly acknowledges to Irene when she warns her ominously: "Why, to get the things I want badly enough, I'd do anything, hurt anybody, throw anything away. Really, 'Rene, I'm not safe" (240). Interestingly enough, Clare stops short of the lengths to which her own mother was reputedly willing to go—she refuses to abandon her daughter. Though she claims she lacks "any proper morals or sense of duty," her concern for twelve-year-old Margery is "all that holds [her] back" from deserting her white husband and moving to Harlem (240, 266).

Irene, on the other hand, grew up in a solidly middle-class two-parent home. She had what she considers an ideal childhood—her life was predictable; her father still lives in the same house she knew as a child. She was comfortable and secure, associated with the right people, and was in a position to be courted by a man of co-equal social status with the elite Westovers. When Irene marries Brian Redfield, a young doctor, she fully expects to replicate the life she perceives her parents to have provided for her. She and Brian move to New York and proceed to have two sons while he is establishing his practice. Recalling the smooth operation of the household of her youth, Irene attempts to institute the same order in her own home. She wants to be the type of wife and mother Mrs. Westover was, but contrary to the fulfillment of her illusions, Brian Redfield is not at all interested in becoming a clone of Irene's father. Brian despises the hypocrisy and hostile racial climate of America and wants to move his family to Brazil, where he believes they can enjoy a better quality of life. Irene, however, will not hear of it. Instead, she deludes herself into the conviction that she and Brian are enjoying a companionate marriage akin to the one her parents shared. Brian eventually gives up his campaign to emigrate to South America, but "his dissatisfaction had continued, as had his dislike and disgust for his profession and his country" (218). Irene rationalizes her absolute refusal to abide by Brian's decision by convincing herself that she can discern Brian's true needs better than he himself, and though he may not be able to recognize it, it is actually in her husband's best interest, as well as their sons' and her own, that she resist him. Larsen's repeated narrational emphasis on qualifying phrases like "so she insisted," "she assured herself," and "as she saw it" make it impossible to overlook that this account is Irene's interior monologue and not an impartial observation of the state of affairs between the Redfields. In fact, the narrative sequence immediately preceding Irene's inaudible soliloquy describes the usual morning routine in the Redfield household, and it seems anything but warm and loving. Brian rises and drives the boys to school before Irene manages to get out of bed, they are both on edge due to the fact that Irene is chronically late; their buried conflict over Brazil manages to resurface, and again gets promptly suppressed in their breakfast conversation, and Brian speaks to Irene in "his usual slightly mocking tone," suggesting that he has long resigned himself to a lifetime of bitterly playing out a charade of a marriage (217). Brian may be able to furnish a spacious home, servants, fine clothing, and the means for Irene to assume her role as a popular society matron, but their quality of life is patently superficial. Compared to the prototypical Westovers, who habitually share confidences "in the privacy of their own room," the Redfields' separate bedrooms, terse conversations, and violently conflicting ideologies all demonstrate that Irene is completely misguided in her belief that she is the competent mistress of a model middle-class household.[7]

Even more disturbing than the effect Helga's, Clare's and Irene's relationships with their mothers have on their interactions with men, is the effect they have on their attitudes toward raising children. As a result of their traumatic—and for Irene, traumatically idealized—childhood experiences, none of the women is emotionally equipped to function as a good mother.

Maternal Effacement in *Quicksand*

Helga Crane's extreme wariness of motherhood is ultimately justified by her experience—the enormous personal toll maternity exacts from her all but obliterates her as an individual. *Quicksand* inscribes the conflict between Helga's shifting attitudes toward the rationality of maternity in the black community and her own unfulfilled desires to establish a home and family. In addition to the sociocultural factors, Helga has two major psychological impediments that prevent her from wholeheartedly embracing her maternal instinct[8]: her biracial heritage causes her to be deeply troubled by America's racial hierarchy, and her emotional alienation from her mother compels her to isolate herself emotionally from other people. From the outset of the story, Larsen presents Helga as an aloof young woman who routinely substitutes the fetishization of material belongings for the development of close interpersonal relationships. Helga as we first see her is an isolated figure surrounded by an assortment of her cherished objects:

> [A] single reading lamp, dimmed by a great black and red shade, made a pool of light on the blue Chinese carpet, on the bright covers of the books which she had taken down from their long shelves, on the white pages of the opened one selected, on the shining brass bowl crowded with many-colored nasturtiums beside her on the low table, and on the oriental silk which covered the stool at her slim feet. (35)

Larsen's deliberate attention to the minute details of Helga's surroundings and the precise description of her personal habitat establish Helga both as an expert consumer and an alluring spectacle. It is as if Helga is on public display, and she herself designed the set. She is in her living quarters at Naxos, the Southern black school where she is employed as an English teacher, plotting her escape from the educational institution she has grown over the course of nearly two years to violently abhor. The next morning, her colleague Margaret Creighton comes to find out why Helga has not emerged from her room for breakfast, ultimately reifying her friend's objectified status on the sober campus: "I do wish you'd stay. It's nice having you here, Helga… . We need a few decorations to brighten our sad lives" (49).

Despite Helga's compassion for the Naxos students—"those happy singing children whose charm and distinctiveness the school was so ready to destroy"—she is determined to resign her position immediately, convinced that her attempts to help them are completely futile (40). The very name Naxos, an anagram of "Saxon," is a wry reference to the bungled attempts of the institution to recondition its student body into imitations of its white benefactors.[9] In choosing the name Naxos, Larsen might also be demonstrating her derision, having been a student at Fisk University's high school and a staff member at Booker T. Washington's Tuskegee Institute, for the restrictive policies and militaristic regime mandated within black schools that effectively replicated the very social system they ostensibly sought to dismantle. "[Naxos] was, Helga decided, now only a big knife with cruelly sharp edges ruthlessly cutting all to a pattern, the white man's pattern" (39). Larsen's satiric portrait of Naxos makes the school complicit in the implementation of a white supremacist agenda—an agenda very clearly articulated by the visiting white preacher whose address from the school's chapel the entire "educational community" is required to attend one spring afternoon. Witnessing his paternalistic speech and the enthusiastic outpouring of appreciation which it elicits galvanizes Helga's decision to submit her mid-term resignation to the president of Naxos. "She could no longer abide being connected with a place of shame, lies, hypocrisy, cruelty, servility and snobbishness" (48). Having no family to welcome her return, she returns to her native Chicago to try building a life for herself in the urban North. She seeks an inroads into the closed circle of Chicago's black elite society by attending the "very fashionable, very high services" of an exclusive black Episcopalian congregation, but none of the parishioners dares to breach "that faint hint of offishness which hung about her and repelled advances, an arrogance that stirred in people a peculiar irritation" (66). Helga's unapproachability is attributed to a defense mechanism acquired during her youth, which she spent living among people who resented her presence. In a pathetic display of self-deprecation, Helga even acknowledges that "she understood and sympathized with … her mother's, her stepfather's, and his children's points of view. She saw herself for an obscene sore in all their lives, at all costs to be hidden" (62). Helga refuses to hold her mother responsible for her inability to reach out to other people, particularly since she is unaware of the uncongenial aura she emanates, but it is clear from the narrative that Karen Nilssen has shaped her daughter's character in a way that has disabled her capacity for initiating and sustaining lasting close relationships.

After several unproductive weeks of living at the YWCA and searching in vain for suitable employment in Chicago, Helga is introduced to Jeanette Hayes-Rore, an avid race woman who hires her to travel with her to New York, where she has a speaking engagement at a convention. Helga sees this as a prime opportunity to relocate to the larger city; she becomes excited at the prospect of the wider opportunities New York has to offer, and "life ceased to be a struggle and became a gay adventure" (68). Fortuitously, Mrs. Hayes-Rore proves to be an invaluable acquaintance—she negotiates a secretarial job for Helga at the newly-formed black insurance company courting an investment from the wealthy widow and introduces Helga to her niece, Anne Grey, a Harlem socialite who eventually invites Helga to share her "unobtrusively correct" home (75).

Helga quickly becomes engrossed in her new cosmopolitan lifestyle; within weeks of her initial arrival, she is imagining a permanent life in the city: "Someday she intended to marry one of those alluring brown or yellow men who danced attendance on her. … Helga Crane meant, now, to have a home and perhaps laughing, appealing dark-eyed children in Harlem" (77). While yet enchanted with her life in what James Weldon Johnson termed "Black Manhattan," Helga nurtures these romantic fantasies of a domestic haven immersed in the black community. The New Yorkers please her because they share her contempt for Naxos and the accommodationist philosophy fueling the institution's purported mission of racial uplift, and she cheerfully anticipates firmly establishing herself in Harlem society by wedding one of her "financially successful" suitors who could provide "a home like Anne's, cars of expensive makes such as lined the avenue, clothes and furs from Bendel's and Revillon Fréres, servants, and leisure" (77). Into such a setting Helga happily envisions bringing children. Unfortunately, her fantasy turns out to be a fleeting one; Helga's inevitable disillusionment cannot long be held at bay, and after a turbulent night at an underground Harlem jazz club, Helga books passage on a ship bound for Denmark, her mother's European homeland.

In Denmark, taking up residence with her mother's childless sister opens the doors to the world of white privilege for Helga. She is a novelty, certainly the object of "massed curiosity and interest, so discreetly hidden under the polite greetings," but nevertheless treated with all of the genuine courtesy extended to any Danish citizen of the privileged socioeconomic status enjoyed by her Aunt Katrina and Uncle Poul (100). Living in Copenhagen grants her all of the desires she had once believed she would obtain through marrying a prosperous young Harlemite "—not money, but the things which money could give, leisure, attention, beautiful surroundings. Things. Things. Things" (97). As a Danish resident Helga is able to circulate among the general populace without question or restriction; she suffers no acts of prejudice or discrimination at restaurants, shops, theaters, private parties, or anywhere else. The freedom from racial hostility compels Helga to retract her earlier expression of optimism about the prospect of building a life in America: "She saw, suddenly, the giving birth to little helpless, unprotesting Negro children as a sin, an unforgivable outrage. More black folks to suffer indignities. More dark bodies for mobs to lynch" (104). Helga's sentiment echoes that of the many of her enslaved foremothers who used whatever folk art or method at their disposal, including celibacy, herbal contraceptive potions, induced miscarriage, and infanticide, to prevent having babies who would be deprived of their humanity and cruelly exploited as the property of their white masters. Historian Darlene Clark Hine notes that "A woman who elected not to have children … negated through individual or group action her role in the maintenance of the slave pool." The former slave William Craft underscores Hine's observation by explaining his wife Ellen's rigid opposition to risking childbirth before their planned escape: "[T]he mere thought of her ever becoming a mother of a child, to linger out a miserable existence under the wretched system of American slavery, appeared to fill her very soul with horror."[10] While Helga's rationale mirrors that of Ellen Craft, her vehemently expressed refusal to render herself complicit in the subjugation of her people by consciously choosing to augment its persecuted population effectively dismisses the inevitable long-term result of planned childlessness, which is race extinction.

Once Helga declares she will remain in Denmark and never return to the United States, her Aunt Katrina begins in earnest to play the matchmaker and plan for Helga to wed one of the several eligible Danes comprising her niece's circle of admirers. However, this frenzy of speculation and activity causes Helga to again become disillusioned with her prospects, and she asks her aunt's opinion about whether "miscegenation was wrong, in fact as well as principle." Aunt Katrina quickly denies that her countrymen "think of those things here," but the unsettling doubt has firmly lodged itself in Helga's mind (108). So when the highly regarded artist Axel Olsen finally proposes to Helga, she decisively rejects him, based in part upon her own adverse personal experience as a child of an interracial union, and her unwillingness to expose herself or any potential children to the risk of emotional rejection.

In the brief space of time subsequent to her final confrontation with Olsen, Helga begins to form a definite scheme of returning to America, to the black community she had abandoned so abruptly two years earlier. Interestingly, it is in her mother's homeland that Helga is finally able to make peace with her father: "She understood and could sympathize with his facile surrender to the irresistible ties of race, now that they dragged at her own heart" (122). Though Helga discovers a point of identification with the father she does not appear to remember, she never questions his motivation for leaving her behind with her white mother. Perhaps, however, Karen Nilssen would not have permitted a separation from her daughter; her sister Katrina pronounces her a foolish, impractical woman: "She wanted to keep you, she insisted on it, even over [her second husband's] protest, I think. She loved you so much, she said. ... And so she made you unhappy. Mothers, I suppose, are like that. Selfish" (108). Helga's censure of the selfishness inherent in maternity persists even after her return to Harlem. She staunchly denounces the idea of indulging oneself by having children who will inevitably end up miserable.

Helga clarifies her position in a speech to her former fiancé James Vayle, now the assistant principal of Naxos, whom she meets unexpectedly at a social gathering in Harlem. When he asks whether she ever plans to marry, Helga replies, "Someday, perhaps, I don't know. Marriage—that means children, to me. And why add more suffering to the world? Why add any more unwanted, tortured Negroes to America?" (132). James Vayle is shocked at Helga's position and returns a class-based argument replete with eugenicist undertones. He maintains that since only the "better class" of black people practices controlled fertility, "each generation has to wrestle again with the obstacles of the preceding ones: lack of money, education, and background. ... We're the ones who must have the children if the race is to get anywhere" (132). Larsen uses this exchange between Helga and James Vayle to rehearse a debate which was then being waged in the black community. There was a concern that the members of the so-called Talented Tenth failed to reproduce themselves, when they were clearly in the optimum position to give their children the advantages of wealth, prestige, and access to the exclusive resources of the elect, thereby virtually ensuring their success. Motherhood in the 1920s, however, was considered an impediment to female achievement, and many women who were politically active and/or career oriented opted to remain childless.[11] Though Helga reasserts her personal conviction that rearing black children is wrong, the close of the narrative finds her in rural Alabama, the wife of a small-town minister, suffering under the anguish of recurring pregnancies: "[W]as it only she, a poor weak city-bred thing, who felt that the strain … was almost unendurable?" (152). Helga reverses her position from being adamantly opposed to motherhood to embracing her dutiful role as a wife and mother literally overnight; she is in the midst of a borderline-suicidal depression after her mortifying tryst with Robert Anderson, the former president of Naxos she had secretly loved for years despite her inability to admit it even to herself, but who had recently married her best friend. When Dr. Anderson suggests they meet alone, the heretofore demure Helga is prepared to begin an extramarital affair with him, but she subsequently realizes that he has summoned her only to apologize for an impulsive, inappropriately passionate kiss he surprised her with at the same party where Helga had her conversation with James Vayle. Helga takes to the rainy Harlem streets, trying to escape the turmoil of her own self-recriminations, but the storm ultimately drives her indoors to the nearest shelter—a storefront church in the midst of a service. Helga makes an unusual entrance; she walks into what she assumes is a place of business, is struck by the oddity of her predicament, and reacts of a piece with her fragile state of mind: "She sat down on the floor, a dripping heap, and laughed and laughed and laughed" (139). The congregation immediately targets her as a woman in desperate need of salvation, and Helga leaves the gathering at the end of the evening on the arm of the Reverend Mr. Pleasant Green as a redeemed sinner.

Religion is depicted as a belief system that temporarily occludes Helga's senses. Right before she succumbs to the ministrations of the believers crowding in upon her, she is planning her final attempt to leave the building. Larsen emphasizes the details that contribute to Helga's vulnerability to religious transformation: her physical weakness from fatigue, her ordeal in the storm, her recent alcoholic overindulgence, and her lack of nourishment. Furthermore, she is emotionally drained from her confrontation with Anderson and the incessant replay of the scene and its attendant implications through her head. Dissatisfied with her own botched attempts to manage her life, she resolves to abdicate control of it completely in accordance with the spiritual teachings of her husband. "Actually and metaphorically she bowed her head before God, trusting in Him to see her through. Secretly she was glad that she had not to worry about herself or anything. It was a relief to be able to put the entire responsibility on someone else" (153). Some years later when her mind is finally cleared, "the obscuring curtain of religion rent," during the aftermath of the horrific delivery of her fourth child, Helga discovers herself embroiled in a situation that she would never in her "right" mind have consciously chosen (157).

Once the "long frightfulness" of her son's birth has subsided, Helga is plunged into an "appalling blackness of pain" where "the ballast of her brain had got loose and she hovered for a long time somewhere in that delightful borderland on the edge of unconsciousness, an enchanted and blissful place where peace and incredible quiet encompassed her" (154–55). As she revels in her nirvana of complete lack of responsibility, the religious faith to which she had clung so desperately gradually loses all of its credibility. "For had she not called in her agony on Him? And He had not heard. Why? Because, she knew now, He wasn't there. Didn't exist" (157). Helga is unable even to summon sufficient emotion to grieve for her newborn son when he fails to survive past the first week of his life. In fact, she hides the "telltale gleam of the relief which she felt" at the news of his death, since her latent feelings of hopelessness in the quality of life accessible to black people in America have been revived (158). She mourns for the futures of "[h]er sons. Her daughter. These would grow to manhood, to womanhood, in this vicious, this hypocritical land" (157). At the same time, she is relieved that she has fewer children to worry about when she begins to formulate a plan of leaving her husband and returning to Northern urban civilization, because Helga "wanted not to leave them—if that were possible. The recollection of her own childhood, lonely, unloved, rose too poignantly before her for her to consider calmly such a solution" (161). The pivotal factor which leads Helga to dismiss the notion of leaving without her children is the memory of her own emotional desertion by Karen Nilssen. She cannot abide the thought of her children believing that she never loved them. In this way Helga seems to reenact the predicament faced by her own mother, and she makes the same "selfish," according to Katrina Nilssen, resolve to retain custody of her children. Motherhood to her is a sacred, unbreakable bond. However, it is precisely the strength of the maternal bond that makes being a mother so unendurable for Helga. Her commitment to her children as well as her tenuous health due to having given birth to the children keep Helga trapped in the domestic prison of her Alabama home. Then Larsen seals her heroine's tragic fate with the implication that her cycle of reproduction is just as unbreakable as the bond she feels with her children, for just when she is beginning to feel well enough to make plans for their departure in earnest, she discovers she is pregnant again.

Sexual Repression and Race Confusion in *Quicksand* and *Passing*

Critics are divided on the issue of whether Nella Larsen's heroines can truly be classified under the rubric of the "tragic mulatto." Marita Golden is emphatic in her pronouncement: "No tragic mulattoes here. These prim, proper colored ladies ... are driven by the impulse to shape their lives rather than suffer them. ..."[12] The tragic mulatto, then, is figured as a victim of circumstance, powerless to resist the multiple degradations of a racist society, despite her intimate ancestral connections with the dominant racial group. Nella Larsen's women become exempt by virtue of their independent action to determine their own futures.

Charles Larson implies that Larsen's version of the tragic mulatto figure is simply more culturally sophisticated than those of her literary predecessors, including Frances Harper's Iola Leroy. "The depth of her characterization, as well as her superior narrative technique" distinguish the novels of Nella Larsen from earlier treatments of the stock female character.[13] Here, Larson is clearly arguing that the designation "tragic mulatto" elicits an image of a flat, one-dimensional, predictable character, and Larsen's take is a much richer and more compelling one.

Deborah McDowell cleverly sidesteps the argumentative issue by pointing out that, given that Larsen depicted heroines who can obviously be designated tragic mulattos, to concentrate on that singular aspect of their representation diverts attention from the more interesting literary themes Larsen engages. "In other words, in focusing on the problems of the 'tragic mulatto,' readers miss the more urgent problem which Larsen tried to explore: the pleasure and danger of female sexual experience."[14]

McDowell makes an excellent point. It is deceptively easy to subsume every issue explored within *Quicksand* and *Passing* under the umbrella of racial difference, but I contend that this is a trap snaring not only Larsen's readers but also her heroines. Helga Crane, Irene Redfield, and Clare Kendry all show a decided tendency to conflate their attitudes toward sexuality and desire with the mythical racially encoded dichotomy between pristine white women and, to borrow a term from Irene, "having" black ones, perpetuated by the dominant social order. They mistakenly associate their ideological battles between sexual innocence and wanton carnality with the interracial mixture of their genetic inheritance. Anxiety over "pure womanhood" pervades the novels of Nella Larsen, and it is invariably wrapped up in confusion over racial identity.

This phenomenon of attributing conflicting sexual impulses to a mixture of black and white ancestry is pointedly exemplified in the scene in *Quicksand* where Helga Crane, with her Scandinavian first name and the surname of the white stepfather who despised her, is both fascinated and drawn in by the unfamiliar atmosphere of a jazz cabaret, a center of black social life in 1920s Harlem:

> [W]hen suddenly the music died, she dragged herself back to the present with a conscious effort; and a shameful certainty that not only had she been in the jungle, but that she had enjoyed it, began to taunt her. She hardened her determination to get away. She wasn't, she told herself, a jungle creature. (89–90)

The music in the cabaret, like quicksand, sucks Helga under its influence. On the dance floor she is unable to maintain her reserve nor resist the sexual stirrings excited therein. When she "drag[s] herself back to the present," it becomes clear that Helga associates this devolution into a "jungle" mentality—a euphemism for wild amorality and pleasure-seeking indulgence—with a black ancestral past: her legacy from the black biological father who deserted her. Helga convinces herself that a removal from the Harlem community would enable her to avoid fully becoming the "jungle creature" which is one avenue of her potential destiny. The very next chapter following her desperate escape from the smoky cabaret opens with her flight to the imagined salvation of her mother's people—the homogeneous white society of Denmark.

Deborah McDowell argues that Nella Larsen's narrative choices were largely influenced by the attitudes toward sexuality prevalent during the Harlem Renaissance. The community was divided between the two major movements involved in disseminating thought—the artists and the intellectuals. The artists, following the bold lead of the age's female blues singers, wanted to celebrate, or, in some cases, exploit the sensuality of black female sexuality, while the intellectuals, struggling against the projected lascivious nature that was a legacy of slavery, were committed to presenting a wholesome, chaste picture of black femininity.[15] McDowell contends that, caught in this dilemma, Nella Larsen tried "to hold the two virtually contradictory impulses in the same novel. [She] wanted to tell the story of the black woman with sexual desires, but was constrained by a competing desire to establish black women as respectable in black middle class terms."[16]

The problem is further compounded, however, by the duality between the artistic and intellectual worlds inherent in Larsen's intergroup status as a fiction writer. This duality finds a parallel in Larsen's own biracial heritage. The tension embodied in the simultaneous existence within two contrary identity circles plays itself out upon the pages of her fiction, where internal conflicts over competing natural impulses are often codified as racial, rather than gendered, class, regional, socialized, individual, or even fundamentally human instincts.

Helga Crane's preoccupation with sexual freedom finds an outlet in her admiring fascination with Audrey Denney, the racially ambiguous object of male attraction who disdainfully ignores social convention in order to indulge her own desires. Audrey's oppositional model of black womanhood, the "brownly beautiful" Anne Grey, is a gentle, respectable widow (76). While Helga seeks to emulate Anne's demeanor, she bristles at Anne's preoccupation with "the race problem." Audrey, who openly challenges the boundaries of the color line through her liberal social interaction on both sides, is also allowed the privilege of open and liberal sexuality. Anne Grey's repressed sexuality is a manifestation of her need to demonstrate the superior nature of her own race and refute the negative image of black femininity perpetuated by white society. Anne's first marriage was childless, and it is implied that the demise of her husband caused her little grief; Helga suspects that her professed unwillingness to speak of death "was a bit of a pose assumed for the purpose of doing away with the necessity of speaking regretfully of a husband who had been perhaps not too greatly loved" (75). Anne's distance from sex is further emphasized by the length of her widowhood (her husband was killed in World War I), and by the virginal aspect of her physical description: "[S]he had the face of a golden Madonna, grave and calm and sweet" (76).

The mundane quality of marital sexual relations is vividly contrasted against the lively excitement of such openly sensual characters as Audrey Denney and Clare Kendry, and the sordidly tantalizing kiss shared by Helga and Dr. Robert Anderson, once he has become the husband of Anne Grey. When Helga walks out into the hall at a party and literally bumps into Dr. Anderson, on impulse he kisses her passionately. Though Helga's first instinct is to resist him, "strangely, all power seemed to ebb away, and a long-hidden, half-understood desire welled up in her with the suddenness of a dream. Helga Crane's own arms went up about the man's neck" (133). The kiss rouses and clarifies in Helga the dormant emotional response to Dr. Anderson she has never been able to recognize as physical desire. Such an intense mutual attraction never occurs within a Larsen marriage, however. The functionalism of marital sex within a reproductive or perfunctory context serves to purify the base carnality of illicit sexual encounters and render the act of intercourse passionless and distasteful.

Such a scenario obtains in "Long Black Song," a short story by Richard Wright; Sarah, the story's central character, is trapped in a loveless marriage of convenience to her husband Silas, while she dreams constantly of Tom, her former boyfriend who went away to war. Sarah becomes essentially desexed in her role as wife to Silas and mother to Ruth, her baby daughter. Her breasts become the "teats" used to provide milk for her child, and her dissatisfaction with Silas is apparent from her incessant fantasies about Tom, whose "leaving had left an empty black hole in her heart."[17] Sarah's feeling of hollowness is compounded by her uncertainty as to whether or not Tom is alive and the knowledge that, even if he has survived, by her interim marriage she has rendered the resumption of their relationship impossible. At this moment of despair and longing, a white traveling salesman who forces himself on her becomes a surrogate for the sexual passion Sarah might have experienced with Tom. The white man's ardent desire for her temporarily reconfirms her as a vibrant woman instead of an animalized drudge carrying out the functions necessary to perpetuate life. She achieves freedom from her suffocating existence with Silas, albeit unintentionally, through her ultimate transgression against him by having sex with a white man.

The long history of sexual disrespect and abuse of black women by white men is a point of discussion between Irene Redfield and her friend, the white writer Hugh Wentworth. Irene explains the attraction between black and white people as fundamentally insincere curiosity. In response to Wentworth's inquiry as to whether she finds a particularly dark-skinned black man "ravishingly beautiful," she responds emphatically: "I do not! And I don't think the others do either. Not honestly, I mean. I think what they feel is—well, a kind of emotional excitement. You know, the sort of thing you feel in the presence of something strange, and even, perhaps, a bit repugnant to you" (236). Irene's tendency towards self-delusion has earned her the label of an unreliable narrator. Here, her denial of legitimate sexual attraction across racial lines implicates herself because the lightness of her skin, her ability to "pass" for white, is a visual testament to the reality of the frequent consummation of that "emotional excitement" existing between the races. Irene's fear of her own sexuality is manifested in her obsession with "security." She and her husband Brian have separate bedrooms. She views their two sons as assurances that their marriage will remain intact and as her own excuse for celibacy. Like *Quicksand*'s Anne Grey, Irene does not want passion. She wants the appearance of happiness and superficial contentment.

Clare Kendry is also involved in a sexless union, though for different reasons from Irene's. Because marital sex is linked with the probability of reproduction, Clare abstains. She cannot endure the unpredictability of genetic combination and the uncertainty of what could emerge from her womb. She rejects motherhood and attributes her abhorrence at the thought of becoming a mother again to her fear of producing a dark-skinned child who would innocently betray her true racial origins. Although her disgust for her white husband grows proportionally with the increasing amount of time she spends in black Harlem, Clare, like Irene, lives constantly under the anxiety of detection and rejection and the disruption of the unstable foundation supporting her fragile lifestyle.

Anne Grey, as well, is depicted as being involved in a superficial marriage to Robert Anderson. Even as a newlywed just returned from her honeymoon, she feels threatened by her husband's uncontrollable attraction to Helga. The virtually sexless, though beautiful, Anne fails to excite in her husband "that nameless and to him shameful impulse, that sheer delight, which ran through his nerves at mere proximity to Helga" (124). Sex to Anne is an unpleasant necessity in marriage, an indecorous act that she resigns herself to perform in order to sustain a successful relationship. "She could carry out what she considered her obligation to him, keep him undisturbed, unhumiliated. It was impossible that she could fail. Unthinkable" (124). In this passage Anne introduces the distinction between a "civilized" sexual reservation and the "lawless," "shameful" impulses of sexual abandon. Though she has not to struggle against her libidinal passions as her new husband does, she understands and embraces the expectation that controlled desire will be the avenue chosen by the elite.

Distaste for the carnal aspect of marital coupling is claimed as the province of genuine ladies early on in *Quicksand*. While Helga is still at Naxos she contemplates the model of true womanhood proposed by the matron of the dormitory where she lives among the students. Miss MacGooden claims to never have considered taking a husband because "[t]here were, so she had been given to understand, things in the matrimonial state that were of necessity entirely too repulsive for a lady of delicate and sensitive nature to submit to" (46). Though Helga is amused by Miss MacGooden's prudishness, especially considering she implies the older woman's attitude may be a pose assumed to derail speculations about her obvious lack of appeal to the opposite sex, she is herself ambivalent about her sexuality and has an obvious fear of intimacy. Helga's apprehension regarding the prospect of consummating a relationship accounts for the violent reaction she has to her final, fateful encounter with Robert Anderson.

Living under a shroud of illegitimacy, reeling from the rejection of the one man to whom she could have surrendered herself in the pursuit of sexual fulfillment, and suffering the shame of feeling herself judged a "jungle creature," Helga Crane seeks absolution in the sanctity of marriage with a Christian minister. As a preacher's wife, Helga can accept her sexuality as a form of socially sanctioned labor, a responsibility to her husband. Their nocturnal sexual encounters become her daily reward for performing the "humble tasks of her household, cooking, dishwashing, sweeping, dusting, mending, and darning," in addition to her gardening and church responsibilities (148). The distinction Helga makes between the desire for sex and the desire for an individual is evident from her personal distaste for her husband. Though she regards him as fat and dirty, she eagerly anticipates their nocturnal adventures. The contrast of night and day for Helga represents anonymity and abandon under the cover of darkness, versus the disappointing reality of what the light reveals to be her husband, perpetually unencumbered by the fetters of personal hygiene. Her ability to indulge in guilt-free sex temporarily occludes her instinctive repulsion toward her partner, which surfaces with a vengeance when sex ceases to be an experience of pleasure and becomes the necessary precursor to the discomfort and pain of childbearing.

The body as a site of loathing is not peculiar in Larsen's novels to Helga's reverie upon her husband, the Reverend Mr. Pleasant Green. Helga has the same sort of nagging aversion to her first suitor, James Vayle, and her remembrance of "the slight quivering of his lips sometimes when her hands had unexpectedly touched his" and "the throbbing vein in his forehead" occasioned by a flurry of kisses (58). In *Passing*, Irene Redfield similarly reflects mildly upon the displeasing bodily manifestations of her husband, Brian. Over breakfast, Brian takes a slice of toast and bites it "with that audible crunching sound that Irene disliked so intensely" (216). Sexual intimacy breeds a type of revulsion for men which suggests that the feelings must be at least in part self-directed; women either develop a repugnance to their own sexuality, or they grow increasingly uncomfortable with being objectified as a sexual plaything. Helga resents her suspicion that men want little more from her than sex. Early in the novel, she breaks her engagement to the intellectual, socially entrenched James Vayle, at least in part because "the idea that she was in but one nameless way necessary to him filled her with a sensation amounting almost to shame" (42). Now, however, despite her sincere attempt to fill flawlessly the role of first lady of the small Alabama church community, she again must try "not to see that [her husband] had rather lost any personal interest in her, except for the short spaces between the times when she was preparing for or recovering from childbirth" (151).

Helga's quest to combine personal respectability with the freedom to express her sexuality leads her to refuse Axel Olsen's offer of marriage after he had originally suggested a less binding, less honorable, "more informal arrangement" (118). The portrait he paints of her is an adequate reflection of his perception of Helga, and Helga will not submit to a relationship with a man who considers her morally suspect. While she and her Danish relatives disapprove of the painting of the "disgusting, sensual creature with her features," "collectors, artists, and critics had been unanimous in their praise and it had been hung on the line at an annual exhibition, where it had attracted much flattering attention and many tempting offers" (119). As Helga in effigy, the portrait acts the role of the call girl going to the home of the highest bidder—much in line with Olsen's assessment that Helga has "the soul of a prostitute" (117).

Until their dissatisfaction with the commissioned portrait, Helga's Aunt Katrina and Uncle Poul had been the leading advocates of the excessive adornment of Helga's body. In Denmark she had become a living, breathing, mobile exhibit, with her showy, revealing clothing and flashy, expensive jewelry. Aunt Katrina's explanation to her niece for the distinct difference in their respective presentations is transparent: "Oh, I'm an old married lady, and a Dane. But you, you're young. And you're a foreigner, and different. You must have bright things to set off the color of your lovely brown skin. Striking things, exotic things. You must make an impression" (98). The objectification of Helga is only complete with the exhibition of the portrait, which effectively communicates the opinion of black femininity articulated by Olsen and obviously shared by the Danes who enthusiastically receive the painting: Helga embodies "the warm, impulsive nature of the women of Africa" (117).

Helga does not refute this characterization; in fact she, along with Larsen's other heroines, internalizes it. They associate the expression of sexuality with a sort of libidinous abandon to their natural black ancestral impulses, the particular inheritance of the women of Africa, instead of recognizing sexual desire as a drive common to all women. Through such portrayals Larsen displays her contempt for the repression of passion middle-class black women believed refuted stereotypes of aggressive oversexuality and established their claim to respectability. The various women in these novels are involved in a project of avoiding the confrontation of their own sexuality by projecting their desires onto others. Aunt Katrina projects hers onto Helga; Irene projects hers onto Clare; Helga lives vicariously through Audrey Denney, and the elusive experience of sexual satisfaction remains an extramarital phenomenon liberated from the restrictive constraints of racial considerations. The sanctity of sex within marriage is perceived as the deceptive quicksand, quickly obliterating feminine identity and sexual fulfillment under the shifting muck of family obligations and the prison of reproduction.

In her discussion of *Quicksand*, Claudia Tate makes the compelling point that Helga "is not simply an innocent victim of racial oppression and sexual repression. Rather, she is also an aggressive and defensive seductress, implicated in her own tragic fate."[18] On the night that they meet in the storefront religious revival meeting, Helga, devastated by Robert Anderson's casual deflection of her intent to consent to an affair with him, does indeed seduce the man who later becomes her husband. As Pleasant Green is walking her back to her hotel a fleeting moment of dizziness causes her to lean into him, and as she retrospectively registers his visceral response to their momentary proximity, she has an epiphany; Helga realizes that Green is physically attracted to her and that she therefore has some measure of control over him. She experiences a resurgence of the thrilling, yet disconcerting, sensation she once felt back at Naxos before she broke off her engagement to James Vayle, whose "mute helplessness against that ancient appeal by which she held him pleased her and fed her vanity—gave her a feeling of power. At the same time she shrank away from it, subtly aware of possibilities she herself couldn't predict" (42–43). Though the full extent of the repercussions are still unknown to her, Helga does not shy away from testing the potency of her feminine allure on Green.

Having defiantly renounced Harlem's high society and the class-based rules of conduct prohibiting such illicit activity, Helga silently considers whether or not to use her newly recognized power over her escort to indulge in a sexual indiscretion which will irrevocably sever, so she believes, her link to black elite culture. Her act of transgression has nothing whatsoever to do with reciprocal desire, for the identity of the man walking beside her has ceased to be at all relevant. Larsen reveals that her heroine cannot even identify him by name when she "had deliberately stopped thinking. She had only smiled, a faint provocative smile, and pressed her fingers deep into his arms until a wild look had come into his slightly bloodshot eyes" (144). In order to follow through with her seduction scheme, Helga must eschew reason entirely and allow herself to be guided by the strength of her companion's passion. By the next morning Helga is determined to marry Green that very same day. Though an impulsive marriage to a country preacher means the forfeiture of her oft-repeated longings for "material security, gracious ways of living, a profusion of lovely clothes, and a goodly share of envious admiration," Helga's unexpected spiritual conversion reveals a sure path to "happiness unburdened by the complexities of the lives she had known" (45, 142). The promise of a simple future with Green suddenly appears very attractive to Helga. At the same time, just as she feels certain he will not reject her when she entices him with her silent indications of receptivity to his desire, Helga becomes Green's wife, Tate argues, because "No doubt, she feels confident that he will not abandon her."[19] Her deep-seated insecurities about her family and her self-worth lead Helga to sabotage relationships with the other men who court her.

Though her purported rationales become conflated with personal revulsion, Helga's self-acknowledged motivations for preemptive desertions are always practical considerations. She disengages herself from James Vayle because she cannot adjust to the world he so comfortably inhabits, though she bitterly acknowledges that his family will heartily approve because they have "never liked" her because her "lack of family disconcerted them" (43). She is concerned, however, about the potential repercussions, the "social suicide," of her action: "The fact that they [the Vayles] were a "first family" had been one of James's attractions for the obscure Helga. She had wanted social background, but—she had not imagined that it could be so stuffy" (43). After Helga decides that she cannot become a permanent fixture within the black elite milieu, she also feels out of place casting her lot among white Europeans. Axel Olsen, the Danish artist who finally proposes marriage to her, Helga refuses on ethnic grounds: "We can't tell, you know; if we were married, you might come to be ashamed of me, to hate me, to hate all dark people. My mother did that" (118). Helga manages to elude Robert Anderson's social calls and other efforts to spend time with her by first foisting him upon her housemate, Anne Grey, and ultimately disappearing across the Atlantic to Denmark for almost two years. When she receives word of his plans to marry Anne, she feels as if she can safely return to Harlem, knowing she has escaped the possibility of a serious relationship with him. Helga's flight from the middle-class respectability embodied by Robert Anderson, sends her careening into her hastily arranged nuptials with Pleasant Green. Through her marriage she indeed experiences the psychological freedom of sexual abandon, but she also suffers the consequences of a physically debilitating, mentally fracturing, emotionally draining series of problematic pregnancies.

Maternity and Domestic Entrapment in *Passing*

Larsen complicates the representation of maternity in her novels by exploring the conflicting attitudes women develop in response to their own positions as mothers. The selflessness and sacrifice indirectly required of them by their children are more than the women are capable of sustaining over time, and they gradually begin to self-destruct. With the pathos evoked by Clare Kendry's lament in *Passing*, Larsen confirms her character's view of motherhood as an unnatural, but curiously necessary, cruelty.

In *Quicksand*, Larsen centers the narrative on Helga Crane, a character who found it impossible to be content in any single social environment because of her biracial heritage. Helga never manages to meet the one person whose behavioral model she might have comfortably emulated: Audrey Denney, "the beautiful, calm, cool girl who had the assurance, the courage, so placidly to ignore racial barriers and give her attention to people," (92). Because Audrey is the "particular pet aversion" of Helga's former best friend, Anne Grey, it would have been tantamount to treason for Helga to have actively sought out the woman's acquaintance (128). Anne, along with most of the other women in their exclusive social circle, bitterly resents Audrey's abandonment of Harlem in favor of residence in a predominantly white New York neighborhood, her cavalier association with black and white people alike, and her immense popularity with men. A lifestyle similar to Audrey's could have been ideal for Helga, who was never able to embrace both components of her racial identity simultaneously. Instead, in a desperate attempt to find meaningful stability in her life, Helga engineers a marriage with a man she barely knows and thus consigns herself to a role she is both physically and emotionally unfitted for—mother to one of "the proverbially large families of preachers" (148).

In *Passing*, Larsen shifts her trenchant focus from the debilitating physical and psychological effects of pregnancy and childbirth to the superficial worlds arranged by women dependent upon a nuclear family to establish their social identities. After twelve years of separation, Irene has assumed her expected place in the black bourgeoisie, while Clare has crossed the color line into the white world. Then Clare becomes bored with her life as a white woman and wants Irene to act as her passport back into the black community. The ensuing series of events is told from the point of view of Irene, who from the beginning maintains serious reservations about Clare's multifaceted potential to upset the delicate balance of the life Irene has very methodically constructed around her husband and children.

When Irene and Clare meet, purely by chance, at the rooftop restaurant of Chicago's select Drayton hotel, both women have secured seemingly enviable lifestyles; each has married well—their husbands are professionally successful—and has become a mother. While each woman glibly gives the other the impression that she is perfectly content with the life she has chosen, the course of the narrative reveals that neither is truly satisfied. Clare wants to desert her husband to assuage her yearning for the excitement and camaraderie of living among black people again. Irene has a false confidence in her marital commitment, based upon her faith in the bond she and Brian share as the parents of their two sons. She is completely oblivious to the threat to her marriage posed by other women, most pointedly, Clare Kendry. When Clare's husband, Jack Bellew, learns that Brian is a doctor and crudely jokes that his profession must routinely throw him in the company of "so many lady patients," Irene smoothly dismisses the suggestion that her husband might be tempted into an infidelity: "Brian doesn't care for ladies, especially sick ones. I sometimes wish he did. It's South America that attracts him" (203).[20] Irene believes that the greatest threat to the stability of her family is not Brian's potential desire to leave her, but his desire to leave the United States.

Their conflict over Brian's proposition of relocating to Brazil emblematizes the Redfields' dissension regarding how best to raise their sons. While Brian is convinced, as Helga Crane was throughout the bulk of *Quicksand*, that America is the most toxic of environments into which to thrust a black person, Irene believes that, if one is properly equipped, it is the best of all possible worlds. Brian's expressed wish to emigrate to South America is not a selfish one; he thinks it would be best for his family, especially his sons. "I wanted to get them out of this hellish place years ago," he hurls at Irene in the midst of a heated argument about whether lynching is an appropriate topic for discussion over dinner with the children. "You wouldn't let me" (264).

Irene is certain she can prevent her boys, the older of whom is only ten, from discovering the "horrible" social reality of racial hostility in America until "they're older." To that end, she enrolls them in private school, worries that Brian Junior might be learning about sex from his older classmates, refuses to discuss issues that expose white animosity toward black people in the presence of the boys, and forbids her husband "to talk to them about the race problem." Irene's goal is for "their childhood to be happy and as free from the knowledge of such things as it can be" (263). Having enjoyed a sheltered childhood in the Westovers' South Side Chicago home, with her family's comfortable affluence, circle of similarly situated friends, and summers at Idlewild, an exclusive black vacation community in Michigan, Irene has no reason not to believe that she can replicate such a homelife for her own children. In addition, because Irene herself seems by all appearances to be a white woman, she cannot appreciate what it is like to experience the interminable acts of prejudice and discrimination routinely leveled against black people solely because of their skin color. Irene is so accustomed to being treated in public as if she were white that she shrugs off the very palpable liabilities attendant to showing color in America. Her futile effort to repel the intrusion of the atrocities inherent in a racially polarized society into the confines of her household is yet another example of Irene's delusional machinations to create her own reality and exist in her own artificial universe.

While Irene seeks to keep her children ignorant of the animosity toward black people, Brian is equally insistent that the boys be familiarized with the dismal condition of American race relations: "If, as you're so determined, they've got to live in this damned country, they'd better find out what sort of thing they're up against as soon as possible. The earlier they learn it, the better prepared they'll be" (263). Brian's contempt for his wife's position becomes clear as she stubbornly continues to assert her fundamental point—she wants the boys to be happy, to enjoy their peaceful fantasy world for as long as she is reasonably able to maintain its inviolability. In complete disbelief, Brian resorts to a personal insult: "I can't understand how anybody as intelligent as you like to think you are can show evidences of such stupidity" (264). Certainly, Larsen privileges Brian's perspective over that of her beleaguered heroine, who is represented throughout the narrative as having a less-than-desirable approach to motherhood.

Brian accuses Irene of "forever fretting about those kids" and "trying to make a mollycoddle out of" Junior (219–20). Irene does seem to expend a great deal of energy cogitating elaborate solutions to the problems she perceives as threatening to disrupt her children's lives. However, when she is involved in developing one of her remedial schemes, it appears that she is more concerned with controlling her husband, and she uses her sons as expedients to manipulate Brian's submission to her will. Irene's unsuccessful attempt to persuade Brian that Junior would benefit from changing schools distresses her because her covert agenda is to provide a rationale for Brian to take a foreign excursion which would temporarily mollify what she believes is nothing more than his recurring restiveness. Irene may feel that educating her son in Europe might be to his advantage, but she is clearly more concerned about finding a way to pacify Brian's resurging agitation. Irene's sons are often an afterthought to her, meaningful in their practical utility as symbols of her rightful claim to a position of prominence in the black middle class. In this way, Irene's sentiment for her sons is akin to that of the pale-skinned Olivia Cary for her equally pale firstborn child, Teresa, in Jessie Fauset's *Comedy: American Style*. Olivia, who harbors an intense desire to pass completely into white society, cherishes her daughter because "Every time she appeared in public with the little girl she was presenting the incontestable proof of her white womanhood."[21] Irene may not be interested in using her sons to demonstrate her claim to whiteness—in fact Junior, like his father, has "deep copper" colored skin—but they are instrumental to her crafting of herself into a middle-class lady, and she does seem to have more of an abstract than personal interest in the boys as individuals (214).

Irene never manages to emerge from her bedroom in the mornings until after the boys are awakened, dressed, fed, and driven to school by their father. When they are home in the afternoons, they are confined to "their own floor," and Irene is never depicted as having any sustained interaction with them (263). Once, she is on the verge of calling upstairs to their playroom to entreat them to be a bit less noisy, but the sudden entrance of Clare distracts her from her purpose. Later the same afternoon she takes Clare up to meet the boys, and the awkwardness of the moment is palpable; their wariness of Clare is understandable, considering she is a stranger to them, but they also seem to be discomfited by the apparently uncommon intrusion of their mother.

Irene's brief introduction of Clare, prefaced by a sharp reprimand to her younger son for picking up a book and sitting down to read it in Clare's presence, is the only scene in the novel in which Irene actually speaks directly to her sons: "Get up, Ted! That's rude. This is Theodore, Mrs. Bellew. Please excuse his bad manners. He does know better. And this is Brian junior. Mrs. Bellew is an old friend of Mother's. We used to play together when we were little girls." Irene's exactitude and formality is a striking contrast to Clare's easy familiarity with Ted and Junior. When Clare perceptively realizes she has violated the boys' expectation of privacy, she tries to be accommodating and conciliatory. "Please don't be cross. Of course, I know I've gone and spoiled everything. But maybe, if I promise not to get too much in the way, you'll let me come in just the same" (232). Irene's sense of the fundamental impropriety of relating to children socially is agitated by what she perceives as Clare's misconduct toward the boys. Even in Irene's absence, "Clare could very happily amuse herself with Ted and Junior, who had conceived for her an admiration that verged on adoration, especially Ted."[22] Irene "secretly resent[s]" the time Clare spends with her sons; she feels that Clare's constant attention "spoiled" the boys "outrageously" (238).

Irene's response to the relationship Clare develops with her sons is telling. Irene herself is guilty of no such transgression of what she believes should be the proper boundary between the respective realms of children and adults. Irene is portrayed as very fussy and particular about the welfare of her sons but never loving and affectionate. She is insensitive and inattentive to their feelings. While Clare immediately senses the boys' discomfort when she and Irene unexpectedly appear in the doorway of the playroom and attempts to tease them into letting their guards down, Irene seems completely oblivious to her sons' states of mind. At the dinner table on the night Brian talks about the recent lynching and Ted evinces so much interest in the subject,

Irene manages to derail the discussion without ever once addressing a word to anyone except her husband. She reserves the open expression of her opinions until the boys have left the table and are safely ensconced upstairs. When Clare teases her about her obsessive-compulsive investment in maternity—"Children aren't everything. ... There are other things in the world, though I admit some people don't seem to suspect it"—Irene becomes defensive: "I know very well that I take being a mother rather seriously. I *am* wrapped up in my boys and the running of my house. I can't help it. And, really, I don't think it's anything to laugh at" (240). The joke, however, is on Irene, because while she is so intensively occupied in her "boys and the running of [her] house," she fails to recognize that the one entity in her life upon which all the others depend—her marriage—is disintegrating.[23]

Irene is certain that her marriage will remain intact because of the children she and Brian share; she believes her husband owes her his allegiance because she is the mother of his sons. When they have their protracted battle early in their marriage due to Brian's desire to emigrate from the United States, Irene resorts to threatening a divorce if he continues his campaign to move them all to Brazil, only because she is fairly confident she will never have to carry it out. Then, as the years pass, her certitude of Brian grows unshakable. She no longer fears "he would throw everything aside and rush off to that remote place of his heart's desire," partly because of his "slightly undemonstrative" affection for her but mostly because of Ted and Junior (221). On some level of her consciousness, it is apparent that Irene realizes that Brian's feelings for her are less passionate than they should be. In Irene's mind, however, she and the boys are a package deal, and therefore her sons are a guarantee that Brian will never desert her. Nevertheless, she needs the assurance of being in control of the trajectory of their lives, so that she can forestall any disturbance of "that security of place and substance which she insisted upon for her sons and in a lesser degree for herself" (221). Once she begins to suspect that Brian may be considering leaving her for Clare, she desperately clings to her conviction that Junior and Ted will ensure Brian's loyalty. As she begins to regard him objectively, as a man she could potentially lose instead of the husband she takes for granted, Irene calmly reassures herself of the claim she has upon "Brian, the father of Ted and Junior" (253). Then, the momentary reassurance dissipates when she considers Clare's seductive hold over men like her husband and realizes that her significance to Brian is confined to her role as his children's mother: "Alone she was nothing. Worse. An obstacle" (254). In this sensitive exploration of the complex psyche of a woman who has based her entire identity on the presence of a husband and children, whose entire sense of herself as an individual is only in relation to a family, and whose blind faith in the permanence of that family is shattered, Larsen provides a compelling portrait of the emotional turmoil raging almost imperceptibly behind the cool mask of a gracious hostess.

Having accepted that she has been displaced in Brian's affections, based entirely upon her own conjecture, Irene shifts her attention to how she can hold on to Brian, albeit nominally, and preserve her family for the sake of her children. She decides that if she feigns complete ignorance of the supposed affair between Clare and Brian, there will never be any need to confront the issue. Afraid that Hugh Wentworth, the guest of honor at her tea party, discerns the reason for her agitation, Irene's mind springs into action and she resolves to control what is within her power to control: She may not be able to prevent others from discovering the indiscretion, but she can prevent them from suspecting she herself is aware of any impropriety between her husband and her best friend. In the instant she makes this decision, Irene constructs herself as the quintessential suffering mother, sacrificing her very dignity in order to protect her children. Irene does not care if people think she is blindly oblivious as long as they do not consider her knowingly pathetic. Later, in a moment of self-righteous indignation, Irene reminds herself of her rights to her husband, that "[h]is duty was to her and to his boys" (267). The inviolability of the family unit is one of Irene's guiding tenets.

In their frequent conversations regarding the wisdom of Clare's secret trips to Harlem, Irene tries to impart to her friend her personal conviction that once established, families belong together. Whenever it sounds as if Clare might be seriously considering leaving her husband and reintegrating herself into black society, Irene brings up her daughter, Margery. Margery Bellew is older than the Redfield boys; she is twelve years old when her mother begins making her visits to Harlem. In fact, as Irene mentions in an effort to convince Clare to subdue her restlessness and maintain her charade of whiteness, Margery is too old to ever learn that she has "Negro blood." "She'd never forgive you. You may be used to risks, but this is one you mustn't take, Clare" (228). Irene depends upon Clare's maternal devotion, certainly not her nonexistent marital allegiance, to curb her reckless behavior. When Clare despondently contemplates her scheduled return to Europe some months later, Irene is encouraging: "I imagine you'll be happy enough, once you get away. … Remember, there's Margery. Think how glad you'll be to see her after all this time" (240). When Clare frightens Irene with her disclosure that if her husband were to discover her hidden ancestry she would simply move to Harlem, "Irene leaned forward, cold and tense. 'And what about Margery?'" (266). Clare's response is even more frightening to Irene: "She's all that holds me back. But if Jack finds out, if our marriage is broken, that lets me out. Doesn't it?" (266). Though Clare professes an allegiance to Margery, she never has an opportunity to demonstrate it in the novel. Clare's daughter is always conveniently out of the way, incapable of interfering with her mother's freedom. Part of Clare's appeal to entice Irene to stop by her hotel when they are in Chicago is the promise that Irene can "see Margery—she's just ten" (185). However, when Irene arrives at the Bellews' suite at the Morgan, Margery is nowhere to be found; it turns out that Clare and Jack left her, reportedly at her request, with some of his relatives in Wisconsin. Two years later, when Clare makes her fateful appearance in New York, Margery has been safely deposited in a Swiss boarding school.

Margery's protracted absences preclude Clare's obligation to privilege her role as a mother, though Irene labors to keep Clare's child at the forefront of her thoughts. When Clare tearfully agonizes over the unsurpassed injustice of motherhood—"I think … that being a mother is the cruelest thing in the world"—Irene seizes the opportunity to deliver a gentle sermonette designed to guide her friend into the proper mindset of middle-class morality: "And the most responsible, Clare. We mothers are all responsible for the security and happiness of our children" (228). Because Clare's maternal responsibility is deferred, she is able to indulge her immediate desires without internalizing the impact her actions may have upon her daughter. Her conduct mirrors that of Edna Pontellier from Kate Chopin's *The Awakening* (1899), another conflicted heroine who resents the constraints placed upon her by the husband she has never loved and the children who tacitly demand her eternal fidelity and devotion. Edna's most sympathetic confidant, Doctor Mandelet, commiserates with her on the difficult predicament many women eventually face when they blithely enter into the lifetime commitment of motherhood: "The trouble is … that youth is given up to illusions. It seems to be a provision of Nature; a decoy to secure mothers for the race. And Nature takes no account of moral consequences, of arbitrary conditions which we create, and which we feel obliged to maintain at any cost."[24] Mandelet encapsulates the dilemma faced by women who grow to resent the plethora of constrictions imposed by marriage and maternity. Edna opts to commit suicide rather than submit to the suppression of her individuality under her domestic obligations as a wife and mother.

Passing likewise ends with a tragic death that is never explicitly revealed to be a suicide, an accident, or a murder. Felise Freeland gives a party which Irene, Brian, and Clare attend together. Jack Bellew makes a surprise entrance. After having an earlier unexpected encounter with Irene, accompanied by the golden-skinned Felise, on a bustling Manhattan street, Jack realizes that Irene is a black woman, and, by extension, that his wife must be as well. He tells Clare he is going on a business trip to nearby Philadelphia, which frees Clare to meet the Redfields and go to Felise's party. Instead of going to Philadelphia, Jack follows Clare to Harlem and confronts her at the Freelands' sixth-floor apartment. In the ensuing confusion of activity, Clare somehow tumbles out of a floor-to-ceiling window that Irene had opened some time earlier when she had expressed a desire for some fresh air.

Many textual clues, aside from her oft-declared wish for Clare's permanent removal from their lives, point to Irene as the murderer. In a moment of intense rage, a teacup slips from Irene's hand at her tea party, leaving "[d]ark stains" on the carpet below; Irene's unconscious act of destruction foreshadows the later scene when Irene's moment of "terror tinged with ferocity" results in Clare's mangled body being recovered from the pavement beneath the Freelands' window (254, 271). Then, Irene's fabricated confession to an intentional attempt to destroy the cup, a family heirloom she had never liked, provides insight into her later motive for causing Clare's "accident": "I had an inspiration. I had only to break it, and I was rid of it forever. So simple! And I'd never thought of it before" (255). Larsen also includes a narrative parallel between the description of Irene tossing a cigarette butt out of the window: "Irene finished her cigarette and threw it out, watching the tiny spark drop slowly down to the white ground below," and the subsequent description of Clare's tragic descent from the same aperture: "One moment Clare had been there, a vital glowing thing, like a flame of red and gold. The next she was gone" (270–71).

Irene wants Clare dead because she knows that the emotional attachment of motherhood, the one force that Irene had hoped might be strong enough to retain Clare in her white world, is not enough to prevent Clare from stealing Brian away from her. Since Clare is willing to forsake her family, precisely what Irene will not permit herself to do, even by default, Irene takes definitive action to put her beyond Brian's reach and into the inescapably, monolithically white domain of the snow-covered ground below. Though Irene will not admit her responsibility, even to herself—"'It was an accident, a terrible accident,' she muttered fiercely, 'It *was*'"—she is simply involved in another willful self-deception engineered to preserve her peace of mind and good opinion of herself (272). The end of the novel is inconclusive regarding the future of Irene and Brian as a couple, but it does suggest that the Clare fiasco was precisely the catalyst Irene needed to induce her to change her approach to her marriage, perhaps being more sensitive to Brian as an individual rather than an entity.

When she finally makes her way downstairs to the small, shocked group of witnesses to Clare's misfortune, Irene "went straight to Brian. ... She had a great longing to comfort him, to charm away his suffering and horror. But she was helpless, having so completely lost control of his mind and heart" (274). Since the reader recognizes that Irene "lost control" of Brian years earlier, when she so viciously opposed his bid to move to Brazil, this passage invites the hope that Irene has finally rid herself of her matriarchal delusions and is willing to make a fresh start with her husband for the benefit of her family. Instead, Brian comforts *her*, having no reason to believe they do not share their grief over Clare's death. He perhaps feels guilty about his infidelity and contrite about having betrayed his innocent wife; the "strong arms" which lift Irene up from her fainting spell in the penultimate paragraph of the novel are surely Brian's (275).[25] Though Larsen does not provide the Redfields with a healthy foundation upon which to rebuild their marriage—both of them harbor devastating (and in Irene's case, felonious) secrets from one another—she does suggest that, with the elimination of the threat posed by Clare, it may survive, albeit tenuously.

The drastic measures Irene considers herself forced to take to preserve her family, along with the futile resignation with which Helga Green must accept the inescapable repercussions of her impetuous decision to marry a man she did not know, manifest Nella Larsen's scorn for middle-class domesticity, its farcical nature, and how it suffocates the potential of black women. Motherhood in her novels is used to underscore her contempt for the uplift rhetoric of racial advancement being effected through strict adherence to a conventional domestic script. Her portraits of middle-class culture reveal Larsen's lack of faith in the adequacy of the black family, regardless of relative social status, to rear children capable of successfully negotiating the repressive social order of America. Larsen's exposés of the milieu of black privilege disallow attention to the home lives of the female servants in her novels, who are treated as mere accoutrements of an elite lifestyle. In the next chapter, however, Fannie Hurst centers the experience of maternity enacted by the black domestic worker, interrogating the popular mythology of the mammy, an image of black femininity which to this day continues to impact the cultural perception of black women.

4 The Stereotypical Mammy in Fannie Hurst's *Imitation of Life*

Fannie Hurst's connection to the Harlem Renaissance is figured most significantly through her relationship to Zora Neale Hurston, the writer from Eatonville, Florida, who secured her position in the modern construction of the (African) American literary canon with her innovative novel *Their Eyes Were Watching God* (1937). To provide her with a means of financial support, Hurst employed Hurston as her personal secretary after meeting her in the early spring of 1925. Hurston's clerical ineptitude soon resulted in her termination as a secretary, but Hurst retained her as a chauffeur, and Hurston evolved into more of a traveling companion for the better part of two years, until late 1926.

Though their relationship was free of the more blatantly exploitative aspects of other patron-protégé associations which flourished during the Renaissance, Hurston did at times express a sense of being used by Hurst.[1] Hurston felt that Hurst may have valued her presence in public as a means of attracting attention to herself and even suggested to one of her friends that Hurst "liked the way my dark skin highlighted her own lily-white complexion."[2] Nevertheless, the two women maintained their friendship for decades after Hurston left Hurst's employment. Hurst supported Hurston's Guggenheim fellowship applications with reference letters in the mid-thirties, and their collected correspondence contains letters dated through 1949.[3]

The tone of the final letters in the collection indicate that Hurst attempted to distance herself from her former associate in the wake of widely publicized, though untenable, allegations that Hurston had sexually molested a ten-year-old boy in 1948. At the time the crime was avowed to have taken place, Hurston was out of the country—she was collecting folklore in Honduras. Despite her irrefutable alibi, Hurston was dragged through a prolonged trial that resulted in her eventual acquittal but effectively destroyed her reputation in the process.[4] Hurst avoids any reference to Hurston in her autobiography, *Anatomy of Me* (1958), very likely due to the scandal in which the writer had become embroiled a decade earlier. Hurston, on the other hand, remained loyal to Hurst even while the author weathered the fallout of black critical indignation in response to her questionable depictions of black women in *Imitation of Life*.

Fannie Hurst surely felt as if she had created genuinely realistic black female characters. She considered herself quite sympathetic to the African-American experience and was particularly gratified by her representation of the black perspective on the national race problem:

> The second world war had ruthlessly exposed American race relations. Negro troops were not only permitted but drafted to spill blood for their country; were allowed to die but not to live with white troops. Outfits were black or white. Not black and white. Gold star mothers were sent abroad by the government in black and white contingents to visit the graves of their sons.
>
> How shocked St. Peter must have been when our colored heroes asked the way to the Negro pearly gates.
>
> My novel, *Imitation of Life*, was born of this consciousness and quickly made into the first of the "race" pictures. ... (338–39)

Since *Imitation of Life* was composed a full ten years before America even entered World War II, Hurst must be implying that her sensitivity to racial antagonism predated the postwar national focus on the problem; this, in fact, was precisely the case. Hurst had associated herself with many civil rights causes through the 1920s and was touted as an acknowledged "friend of the Negro race." As she declares in *Anatomy of Me*, "Ever since I had emerged from the climate of St. Louis, I had been lifting pen and voice against the second-class status of the American Negro, ashamed that my country should bear the ugly tattoo both here and abroad."[5] However, if *Imitation of Life* is to be taken as a statement in opposition to "the second-class status of the American Negro," then the manner in which Hurst chooses to characterize Delilah Johnston, the narrative's mammy, suggests that the novelist must be implicating black people in their own subjugation and attacking the maintenance of attitudes which operated to uphold the tenets of white supremacy.[6] Hurst was enlisted to serve on the panel of judges for the 1925 *Opportunity* magazine literary contest—a competition established to encourage the efforts of black writers and discover new talents. It was there that she met budding writer Zora Neale Hurston, who won prizes and honorable mentions for four of her submissions that evening. Hurston unwaveringly endorsed Hurst's representations of black people. While Sterling Brown, Renaissance poet and author of *The Negro in American Fiction*, denounced Hurst's depiction of the mammy figure in *Imitation of Life* as that of a "contented slave, brought up to date," in 1940 Hurston wrote to Hurst that Brown's views conflicted with those of many people she encountered in Durham, North Carolina, where she was living while she taught at what is now known as North Carolina Central University:

> You have a grand set of admirers in this part of the world because of "Imitation of Life." So it seems that Sterling Brown is not in the majority. He picks on me all the time now. ... [H]e says that I stand convicted of having furnished you with the material of "Imitation." I let it stand without contradiction because I feel he does me an honor. In so saying, he pays you an unconscious tribute because he is admitting the truth of the work. What he and his kind resent is just that. It is too accurate to be comfortable. ... [7]

Hurston's comments in praise of Hurst's characterizations suggest that, as I will argue more fully later, the mammy figure is not meant to be admirable; *Imitation*'s Delilah Johnston is not intended to be a model of exemplary black female conduct. Instead, when Hurston notes that the "accuracy" of the narrative incites reader discomfort within the black community, she implies that Delilah's character retains anachronistic attitudes that compel her to slavishly worship those with white skins and engage in insidiously destructive forms of self-deprecation. The novel, then, can be read as using Delilah's very pervasiveness to graphically demonstrate the extent of the damage done to the race as a whole, as well as the individual family unit, by the retention of the "contented slave" mentality.

The Cultural Significance of the Mammy

Ever since the irrepressible Aunt Jemima made her dusty debut from a flour barrel at the World's Columbian Exposition of 1893 in Chicago, American culture has indelibly printed the image of the doting black mammy upon our collective imagination with such memorable film and novel characters as Delilah Johnston. In *Imitation of Life*, the novel, the overwhelmingly positive response to the B. Pullman chain of waffle restaurants is due to Delilah's appeal to the public. She is infantilized and patronized by the female customer who calls her "adorable" in obvious adherence to an alternative standard of aesthetic appreciation than what might provoke the woman to append the same label to Bea's young daughter Jessie, for instance.

The customer's comfort in designating Delilah "adorable" resides in the same collusion of race and gender expectations which make Miss Muldoon uncomfortable with attractive black women in Dorothy West's *The Living Is Easy*. Miss Muldoon, fruit merchant Bart Judson's bookkeeper of fifteen years, is an older white woman who resents his wife Cleo's Caucasoid beauty because "She preferred to picture Negro women as fat, black, and plain-faced."[8] Like the customer at the B. Pullman restaurant, Miss Muldoon is pleasingly gratified by black women who conform to this phenotypic norm.

Douglas Sirk, director of the 1959 remake of *Imitation of Life*, neither read Hurst's novel nor screened John Stahl's 1934 film before he shot his version of the story, but he was adamant about providing reasonable motivation for Sarah Jane's (Peola's) rebellion against blackness, which he thought would be missing if he replicated the plotting of her mother's partnership in the lucrative business:

> [N]owadays a Negro woman who got rich *could* buy a house, and wouldn't be dependent to such a degree on the white woman, a fact which makes the Negro woman's daughter less understandable. So I had to change the axis of the film and make the Negro woman just the typical Negro, a servant, without much she could call her own but the friendship, love, and charity of a white mistress. This whole uncertain and kind of oppressive situation accounts much more for the daughter's attitude.[9]

Because Sirk's Annie Johnson is "just the typical Negro" instead of the inspiration behind, and unacknowledged cofounder of, a multimillion dollar company, he is able, on the brink of the Civil Rights Era, to recuperate the drama of the mythical mammy persona which informed Hurst's novel more than a quarter of a century earlier. Black self-deprecation, fear of autonomy, and unrestrained joy in serving white people would have been incomprehensible and unconvincing to a 1959 theater audience, so Sirk altered the plot to create a justification for Annie's loyalty, where Delilah needed no such contrivances. In fact, Sirk's argument about providing a basis for understanding Sarah Jane's resentment is precisely Hurst's point back in 1933. Even then Delilah's dependence upon Bea had no logical motivation after the commercial success of the B. Pullman enterprise, which makes Peola's dissatisfaction all the more reasonable. Though they serve different functions in their respective settings, however, both Annie and Delilah are conspicuous symbols of the long, bizarre history of the American mammy.

The influential black leader Booker T. Washington encouraged the continued presence of mammies in white households after the abolition of slavery. He thought they could act as a sort of fleet of good-will ambassadors between the races. His 1909 publication *The Story of the Negro, Vol. II*, outlines his rationale:

> The simple hearted devotion of the Negro slave woman to their [sic] masters ... was one of the redeeming features of Negro slavery in the South. ... I know of scarcely anything more beautiful than the tributes I have heard Southern white men and women pay to those old coloured mammies, who nursed them as children, shared their childish joys and sorrows and clung to them through life with an affection that no change of time ... could diminish.[10]

Modern black ambivalence about the efficacy of Washington's social philosophy is based upon such assertions as this. However, black suspicions about Washington's loyalties may perhaps underrate his political sophistication and diplomatic instincts. Washington's consciousness that his status as the nationally endorsed spokesperson for American black people was conditional upon his continued appeal to the white majority, coupled with his understandable solicitude to ingratiate the white Southerners alongside whom he and millions of other freedmen had to coexist every day, may have influenced his seemingly nostalgic reverie upon the relationship between black slave women and the white children they cared for so tenderly. Perhaps Washington might also have been interested in centering and sentimentalizing the image of mammy in order to constitute her experience the predominant one typifying the black female condition under slavery.

The promotion of the mammy could be viewed as instrumental in the project to reform the image of black femininity, a task many black schools busily endeavored to accomplish—among them Howard, Hampton, Fisk, and Washington's own Tuskegee Institute. However, the usual route towards image reformation involved the cultivation of genteel female students through intensive etiquette training, strict codes of conduct, and the recruitment of exemplary models of womanhood to serve on the faculty and staff. Mammy was not held up as a woman to be emulated. In fact, she was vigorously denounced by many prominent black leaders. W. E. B. Du Bois believed the black female presence in white households weakened the black family unit and put the women at risk for sexual harassment:

> Let the present-day mammies suckle their own children. Let them walk in the sunshine with their own toddling boys and girls and put their own sleepy little brothers and sisters to bed. As their girls grow to womanhood, let them see to it that ... they do not enter domestic service where they are unprotected, and where their womanhood is not treated with respect.[11]

Despite Du Bois' 1912 expostulations, sixty percent of employed black women worked in domestic service as late as 1940, seven years following the appearance of *Imitation of Life*.[12] The *Baltimore Afro-American* reported in 1945 that the most vehement outcry against black women obtaining jobs at a Naval plant in Macon, Georgia, came not "from management or the employees ... but from white local housewives, who feared lowering the barriers would rob them of maids, cooks, and nurses."[13] Surely, Mammy retained her cultural currency in the public psyche. There was a Black Mammy Memorial Institute operating in the 1910s, known as such because the Black Mammy Association of Athens, Georgia, donated considerable sums of money to the Tuskegee-like industrial evening school on the condition that the institute adopt the absurdly inappropriate name.[14] There was even an ardent but ultimately unsuccessful effort spearheaded by a group of Southern white women to erect a granite memorial to mammies in Washington, DC.

Disappointed by the dismal failure of the grassroots movement to establish a series of mammy monuments throughout the South, the Daughters of the Confederacy solicited a senator from Mississippi to introduce a Congressional resolution for the designation of a site in the nation's capital for a permanent shrine to Mammy's memory. The Honorable John Sharp Williams addressed the Senate in 1924 on behalf of the doomed resolution with impassioned rhetoric: "The proposed monument is intended to express the gratitude of this generation for the unselfish devotion and self-sacrificing service rendered by those Negro women of the days of slavery, to the children of their masters."[15]

Honest postbellum reminiscences of mammies often contradict the traditional image of the hired caretakers as fat, dark, and jolly, and they guiltily acknowledge the emotional abandonment of mammies as the children outgrew their need for them. Writer Ellen Glasgow remembered her "beloved" mammy as

> an extraordinary character, endowed with an unusual intelligence, a high temper, and a sprightly sense of humor.... But she could neither read nor write. ...
>
> "As soon as I learn my letters, Mammy, I'm going to teach you yours," I promised. But I never taught her, and to this day, I regret that I did not.[16]

Playwright Lillian Hellman echoes Glasgow's note of contrition in her memoir of Sophronia, "a tall, handsome, light tan woman ... who was for me, as for so many other white Southern children, the one and certain anchor so needed for the young years, so forgotten after that."[17] In an effort to dodge the reification of simpering, insincere testimonials and collapse the distinction between the labels of "mammy" and "mother," writer Adrienne Rich catalogues the many maternal services her mammy performed for her:

> My black mother was "mine" only for four years, during which she fed me, dressed me, played with me, watched over me, sang to me, cared for me tenderly and intimately. "Childless" herself, she was a mother. She was slim, dignified, and very handsome, and from her I learned—nonverbally—a great deal about the possibilities of dignity in a degrading situation.[18]

Rich's heartfelt words notwithstanding, the mammy was commonly expected to engage in the physical and emotional labor of child care without being granted the socially approved distinction of "mother," which was reserved for the white women for whom they stood as surrogates.

Sentimental tributes to mammies were not restricted to nostalgic or remorseful white people, however. In October 1920, the *Half-Century Magazine*, a Chicago-based periodical that asserted its fiction was "written by Colored people, about Colored people, and for Colored people," printed a story by Leona Gray called "Mammy Sue."[19] Mammy Sue is facing dismissal after several years of service to the Stanton family. Though she is informally bequeathed to Edith Stanton after the young woman's marriage, in an effort to keep pace with their social circle, Edith's newlywed husband, Mr. Jackson, convinces her to replace all of their black domestics with white ones. Despite her forced retirement, Mammy Sue alone remains to care for Mrs. Jackson and her three-year-old son, Bobby, when they contract the deadly influenza virus and the entire staff of white servants stages a full-scale desertion.

Gray employs an avalanche of minstrel stereotypes in her story, describing Mammy Sue as "more than ordinarily homely. Corpulent, ebony-hued, ill featured, she now had the additional defects subsequent upon the ravages of old age and rheumatism" (5). In our first glimpse of Mammy Sue she is "gaily attired in vari-colored calico" and exhibits a curious juxtaposition of tragic and comic attributes: when one of the new white maids informs her that her mistress wants to talk to her, "Mammy tossed her head high and shuffled off in the direction of the living room" (5). Mammy Sue is devastated to hear she is being fired because "For some time she had proudly boasted that she was 'de only cullud pu'son on de place'"; in her response to Mrs. Jackson's explanation for her dismissal, a sequence of what seems to be high dramatic action culminates in comical dialect speech: "I'se old and crippled up, but I kin earn my bread 'n butter 'thout no 'sistence f'om nobody" (5).

Mammy Sue proceeds to prove her claim to competence when she takes charge of the household after Mrs. Jackson and young Bobby succumb to the flu. She promptly engages a fleet of black replacement workers who "rolled their white eyes heavenward and scoffed at the word 'epidemic,'" and wins back the esteem of the Jacksons through her improvisation of a course of treatment for Bobby which the overburdened local doctor later pronounces is responsible for saving his life (5). Mammy is finally back in her element when she is acknowledged to be indispensable to her beloved white family. Gray's portrayal of Mammy Sue might be thought an insider parody of an oft-ridiculed figure until the final resolution of the story, when Mr. Jackson declares his change of heart toward Mammy. He confesses to her that she has revealed to him the true significance of Jesus Christ's ministry through her selfless service to his family. Though "Her black skin blinded him to all her many virtues" before, the "terrible crisis" occasioned by the influenza reveals to him "not the plain, black servant, but the inner woman, the true Christian friend" (12).

Gray's message becomes complicated by this conclusion in which Mr. Jackson experiences a spiritual awakening, which, if duly considered, may point to an interpretation of "Mammy Sue" as an effort to recuperate the legacy of mammies as pious, saintly figures in black history, faithfully following the biblical precepts which instruct servants to serve their masters as zealously as if they were serving God Himself.[20] Gray's rendition of Mammy is then reminiscent of Booker T. Washington's racial reconciliation campaign: the writer helps her predominantly black audience to understand and sympathize with this elderly woman whose entire life has been committed to the service of her white employers and whose natural proclivity toward familial bonding has been channeled into the white people with whom she lives. Gray's story is a gentle encouragement to the black community to reclaim the mammy as a symbol of pride instead of reviling her as a means of expressing opposition to the white Southerners who were not only appropriating Mammy as their exclusive property but actively publicizing their fond recollections of her.

For Washington, Mammy's political expedience lay precisely within the manifold virtues she possessed which endeared her to her white constituency, among them dependability, self-sacrifice, sincerity, and loyalty. Her benign memory, while disturbing to African Americans to the extent that Mammy's performance of maternity was contingent upon a severing of ties with the black community, harbored none of the salaciousness associated with the other problematic manifestation of black maternal links to white people during slavery—the sizable number of mulatto children, which attested to the unbridled frequency of sexual relations between black women and white men. Washington himself was the product of such a liaison, though he never publicly admitted certainty of the identity of his white father. Washington's reference to "old coloured mammies" and his pronounced emphasis on their interaction with white children, however, completely forestall any attempt to link the idyllic domestic scene he evokes to the narrative of sexual misconduct. The alternative scenario of black and white intimacy erases the association of the black female presence in the white household with the threat of sexual rivalry between the white mistress and her black domestic. Indeed, a prudent mistress seeking a servant to function in such an intimate household capacity would certainly have consciously chosen to engage a black woman she did not perceive as a potential object of her husband's affections. Hurst, for instance, adroitly avoids the pitfall of the possibility of Delilah being perceived as sexual competition for Bea by making Delilah almost twenty years Bea's senior and having Delilah project all her expressions of romantic desire onto Bea, her "bigges' baby": "I want some lovin' for you, honey—some man-lovin.' ... I's jes' an ole nigger-woman, honey, but I's had it and I's done wid it, but I's had it while it lasted. ... And knowin' dat, I wants mah Miss Honey-Bea to have it" (220). Any intimations of white male susceptibility to Delilah's "charms" are also defused by the repudiation of miscegenation in the novel. Delilah is emphatic about establishing Peola's non-white paternity, denounces interracial relationships, and keeps a respectful distance from white men. When Bea gets into the habit of inviting her young male regular customers home for wholesome after-hours gatherings when the B. Pullmans close down for the day, Delilah is "not to be coaxed out of the rear end of the apartment," but would on occasion concede to "sit in her dark kitchen, firelight on her eyeballs, cheek bones, and surf of white teeth, and sing through the open doorway" (231).

The mammy figure successfully deviates from the typing of black females as shameless seductresses, but she occupies the strange position of serving as no more than an ambiguously maternal figure to the white family for whom she works tirelessly, while she is displaced from a parallel function in a black family unit. She is only ambiguously maternal, as exemplified in D. W. Griffith's 1915 epic drama *Birth of a Nation*, because the cultural standards for motherhood which undergird the representations in that film are clearly very different depending upon the race of the woman in question. The black mammy deftly assumes the masculine responsibilities of the absent white father, defending the home against assailants, and protecting the white females from harm. She is not viewed as vulnerable to male intruders, most pointedly because she is not considered even remotely sexually desirable. Her allegiance to her white "family" is tested, but remains inviolable, and she will preserve their lives at the sacrifice of her own. Devotion until death is standard protocol in romanticized narratives of mammies.

The characterization of Delilah falls squarely within the purview of Griffith's screen version of the mammy and Gray's textual heroine, Mammy Sue. As a generic type, Delilah functions in place of the traditional wife in what Lauren Berlant has called the "quasi-companionate couple" comprised by Bea Pullman and Delilah Johnston.[21] Bea is amazed by the "red of her easily-hinged large mouth, packed with the white laughter of her stunning allotment of hound-clean teeth; the jug color of her skin with the gold highlights on cheekbones; the terrific unassailable quality of her high spirits, Baptist fervor, and amplitude," all of which characterize the incomparable Delilah (96). She consecrates herself to her appropriated family so completely that her very will to live is predicated upon their need of her: "I's got to live on. I's got babies, one, two, three of 'em ... besides de one God give me out of mah own flesh" (262). Delilah exhausts herself making herself indispensable to her three white "babies," Bea, Jessie, and Mr. Chipley. The result is that her monumental presence, while not coerced, still emancipates Bea from her domestic obligations and enables her to become a successful businesswoman.

Mammy as the Liberator of the White "New Woman"

The major uncertainty driving the various interpretations of *Imitation of Life* is how the audience is supposed to receive Delilah's role in the narrative. In Hurst's text she is clearly presented as the model servant. Angie, the young black girl who appears in the beginning of the novel to assist with the preparations for Bea's wedding to Benjamin Pullman, is suspected of thievery and deliberate malevolence. When Bea returns home from the postnuptial celebration at a restaurant in town, she surveys the room in which she had been married just hours before to ensure that "the little black girl ... had carted nothing away" (48). Later, when she ascends to the master bedroom, which she and her new husband have arrogated from her widowed father, Bea reviews the collection of Mr. Pullman's personal effects. She is shocked by the prominent display of a picture of a semi-nude woman, and immediately assumes Angie is the intentionally crude culprit: "With what seemed actual malice, that picture had been propped up [on the mantelpiece] against one of the china pugs. Those darkies. ..." (50)

Bea's dubious opinion of "darkies" is intensified when she begins her door-to-door "shanty district" search for a live-in housekeeper and finds no one receptive to her needs. "Most of the female domestic help, wives, sweethearts, or what nots of the thousands of negro waiters, chair-pushers, and miscellaneous helpers about town and the Boardwalk, demanded the freedom to return home evenings" (90). Bea appears to be oblivious to the fact that the women whose labor she solicits have personal lives of their own and is annoyed by their unwillingness to forfeit their independence in order to sustain her household.[22] By contrast, Delilah's tractability, along with her uninduced association of her racial identity with a natural propensity to serve white people, endears her to Bea: "We's black, me and mah baby, and we'd lak mighty much to come work for you" (92).

Part of the difficulty bound up in formulating an interpretation of Delilah's character is connected to the question of whether or not Bea is designed to model the proper white response to her servant. Regardless of Hurst's intentions, which are impossible to determine with any absolute precision, Delilah's characterization effectually subverts a positive reception. Even granting that Hurst's audience would have been composed largely of white people who would have approved of a black woman who evinced such fidelity to her white employers, Delilah's presence ultimately sabotages Bea's happiness. She is a disruptive influence to the Pullman home; she supplants Bea's desired place as a mother to her daughter, and she is sorely lacking as a substitute domestic partner for the loving husband Bea longs for but has no idea how to obtain. That Stahl would have toned down the representation of Delilah to make her more palatable to a general audience suggests that the character Hurst depicts is not meant to be regarded favorably.

Louise Beavers, the actress who portrayed Delilah in the 1934 film, was praised by the *New York Daily News* for her "perfectly corking performance," implying that her rendition of the character was akin to a blackface minstrel stereotype.[23] Stahl's Delilah may be unsophisticated and eager to please—for instance, immediately after swearing never to divulge the secret family pancake recipe, she impulsively leans over and whispers it to Bea—but she is far more dignified and self-contained than the wailing, whining, self-deprecating Delilah of the novel. The representation of Bea's mother, Adelaide Chipley, makes the distinction between proper maternalism and melodramatic excess absolutely clear.

Imitation of Life, the novel, opens on the scene of Adelaide Chipley's corpse laid out in her parlor. Bea is overwhelmed by the intricacies of housekeeping when she has to take over the responsibilities after the death of her mother and wistfully reflects upon the time when "icepans had never overflowed, nor laundry accumulated, nor windows grown thick with grime" (6). Mrs. Chipley's life is centered upon efficient housekeeping; she conceives of her utility through her output of domestic labor, and consequently, she requires a dependent family to nurture. The disturbing corollary to her operational equation is that in order to maintain her distinctive position within her household, she must ensure that the members of her family remain totally dependent upon her. Therefore, while Mrs. Chipley's untimely death preserves her from the unkind fate her daughter faces of life as a widow with neither marketable skills nor monetary resources (and the additional burden of caring for her father since Mr. Chipley has a stroke which leaves him permanently confined to a wheelchair), it ironically precipitates the series of misfortunes which plague her beloved daughter.

Adelaide Chipley's sudden, disconcerting absence from the home actuates the shifting of masculine predominance from Evans Chipley to Benjamin Pullman, evidenced by the facility with which he arranges his marriage to Bea. Mrs. Chipley's premature death also compels Bea to assume a function in the household which she is ill-equipped to execute and deprives Bea of the maternal guidance she so desperately needs to initiate her into the enigmatic particulars of becoming a woman. It is curious that Adelaide Chipley, who must have known her death was imminent and who was so paranoid herself about being left with no means of material support, would have so inadequately prepared her only daughter for life without her mother. As Bea later reflects, "Mother's mock-regretful boast had been that Bea could not so much as darn a stocking or boil an egg" (18). Perhaps her preoccupation with financial security eclipsed Adelaide Chipley's attentiveness to the necessity for teaching her daughter the rudimentary skills she would need to adopt the household routine of her inherited responsibilities, and foregrounded her misguided optimism in the certainty of her daughter's economic livelihood.

Mrs. Chipley's life is claimed by a prediagnosed inoperable cancer, but she apparently makes no effort to train her daughter how to act as mistress of the house, to encourage her to interact with members of the opposite sex, to pass on to her any useful information about female sexuality, to even help Bea to cope with her terminal illness and prepare for her death. Even so, Bea idolizes the memory of her mother and perpetually feels her own inferiority to her mother's efficiency and competence. She envisions romantic fantasies about a happy and fulfilling home life in which she functions as a replica of Mrs. Chipley; she dreams of earning enough money to spend "hours in the nursery. Afternoons on the beach or on a Ventnor veranda, sewing for a child who romped as she stitched" (114). Consequently, Bea feels unfitted for the exigencies of bread winning: "The hanker in her was for the doing of little and tidy things. To stack spiced cookies into a painted jar for the cupboard. To hem the dotted-swiss bathroom curtains, were nostalgia indeed" (134). Bea's dainty, idealized domestic visions keep her perpetually within the home, but these particular visions still depend upon another laboring body to perform the less pleasant tasks required to maintain a well-appointed household. Even with enough money to abandon the workforce, Bea would need her Delilah.

Like Mrs. Chipley before her, Delilah stays constantly busy, but she is just as constantly airing concern about the intensity of Bea's work habits. Delilah is very disturbed by what she perceives as her mistress's overexertion, as Bea discovers when she consults Delilah for ideas on how to spend their mounting business revenues. Since Bea fully expects to hear Delilah make a personal request, she is startled by what issues from her housemate's lips: "I'd lak to see you, honey, rest up them achin' bones of yourn" (173). Hurst implies that Bea does indeed work harder than Delilah, in the sense that Bea aspires to the ultimate American dream of prosperity and worry-free leisure, while Delilah is content with a dramatically humbler standard of living. It is Bea who is up nights frantically scribbling figures on the backs of scrap envelopes while Delilah sleeps the peaceful slumber of the insouciant dependent. Delilah is more of a menial laborer who simply performs demanding physical tasks and does what she is told, while Bea is the innovator, the brains behind Delilah's brawn, and the bearer of the burden of the responsibility for their fused household. Because Delilah believes in the ideology contrasting black female ruggedness with white female delicacy, she is convinced that she should work while her young mistress remains idle.

In their consideration of Stahl's 1934 screen adaptation of *Imitation of Life*, film critics Jane Caputi and Helene Vann discuss the scene from the movie in which Delilah refuses a twenty-percent share of the profits from Bea Pullman's pancake empire—a dramatic enactment of Delilah's pronounced anti-materialist stance in the novel. Throughout the text she steadfastly insists upon little more than nominal payment for her essential, immeasurable contribution to Bea's prosperity. The first attempt Bea makes to compensate Delilah for her labor is forcefully repelled. Delilah protests, "We's partners in dis heah shebang, Miss Bea. … We got our chillun to think about before we go squanderin' de fust spare money dat comes in on no-'count suvvant's wages" (95–96). Delilah's so-called partnership with Bea is a strange one, since their arrangement does not include anything approaching an equal division of the profits, nor the credit for the inspiration behind the bustling enterprise. Though it is Bea who devises the clever gimmick of associating the name "B. Pullman" with restaurants designed to resemble railroad dining cars, she recognizes that "Delilah's savory coffee, Delilah's hot waffles, Delilah's Hearts, Delilah's smile, ... the little pampering something that came so readily from Delilah" are what account for the flourishing business (152). In an obvious allusion to the popular Aunt Jemima brand name and public icon, Delilah is portrayed in both Hurst's novel and Stahl's film as having her inbred domestic expertise shrewdly exploited by the resourceful, clever, and hard-working Bea.[24] Delilah willingly submits to this exploitation because she has no desire for wealth nor prestige; she simply wants the security of a permanent place to call home and people around her to work for, because for the simple Delilah, labor is an act of selfless love. Caputi and Vann conclude that

> the implication here, as in so many American films, is that blacks were happiest during the days of slavery, that slavery fulfilled black nature, and that most are actually yearning to return to that state. Thus, although offered her 'freedom,' represented by her own car and home, Delilah views this with dread, openly proclaiming that she desires only to stay and serve.[25]

Delilah needs to be needed. She wants to greet Bea when she comes home from work, help her undress, rub her feet, massage her back, fix her dinner, turn down her bed, and do whatever else she can to make their home a safe, comfortable, inviting haven from the outside world. Berlant's suggestion that Bea and Delilah are reminiscent of an old married couple is substantiated by the routine they settle into over their long years of cohabitation; when Peola unexpectedly returns to the New York apartment and interrupts her mother's "nightly rite of peeling a cold red apple for Bea before she retired," it is a graphic demonstration that fuels her contempt for Delilah's sycophancy (291–92).

Delilah is the only person (with the possible exception of Mrs. Chipley, who could reasonably be accused of both premature abandonment and neglect of her maternal duty to teach her daughter how to function as mistress of her own domicile) in Bea's life who never betrays, undermines, disappoints, or hurts her, whether intentionally or not. Delilah's devotion to Bea is completely disinterested, unconditional, and uncomplicated. While Bea's success is popularly ascribed to her "genius," Delilah is effaced into a symbol of somebody else's achievement. If read as a satire of the Aunt Jemima phenomenon, Hurst may be critiquing the use and widespread conception of the jolly, servile, pancake-flipping black mammy as a legitimate symbol of black womanhood. As Caputi and Vann insightfully contend, "behind the recurring stereotype of the black as servant lurks the recurring fantasy of the black as slave."[26] In the novel, Bea is savvy enough to cater to the pervasive American cultural fantasy of a reversion to slavery by crafting an image of

Delilah as the quintessential mammy—an image which accounts for the phenomenal success of the B. Pullman enterprise.

Delilah's first contribution to the diversification of the maple syrup delivery service upon which Bea builds her empire is the creation of heart-shaped candies made from a large shipment of maple sugar Bea had procured for a customer who subsequently reneged on the order. Delilah originally prepares the candies as a treat for the finicky Mr. Chipley, but Bea quickly perceives the marketability of the sweets and engages a number of retail establishments to sell them on consignment. When Bea suggests they adorn the boxes of "Delilah's Hearts" with a picture of the confectioner, Delilah wants to appear in the colorful headdress she had worn at her wedding to Peola's father, but Bea insists she don a crisp white chef's hat instead. "Why not Delilah's photograph, in her great fluted white cap, and her great fluted white smile on each box? Delilah, who, though actually in no more than her late thirties, looked mammy to the world. ... Delilah beaming and beckoning from the lid" (103). The conception of Delilah as "mammy to the world" seems at first to exist only in Bea's perception. She is conscious of the importance of presentation in achieving sales and thinks about how much the picture of Delilah would enhance the distinctiveness and appeal of her product. Bea realizes that she can profit from consumer attraction to Delilah's caricaturistic appearance and seeks to portray Delilah as completely at ease with her place in the kitchen, gratified by her subservient position, and eager to please: "A campaign of newspaper advertising, dreamed by Bea, ... was about to make Delilah's face, Delilah's name, Delilah's smile, one that reached from coast to coast" (175). Bea even coins the "succinct and magic" slogan "Delilah Delights," supported by a litany of reasons why she does so, such as "Delilah loves to spoil you" (175). Bea even further commercializes and commodifies Delilah's image by promoting a contest to encourage customers to compose their own tributes in appreciation of Delilah: "One thousand dollars to be given away in prizes for best statement not to exceed ten words, why Delilah delights" (175). However, even when the perspective shifts from the interior monologue of Bea to the supposedly impassive narrative voice, the overdrawn embodiment of all of the iconographic attributes of the stereotypical mammy that Delilah manifests stubbornly persists.

Bea is recuperated by her frank acknowledgments that Delilah deserves much of the credit for the triumph of the B. Pullman corporation. She inwardly concedes that her home is not truly her own but "Delilah's, upon whose terrific and willing-to-sweat shoulders rested so much of her success" (168). Bea also feels compelled to somehow recompense Delilah for her devotion: "I owe you so much more than I can ever repay, even if you let me. Do you realize that instead of the hundred-dollar-a-month slave you insist upon being, you could be working for me under any financial terms you name?" (263). What Bea does not ever sufficiently understand is that Delilah does not subscribe to her system of values. Delilah is not interested in wealth, recreation, leisure, or any other of the trappings of material success. She feels that Bea has made her life "a white-satin padded cell," and she is perfectly content to be confined there (263). The prison imagery is telling, however; as simple as Delilah appears to be, she does perceive that "being black in a white world" is tantamount to lifelong incarceration, a sentence her white-skinned daughter cannot abide (297).

Passing as the Modern Black Rejection of the Mammy

Color-line passing in *Imitation of Life* signals a repudiation of reproductive claims to fidelity or even genetic affinity. Though Peola Johnston is indeed her mother's biological child, she feels absolutely no familial connection to her. Peola's persistent rejection of Delilah problematizes a straightforward acceptance of the mammy as a favorable character. Hurst could be easily dismissed as an author so indoctrinated with racist ideology that she faithfully reproduces and endorses the delineation of the willing black subordinate. Bea and Jessie adore Delilah, and even the cantankerous Mr. Chipley responds warmly to her ministrations. But by mobilizing Peola, her own daughter, to repudiate her, even while acknowledging her goodness and generosity, Hurst suggests that Delilah's mentality is both outdated and inappropriate.

Peola Johnston is different from Fauset's Teresa Cary, of *Comedy: American Style*, because of the difference between their mothers and the impact that difference had on their upbringing. While Teresa was pressured against her will to conceal her racial affiliation, Peola was constantly chided to accept her blackness. Teresa and her mother, Olivia, are similar in appearance—both can pass for white women, whereas Peola and her mother, Delilah, have no physical feature in common. There is nothing about Delilah with which Peola can, or would desire to, identify.

While the magnanimous Delilah is supposedly intended to be a sympathetic character, her consistent delineation as a stereotypical mammy is both comical and repulsive in many ways. Scattered throughout the text are graphic descriptions of her monstrous girth and glistening blackness that make the opposition between herself and her slim, pale daughter too great to be bridged. Bea once observes her, avowedly fondly, as "black, gargantuan, a tent, there were suds of white already scattered into the kink of her mossy hair and deep in each breath, like springs coiled about the heart, asthmatic wheezes" (262). The recurring imagery of Delilah conjures up the comparison to the "whales being hauled ashore after a catch" Bea envisions during Delilah's death scene (320); Delilah is constantly massive and awkward and moist—she is often either sweating, crying, or both—and feeling herself out of place and out of her proper element.

Delilah sniffs "with her great flaring nostrils" (112). Delilah's "enormous face" looms over the waffle iron at the B. Pullman (138). Delilah disturbs the quietude of the home with her "ponderous lumbering about" (170). As Delilah stands at Peola's classroom door and asks for her daughter, "sweat began to pour on [her] lak it was rain outdoors" (225). Delilah is discovered "hidden and shuddering in the locker-room" of the magnificent, newly-opened Fifth Avenue B. Pullman in an effort to alleviate the painful discomfort of standing on her feet for more than an hour at a time (249). Delilah possesses a "vast wet surface of a face" and "arms loaded with flesh" (294). Delilah is indeed a nauseating spectacle to her daughter.

Peola's renunciation of her blackness is rooted not so much in an abhorrence of the race as in an abhorrence of her mother. Valerie Smith's "resistant, black feminist analysis" of the *Imitation of Life* narrative is consistent with this interpretation. She argues that because the novel and its celebrated pair of film derivatives "all conflate the light-skinned daughters' rejection of their own subordinate status with their rejection of their mothers, readers or viewers are manipulated into criticizing rather than supporting these light-skinned women."[27] Smith assumes that the American cultural consecration of motherhood will ensure that the daughters are condemned for their disloyalty to the women who gave them life. While Smith's point has merit, Hurst does leave space in the text to find fault with Delilah's maternal tactics.

Delilah conditions her daughter into inferiority practically from birth and certainly from the moment they become members of the Pullman household in Atlantic City, New Jersey. At three months old, Peola is just two weeks older than Bea's daughter, Jessie, when Delilah accepts Bea's offer to work for the Pullmans as a live-in housekeeper. From the very outset of their cohabitation, Delilah begins insistently to underrate little Peola's developmental progress in order to document, promote, and applaud Jessie's "natural superiority." Delilah is appalled by the sight of the nub of a tooth in her daughter's mouth before Jessie has reached that threshold, and even the combined nightly cries of the babies cause Delilah to come "running intuitively to her own, but the switch was without hesitancy to the white child, every labor of service adhering rigidly to that order" (101).²⁸ Peola is raised to believe that being black necessitates eternal deference to white people, because Delilah refuses to grant her supremacy in anything, including punishment, in order to appease "Miss Honey-Bea" and coddle her golden-haired child: "Gimme dat white ear, Jessie, for to twist. Gimme dat yaller ear, Peola, for to twist. Stop pushin', Peola. You cain't git your ear twisted befoh white chile has had her'n" (116). She will not allow Peola to apologize first when the girls conspire in mischief: "Peola, will you stop bein' sorry before Jessie is sorry? Ain't you got no way of keepin' yourself in your place?" (120). Delilah fails to defend and console her daughter even when Jessie cruelly taunts her in the heat of a dispute over a toy; after her particularly vicious outburst of "Nigger! No fair! You pushed! You're a little nigger and you've got no half-moons on your finger nails. Nig-nig-nig—ger!" little Jessie acts rather unconvincingly perplexed by Peola's fury (179). Bea commands her daughter to mollify Peola's wounded feelings, but Delilah thwarts her intentions: "No white chile cain't be comin' apologizin' to a black and puttin' ideas into her ahead. Stop dat tremblin', Peola, and walk over dar, and tell Jessie you're proud of bein' a nigger, 'cause it was de Lawd's work makin' you a nigger" (181). Peola, as our twenty-first century sensibility makes us gratified to learn, refuses to obey her mother and loudly proclaims her determined refusal to "be a nigger." While Delilah seems to have at heart the honorable intention of preparing Peola for the unfortunate reality of American race relations, her insistence upon her daughter not only humbly accepting but professing glory in an offensive label is fundamentally misguided. Only because Delilah herself welcomes suffering as part and parcel of her religious ethic and has internalized the tenets of white supremacy so thoroughly is she capable of encouraging Peola to appropriate the single most derogatory racial epithet as an expression of pride in her racial ancestry.

 Peola's resistance to her mother's inappropriate commands is rooted not in a natural aversion to blackness but in her mother's stereotypical embodiment of blackness. Peola has no other available model of black womanhood because she is isolated from the black community and raised as an inferior in a white household. Peola has no conception of what it means to be black other than the example of her mother, and she is unwilling to replicate her mother's persona, unlike the horde of imitation "Delilahs" her mother personally trains to preside over the waffle irons of the various eateries in the B. Pullman restaurant chain. Peola has no sense that she is tangibly linked to a black identity except through the overwhelmingly black body of her mother—when Peola passes for white for over two years at her public elementary school, it is only when Delilah unexpectedly materializes at the classroom to walk her daughter home one rainy day that Peola's racial difference from her classmates is betrayed.

From early infancy, Peola is raised in an environment in which there is no perceivable difference between herself and the affluent white people with whom she lives, and the lone obstacle between herself and freedom from the stigma of blackness is her mother. It is Delilah herself who makes the distinction between black and white an issue by actively grooming Peola to assume a subservient position without question or resistance, an act of capitulation against which Peola understandably rebels, especially in light of the complete absence of racial markings to identify Peola as a black person. Though Delilah claims "I wants mah chile full of nigger-love and lovin'-to-be-nigger," she has absolutely no idea how to achieve, or even properly phrase, her desired outcome (142).

A similar situation to Peola's obtains in the case of Phebe Grant, also of Fauset's *Comedy: American Style*, though with a entirely different end result. Like Peola, Phebe is the white-skinned daughter of a brown-skinned, dialect-speaking black woman. However, Mrs. Grant (some of her neighbors disapprove of her use of the title despite her lack of a husband) has her own home. She is a domestic day worker for a wealthy white woman, and she takes in a lodger to help cover the expenses of the modest household she provides for her daughter. Phebe's case also differs from Peola's in that the blond Phebe openly acknowledges her racial ancestry, largely because of her loyalty to her mother. She once confides to a childhood admirer that "white people haven't treated my mother very well. Perhaps that's why I can't get excited about them."[29] Phebe can also perceive a genetic connection to her mother, as she explains to a white man on the verge of proposing marriage to her when she finally confesses her racial identity:

> I am colored. My mother is the ordinary brown mulatto type, with rather straight hair. My father was very white, blond with hair so light it was almost white, the color of untinted butter. They call it platinum blond now. I happen to take after my mother in looks, she really was remarkably like me before life took it out of her. But my color is my father's gift. (286)

Peola's coloring was a "gift" from her father as well. The late Mr. Johnston was light like his daughter, a black man who could easily pass for white, as Hurst emphatically reiterates throughout the text, usually through Delilah's frequent recollections of him as "a white nigger." Phebe's father was a white man, and though there is no detailed narrative of the relationship between her parents, Phebe's disclosures to various characters in the novel indicate that her parents were rural Southerners (her father was "the son of a country grocer"), and that their attraction was mutual, their affection very real (288). When her mother becomes pregnant, Phebe's paternal grandparents realize their son's involvement is more than a fleeting dalliance and promptly intervene; Phebe's father has not the strength, resolve, or will to resist, and his marriage to a local white woman is speedily arranged. After Phebe's birth, her mother takes her newborn and joins the great migration North to better job prospects, better living conditions, and the rejuvenating bliss of urban anonymity. Unlike Peola, Phebe never expresses disdain for her mother but reserves her contempt for the man who abandoned his lover to raise their child all alone. Furthermore, unlike Delilah, Phebe's mother never suggests that being black is an anomalous curse of inferiority to which one must reconcile oneself in order to live peacefully in American society. Instead, Phebe derives the benefits of her mother's universalistic doctrine that "Everybody had trouble," but "It don' make much difference about trouble if you has someone who you can always depend on" (62). Phebe embraces the wisdom of her mother's precepts, and she shows her love for her mother by refusing to consider her African ancestry an intolerable liability. As she explains to her white suitor when he is frankly puzzled by her lack of desire to marry a white man, "I just prefer being colored. The best of us are not to be equalled, I'm convinced, throughout the world" (289).

Delilah attributes Peola's bitter resentment of her racial classification to an inherited aversion to life among the downtrodden black race—the restless "white horses" which had run in her late husband's bloodstream and were now running in Peola's. However, Delilah herself replicates her role as an enabler through her own inherent sense of inferiority and her grateful servility to those bearing white skins. She happily slaves for Peola and Bea Pullman's family just as she had, by her own admission, slaved for Peola's dead father, demanding nothing in her return for her labor: "I's laid wid a no-'count nigger, knowin' I was no moh to him dan a washin' machine and a ironin'-board dat he married to save ever havin' to shuffle a bone again" (221). For a time she even refuses to accept her earned wages from Bea, preferring instead to be cared for as a dependent member of the household whose needs would be met in due course with the other members of the family. In an effusive declaration of maternal self-sacrifice, Delilah professes the insignificance of her life apart from her usefulness to Peola.

"Oh, mah baby, a-givin' you has been the meanin' of livin'. A-givin' you, seein' you git fine and educated an' into what you are now, even if in de end it crucify me, is God's meanin' for puttin' breath of life into dis black hulk" (296). Delilah is symbolic of all that is undesirable from a progressive view of blackness. She represents all that the modern black subject wants to sublimate and suppress, but the very qualities she possesses that black people find so shameful and revolting are precisely those that white people cherish and advocate. Delilah's character is perfectly nonthreatening and capably sustains a white supremacist lifestyle and worldview.

In a novel that chronicles the determination of Bea Pullman to overcome traditional ideas of separate public and private spheres and the unsuitability of women for entrepreneurial ventures, it is curious that Delilah remains so stubbornly stagnant. In fact, as Lucy Fischer has observed, *Imitation of Life* "fabricates a suspect solution to the dilemma of the middle-class professional [white] woman: a deferent black double who assumes the position she vacates."[30] Delilah revels in her degradation, believing that cheerful acceptance of her low status, her earthly "cross," will win her eternal glory. She provides her daughter no space to aspire to anything other than a life that invites perpetual insult and subjugation to which she must willingly and eagerly submit in all humility in order to earn a heavenly reward.

Delilah seems to perceive no defect in her childrearing philosophy—it is to do the interpretation of her character a disservice to believe that she is not convinced she is preparing her daughter in the only reasonable, responsible way imaginable for the treatment she can expect to receive from a world contemptuous of black womanhood. At the same time, however, Delilah is unconsciously sending an antithetical message to her daughter, resulting in the confusion Peola finally resolves through her denial of her African ancestry. From the time of the children's infancy, Delilah begins to forcibly assimilate Peola into white culture by patterning her daughter's life after Jessie's. She replaces "Peola's colorful and fantastic little wardrobe of checks and bright calicos" with "a coarse replica of the sheer and dainty" layette Bea has sewn for Jessie and abandons her accustomed method of feeding Peola in order to obediently follow "Dr. Merribel's carefully devised scheme" for Jessie's early nutrition (100–1). When the girls reach their early teens and Jessie continues to openly display her affection for Delilah, Delilah pays Jessie "the perfect tribute of reciprocal devotion by emulating in Peola, as far as her sense of propriety dared, Jessie's clothes, hair-dress, and color schemes" (212–13). By seeking to produce in her daughter a veritable carbon copy of Jessie, Delilah overzealously adheres to the popular adage that imitation is the sincerest form of flattery and sends yet another contradictory message about Peola's intrinsic worth and the availability of positive black role models. Delilah effectively reinforces to her daughter that being white is better than being black, that black people can aspire only to enjoy life vicariously through white people by taking advantage of the opportunity to play supporting roles in their lives, and that Peola can hope to constitute no more than a flawed impostor of Jessie's validated magnificence.

Peola's rebellion against her mother's mixed signals takes the form of a series of violent outbursts, fainting spells, and various other manifestations of a persistent nervous condition. When she finally confronts her mother with her intentions to marry a white man and live as a white woman, she explains to Delilah how tortured her life has been on the threshold between the black and white worlds: "I've prayed same as you, for the strength to be proud of being black under my white. ... But I'm not. I'm light. No way of knowing how much white flows somewhere in my veins. I'm as white under my skin as I am on top" (297). Peola inevitably views blackness and whiteness as mutually exclusive categories, refined reason versus emotional excess, and she identifies with Bea throughout her final confrontation with her mother. As Jessie had done many times before her, except in reverse, Peola enlists Bea to serve as her ally and intermediary with Delilah, who repeatedly loses her composure and wails prayerful appeals that interrupt Peola's confessions. Peola is understandably disgusted by the sight of her mother, with the "wide expanse of her face slashingly wet, the whites of her eyes seeming to pour rivulets down her face like rain against a window pane, her splayed lips dripping eaves of more tears, her throat even rained against" (293). As a young woman Peola has gained control of her own emotions and has nothing short of revolted disdain for the demonstrative exhibition she believes to be an intrinsically black racial trait.

Each film version of *Imitation of Life* sentimentalizes the death of the Delilah character by scripting it as a direct consequence of her daughter's desertion. Then a belatedly contrite Peola or Sarah Jane can be disciplined for her attempt to pass by the guilt and remorse she feels for causing her mother's death. Hurst's novel, however, not only establishes that Delilah had a preexisting medical condition about which she informed neither Peola nor the Pullmans, and for which she neglected to seek treatment, but suggests that Peola would have had no knowledge of her mother's dying, much less reconsidered her decision to sever all ties with her. While the critical consensus in regard to this plotting sequence has been that Delilah's death is her daughter's punishment for passing and is the tragic event which brings Peola back to her "rightful place" in society, this interpretation does not hold true for the originary narrative of Hurst's novel.

Unlike either of the film adaptations of her text, Hurst provides an extremely ungracious exit for the character of Delilah. The death scene Hurst crafts is nothing like the dignified displays of composed sorrow the screen mammies enact. The novel's Delilah dies on the floor where she has crawled and collapsed in considerable pain, because she is simply too enormous to be lifted and transported anywhere else. The movie characters are in beds, serenely bidding their goodbyes to their assembled devotees, and it is the Bea characters who lose emotional control. In Sirk's film, Annie bids "Miss Lora" to deliver a message to Sarah Jane from her deathbed: "Tell her I know I was selfish, and if I loved her too much, I'm sorry. But I didn't mean to cause her any trouble. She was all I had."

In contrast to the two screen portrayals of an adoring mother who endures the cruel rebuffs of her scheming daughter, Hurst's Delilah is easily condemned for having created the conditions for Peola's ultimate abandonment. Despite her professions of motherly devotion, Delilah is so consumed with her parasitic attachment to Bea that she is completely inattentive to her daughter's psychological needs. She repeatedly demands that Peola embrace her black identity, but she provides no context within which Peola can comfortably do so. While they are living in Atlantic City, which we are informed has a black population of nine thousand, Peola's sole playmate is Jessie Pullman, the white daughter of her mother's employer.

Obviously, Delilah has not the proper background, education, social status, etiquette, or bearing to secure acquaintances among the black middle class, but if Peola had had the contact with members of black society that a Maggie Ellersley had with the Marshall family and their set in Jessie Fauset's *There Is Confusion* (1924), she would have been exposed to a milieu which could have opened up vast, promising possibilities for her future as a black woman. Delilah is a poor advocate for her daughter's interests because she displays a sincere belief in black inferiority; while she encourages Bea to enroll Jessie in "one of them fancy boardin'-schools," and Jessie is subsequently entered into New York City's most exclusive private girls' academy, Delilah insists that the neighborhood public elementary school is good enough for her own child (207). In a description of Jessie's growth into womanhood, Hurst is careful to mention "that quality of golden childishness which had once made it a delight for Delilah to appear with her showy charge among the nursemaids in the park," implying that Delilah considered her own daughter plain or ordinary next to the blond Jessie (208). If Delilah's death is a punitive consequence, it is proper retribution for her own bad mothering rather than Peola's color line transgression.

When Delilah seeks to "atone" for her daughter's concealment of her racial ancestry, she distributes the modest stipend she receives from Bea— most of which she formerly sent faithfully to Peola—among a host of black charities. Delilah hopes that her generous financial gifts to black churches, lodges, and the several funds and organizations which solicit her donations will somehow make up for the racial betrayal represented by Peola's defection from the black community, despite Bea's disapproval of her course of action: "Delilah, you simply can't handle money if you are going to give it out willy-nilly to everyone that comes along. Don't you know those darkies aren't always honest with you? Word of you has gone out among them, and now see this deluge ..." (306–7). Delilah is unmoved by Bea's warning, convinced that the righteousness of her motivation matters more than the legitimacy of the beneficiary. "Honey-chile, dem niggers dat thinks I's jes anybody's easy mark doan' know it, but I's atonin'. Lordagawd won't hold it ag'in' mah chile so long as her black mammy loves Him twice. Once for herself and once for her baby-chile what couldn't see de light" (307). Delilah's resolve demonstrates her attempt to literally pay for her daughter's crime against nature and therefore absolve the mortal sin she has supposedly committed by repudiating her God-given identity. However, her pecuniary generosity is also evidence of her cognizance of her own culpability in her daughter's transgression; she fails to subdue the "white horses" galloping in Peola's veins and eventually submits to her daughter's desperate, prostrate plea that she conceal their blood relationship. "Lordagawd, forgive mah chile, for she knows not what she does. Bless mah chile. Make happy mah chile. Strike me daid Lordagawd, if ever on dis earth I owns to bearin' her" (304).

While Delilah agonizes over Peola's decision to live her life as a white woman, she remains complacent regarding her own integration into black society. Delilah may not be able to deny her racial designation, but her abandonment of her people is nearly as complete as her daughter's. She, not unlike Peola, has withdrawn herself from personal association with the black community. In Harlem, where her funeral is held, the people relate to Delilah as a celebrity, a famous achiever, eccentric philanthropist, and pioneer for the race, even though, ironically, in accordance with her own wishes, she is buried in the puffy white hat which symbolizes her servility: "Harlem, of which she had never been a part, except by gestures of patronage and munificence, poured forth for the spectacle of this dead face of one of the humblest members of its race which had become an affectionate daguerreotype against the consciousness of a nation" (325). The novel includes a lengthy and detailed description of the pomp and circumstance involved in laying Delilah to rest amidst the practiced rituals and costly tokens of a plethora of civic and religious organizations.[31] Hurst's blatant mockery of the elaborateness of funerals in the black community underscores what perpetually gets lost in the discussions of the penitence catalyzed by the death of Delilah—that Delilah herself considers death her reward. Her biggest regret seems to be her imminent separation from Bea. She spends the final moments of her life raining sloppy kisses on her employer's bare feet.

Repeatedly throughout the novel, Delilah fixates upon a magnificent funeral as the only material benefit she desires for herself from the enormous wealth she enables Bea to accumulate. She envisions herself "Ridin' up to heaven in a snow-white hearse wid de Lawd leanin' out when He hears de trumpets blowin' to see if I's comin' in a white satin casket pulled by six white hosses" (173). Delilah's fantasy about a spectacular funeral shows that she has a severe martyr complex. She believes that being black is about being humbled and downtrodden on earth in order to be glorified and elevated in heaven. Her credo is Jesus's biblical promise that "Whoever wants to be first must be last of all and servant of all."[32] Death, therefore, is Delilah's triumph; her funeral is her posthumous celebration of her victory. Delilah's faith that her cheerful endurance of lowliness will be more than compensated in a glorious afterlife is a doctrine to which her proud, svelte, white-skinned daughter simply cannot reconcile herself, and her unwavering refusal to adopt her mother's dogma drives her into her desperation to live as white.

Delilah and Peola represent two opposite extremes on the continuum of a conceptual orientation toward blackness, neither of which is rational within the modern American landscape.[33] That both women are written out of the plot before the conclusion of the novel indicates that, like Harriet Beecher Stowe, who shuttles her entire black cast of characters beyond the borders of America before the resolution of *Uncle Tom's Cabin*, Hurst concedes a place for neither Delilahs nor Peolas in her vision of contemporary black subjectivity. Both constructions of black femininity are detrimental to a positive racial self-image and must be thoroughly expurgated in order to secure the future of the race.

When Peola becomes engaged to her white fiancé, she has herself medically sterilized because racial intermarriage is "not a sin, Mammy, where there won't be children" (302). In light of the understanding of Peola as counterproductive to the movement towards racial uplift, however, her self-imposed sterility can then take on the additional significance of being not only a necessary precaution to ensure that the secret of her ancestry is not betrayed by her progeny potentially exhibiting tell-tale racial characteristics, but also a way to irreversibly exclude her from participation in the black diaspora as well as forestall the possibility of her producing any more "counterfeit" white people. For although Hurst grants Delilah's daughter her freedom from being identified as a black woman, Peola's liberation comes with strict parameters—Peola is alone in her deception, which is ironic considering her intended husband, a veteran of the Great War, had been the front-runner of the spirited young "doughboys" who adopted the newly opened B. Pullman restaurant in New York's Grand Central Station as their personal sanctuary and the one whom Delilah had helped nurse through a bout with influenza and adjudged her "sweetest boy from all de war" (169). Strangely enough, Allen Matterhorn might have been pleasantly surprised to discover that the woman with whom he had fallen in love was the daughter of the woman to whom his ailing mother had written: "Darling Mammy Delilah, My boy Allen has told me all about you. He is not ashamed to say that without your kind substitution for his old mother, he could not easily have found the courage to face the dreadful days following his sailing from New York. Bless you" (233).

Hurst introduces the improbable coincidence of Peola moving to Seattle, Washington, and becoming involved with the very young man to whom her mother had served as a surrogate mother, not simply to unify the plot but to suggest that the tragic lengths to which Peola goes to accomplish her subterfuge—including perpetually deceiving the man she professes to love, estranging herself from her mother and the Pullmans, and undergoing a horrific surgical procedure to make it impossible for her to ever conceive a child—were likely unnecessary. Still, Peola cannot look forward to the promising future Jessie anticipates at the end of the novel. Peola's husband may be white, but since he is "gassed, to say nothing of half a hand he lost in Flanders," he is not a wholly perfect male specimen (302). Furthermore, she is exiled from the United States to the "white man's jungle" of Bolivia, and even if she eventually repents of her decision to conceal her racial heritage, she can never have children of her own.

Jessie Pullman marries Frank Flake, her mother's business operations manager, at the end of the novel, never realizing that Bea is in love with him and had planned to marry him herself. Having made her choice to pursue masculine success, Bea cannot now enjoy her feminine dream of domestic fulfillment. The house she had intended to share with Frank and Jessie as a conventional wife and mother, respectively, ends up being her wedding gift to them, and she travels between her international restaurants in bitter exile from the place and the people she so desperately wanted to be her home. Her plans for early retirement and the realization of her heretofore elusive working woman's fantasy of "more income and more leisure" evaporate at the moment she finally discerns that Frank and Jessie have fallen in love (114).

Bea's life begins to fall apart once Delilah dies. Delilah is the ordering influence for Bea without which she cannot effectively function. Hurst's condemnation of the mutual interdependence of the mammy figure and the white woman who employs her as a surrogate laborer is made complete with the estrangement each woman suffers from her daughter. *Imitation of Life* suggests that the mammy is a twisted type of maternity—she wreaks havoc in the household she is engaged to infiltrate and in the household she is required to abandon. Delilah's compromised position in the Pullman household cost her her own daughter and cost Bea hers as well. For these unfortunate mothers, there are no happy endings.

Notes

Introduction

1. Description found on back cover of Benilde Little, *Good Hair* (New York: Simon & Schuster, 1996).
2. Dorothy West, *The Living Is Easy* (1948; New York: The Feminist Press, 1982), 27; Leona Gray, "Mammy Sue," *The Half-Century Magazine* 9.4 (October 1920).
3. Jessie Redmon Fauset, *Comedy: American Style* (1933; New York: G. K. Hall & Co., 1995), 35. Further quotations will be cited parenthetically.
4. Nella Larsen, *Quicksand*, 1928; *An Intimation of Things Distant: The Collected Fiction of Nella Larsen* (New York: Doubleday, 1992), 152–53.
5. Larsen, 152.
6. Fauset, *There Is Confusion* (1924; Boston: Northeastern University Press, 1989), 26. Further quotations will be cited parenthetically.
7. Fauset, *The Chinaberry Tree & Selected Writings* (1931; Boston: Northeastern University Press, 1995), 61–62. Further quotations will be cited parenthetically.
8. Ross Brown, *Afro-American World Almanac: What Do You Know about Your Race, with Unusual Historic Facts about Prominent People of African Descent from A to Z* (Chicago: Bedford Brown Edition, 1942), 6.
9. Jacquelyn McLendon, *The Politics of Color in the Fiction of Jessie Fauset and Nella Larsen* (Charlottesville: University Press of Virginia, 1995), 7.

1. Conceiving Class and Culture: A Contextual Retrospective

1. See, for instance, Shari L. Thurer, *The Myths of Motherhood: How Culture Reinvents the Good Mother* (Boston: Houghton Mifflin Co., 1994); E. Ann Kaplan, *Motherhood and Representation: The Mother in Popular Culture and Melodrama* (New York: Routledge, 1992); Pamela Ryan, "A Woman's Place:

Motherhood and Domesticity in Literature," *Unisa English Studies* 29.1 (April 1991): 24–34; *Marianne Hirsch, The Mother/Daughter Plot: Narrative, Psychoanalysis, Feminism* (Bloomington: Indiana University Press, 1989).

2. Marianne Hirsch, "Maternity and Rememory: Toni Morrison's Beloved," *Representations of Motherhood*, ed. Donna Bassin, Margaret Honey, and Meryle Mahrer Kaplan (New Haven: Yale University Press, 1994), 93.
3. Quoted in Hirsch, "Maternity and Rememory," 96.
4. Gloria Wade-Gayles, "The Truths of Our Mothers' Lives: Mother-Daughter Relationships in Black Women's Fiction," *SAGE: A Scholarly Journal on Black Women* 1.2 (fall 1984): 12.
5. See Patricia Hill Collins, "Shifting the Center: Race, Class, and Feminist Theorizing about Motherhood," *Representations of Motherhood*, ed. Bassin et al., 59–61.
6. Anna Julia Cooper, *A Voice from the South* (1892; New York: Oxford University Press, 1988), 254.
7. In her autobiography, race leader Mary Church Terrell repeats a comment made by one of her white friends which underscores the theme presented in Rachel: "'I do not see,' she said, 'how any colored woman can make up her mind to become a mother under the existing conditions in the United States. Under the circumstances,' she continued, 'I should think a colored woman would feel that she was perpetrating a great injustice upon any helpless infant she would bring into the world.'" *A Colored Woman in a White World* (1940; Salem, NH: Ayer Co., 1986), 108.
8. See Jean Fagan Yellin, *Women and Sisters: The Antislavery Feminists in American Culture* (New Haven: Yale University Press, 1989), for more on the efforts to rally white female support behind abolition. The quote from Grimké is found in Claudia Tate, *Domestic Allegories of Political Desire: The Black Heroine's Text at the Turn of the Century* (New York: Oxford University Press, 1992), 219.
9. Frederick Douglass, *Narrative of the Life of Frederick Douglass, An American Slave, Written by Himself* (1845; New York: Penguin, 1968), 22.
10. Tate, 32.
11. Betty Deramus, "Some of Us Are Brave," *Essence* 28.10 (February 1998): 85.
12. Martin Robison Delany, "The Condition, Elevation, Emigration and Destiny of the Colored People of the United States Politically Considered," 1852. Quoted in Paul Gilroy, *The Black Atlantic: Modernity and Double-Consciousness* (Cambridge: Harvard University Press, 1993), 26.
13. Toni Morrison uses this idea in "Unspeakable Things Unspoken: The Afro-American Presence in American Literature," *Criticism and the Color Line: Desegregating American Literary Studies*, ed. Henry B. Wonham (New Brunswick, NJ: Rutgers University Press, 1996), 16–29, to talk about the ways in which African-American identity is crucial to the understanding of the development of Anglo-American literature. In her argument that African-

American presence is the "ghost in the machine" haunting the literary works which purport to exclude it, she emphasizes that "certain absences are so stressed, so ornate, so planned, they call attention to themselves; arrest us with intentionality and purpose, like neighborhoods that are defined by the population held away from them," 23, 24.

14. Collins, *Black Feminist Thought: Knowledge, Consciousness, and the Politics of Empowerment* (Boston: Unwin Hyman, 1990), 118.
15. Kevin Kelley Gaines, *Uplifting the Race: Black Leadership, Politics and Culture in the Twentieth Century* (Chapel Hill: The University of North Carolina Press, 1996), 230. For a complete account of the Rhinelander case, see Mark J. Madigan, "Miscegenation and 'The Dicta of Race and Class': The Rhinelander Case and Nella Larsen's Passing," *Modern Fiction Studies*, 36.4 (winter 1990): 523–29.
16. Gaines notes that the discourse surrounding reproductive concerns "was partly a response to declining black fertility rates in cities since the turn of the century, as black women and families increasingly exercised birth control for economic reasons" (230). The effort to curtail fertility was linked to the shift from an agrarian to an urban landscape in Jessie Rodrique's assessment of the phenomenon as well: "Contraceptive use was one of a few economic strategies available to black people, providing a degree of control within the context of the family economy. Migrating families who left behind the economy of the rural south used birth control to 'preserve their new economic independence,' as did poor families who were 'compelled' to limit their numbers of children." Rodrique, "The Black Community and the Birth Control Movement," *Passion and Power: Sexuality in History*, ed. Kathy Peiss and Christina Simmons (Philadelphia: Temple University Press, 1989), 141–42. Paula Giddings notes that part of the mounting tension created by the growing numbers of black female college graduates was due to the "tendency of middle-class Black women to make certain social decisions, no matter what the marriage and baby boom trends of any period." Citing a study performed by Jeanne L. Noble in 1956, Giddings reports that "In a period when the average Black mother had four children and the average White mother had three, 38 percent of the women in Noble's study had one child, 15 percent had two children, and 6 percent had between three and six children. A whopping 41 percent were childless." Paula Giddings, *When and Where I Enter: The Impact of Black Women on Race and Sex in America* (New York: Bantam 1984), 248.
17. Thurer, 231.
18. Darlene Clark Hine, *Hine Sight: Black Women and the Re-Construction of American History* (Brooklyn, NY: Carlson Publishing, 1994), 45.
19. Hine, 46. As has been mentioned before, none of the women novelists in this study became a mother.
20. Nella Larsen, *Quicksand* (1928), in *An Intimation of Things Distant: The Collected Fiction of Nella Larsen* (New York: Doubleday, 1992), 154.

21. Larsen's attention to this figuration may have been linked to her possible inability to give her husband a child. She emphasizes her suspicion that Elmer Imes's mistress was pregnant, suggesting that he may have been disappointed in their failure to conceive.
22. Dorothy West, *The Living Is Easy* (1948; New York: The Feminist Press, 1975), 254.
23. Gloria Wade-Gayles, "The Truths of Our Mothers' Lives: Mother-Daughter Relationships in Black Women's Fiction," *SAGE: A Scholarly Journal on Black Women* 1.2 (fall 1984): 11.
24. Charles Chesnutt, "The Wife of His Youth," *The Wife of His Youth and Other Stories of the Color Line* (1899; Ann Arbor: The University of Michigan Press, 1968), 8. Chesnutt was characterizing the thoughts of a fair-skinned man who sought to marry an even fairer woman in the expectation that their offspring would appear even more Caucasoid, and eventually be accepted, or simply blend into the white race.
25. In addition to the works I reference in this section, see also Stephanie J. Shaw, *What a Woman Ought to Be and to Do: Black Professional Women Workers During the Jim Crow Era* (Chicago: The University of Chicago Press, 1996); Jacqueline Jones, *The Dispossessed: America's Underclasses from the Civil War to the Present* (New York: Basic Books, 1992).
26. I am indebted to Alford A. Young, Jr., of the University of Michigan Department of Sociology, for guiding my research into the class issues relevant to the black community.
27. Bart Landry, *The New Black Middle Class* (Berkeley: University of California Press, 1987), 5–11. Landry addresses the absence of a critical consensus in establishing the meaning of class for the black community and seeks to stabilize his terminology in relation to economic theory in order to avoid imprecision and to create a common language for future scholarly discussion.
28. Landry argues that "[T]he distinction between status groups and classes is an important one, one that is far too often confused or overlooked. Status groups emerge out of the subjective evaluation of community members; classes are based on objective positions within the economic system," 25.
29. Landry, 21.
30. Andrew Billingsley, *Black Families in White America* (Englewood Cliffs, NJ: Prentice-Hall, 1968), 212.
31. St. Clair Drake and Horace R. Cayton, *Black Metropolis: A Study of Negro Life in a Northern City* (New York: Harcourt, Brace, 1945), 714.
32. Drake and Cayton, 529.
33. Drake and Cayton, 527.
34. Drake and Cayton, 529.
35. E. Franklin Frazier, "The Negro Family in America," *On Race Relations: Selected Writings* (Chicago: University of Chicago Press, 1968), 208.
36. Frazier, "The New Negro Middle Class," *On Race Relations*, 257.

37. Frazier, "The New Negro Middle Class," 258.
38. Frazier, "The New Negro Middle Class," 263.
39. Frazier, "The New Negro Middle Class," 266.
40. Fannie Hurst, *Imitation of Life* (New York: Harper & Brothers, 1933), 229.
41. Hurst, 91.
42. West, 24.
43. West, 27.
44. West, 43.
45. Paula Giddings, *When and Where I Enter: The Impact of Black Women on Race and Sex in America* (New York: Bantam Books, 1984), 145.
46. Giddings, 143: "Although it was true that Black women were leaving the kitchen and laundry, they did so only as fast as White women made their way up the employment ladder. ... For example, in Philadelphia, Black women were hired as live-in domestics rather than dayworkers only when White women, the previous live-ins, found work in the factories."
47. Morrison, 23.
48. Tate, 5.
49. By hinging this issue upon a conditional premise, I am deliberately leaving myself an avenue to argue that the black middle class did not simply adopt a system of values dictated by its white counterpart in order to authenticate its existence. I also want to guard against importing Homi Bhabha's widely circulated theory of mimicry here, because I think the different circumstances undergirding American race relations warrant a different understanding of the cultural development.
50. Throughout Willard Gatewood's *Aristocrats of Color: The Black Elite, 1880–1920* (Bloomington: Indiana University Press, 1990), he chronicles the many journalists across the nation who issued column after column of scathing criticism of the "colored aristocracy," especially with regard to their intraracial color prejudice.
51. Quoted in Watson, 44.
52. Gatewood, 338.
53. Watson, 19–20.
54. This brief account of Larsen's life is distilled from Davis's biography of the writer, Nella Larsen, *Novelist of the Harlem Renaissance: A Woman's Life Unveiled* (Baton Rouge: Louisiana State University Press, 1994).
55. Gatewood, 344.
56. Ann Douglas, *Terrible Honesty: Mongrel Manhattan in the 1920s* (New York: Farrar, Straus, and Giroux, 1995), 4.
57. Douglas, 5.
58. Ross Brown, *Afro-American World Almanac: What Do You Know about Your Race, with Unusual Historic Facts about Prominent People of African Descent from A to Z.* (Chicago: Bedford Brown Edition, 1942). James Weldon Johnson, *Black Manhattan* (1930; New York: Da Capo Press, 1991), 246. In

addition, both authors describe at length the "Houston Affair" of August 23, 1917, in which part of a black regiment (the Twenty-Fourth Infantry) that had seen action overseas but was temporarily stationed in Houston, TX, was involved in a skirmish in retaliation for the beating of Corporal Charles W. Baltimore, a black noncommissioned officer, by white Houston police officers. Brown claims that the incident arose when CPL Baltimore and other soldiers came to the aid of a black woman who had been "bathing and protested the invasion" of a policeman who had chased a black youth into her home. "The white policeman arrested and took the naked woman down the street," at which time the soldiers intervened and were beaten. Johnson establishes that prior to this incident the battalion had endured constant harassment from the policemen, that CPL Baltimore was one of the most popular servicemen, and that he had been reported dead instead of wounded. Two black people, five police officers, and twelve other white people were killed in the riot; after a massive series of court-martials, nineteen of the soldiers were hanged, and over fifty were sent to Leavenworth prison, some for life. While Johnson argues that the soldiers' actions were provoked by "a long series of humiliating and harassing incidents, culminating in the brutal assault on Corporal Baltimore," Brown chooses to emphasize that "all were fighting for the protection of a Negro woman." Johnson, 239–44; Brown, 66. Also see Johnson's record of the July 1917 "Silent Protest Parade" staged by black New Yorkers in response to the disturbing trend of violence (236–38).

59. *Ithaca Journal News, Opportunity* 2.14 (February 1924): 61–62.
60. Gaines, 215.
61. *The Birth of a Nation,* which purported to be a historical drama of the Reconstruction South, was based on Thomas Dixon's 1905 novel *The Clansman: An Historical Romance of the Ku Klux Klan.* In *Terrible Honesty,* Ann Douglas talks about the film's impact on the movie industry. It "ran 2 hours and 40 minutes, drew huge audiences, and advanced cinematic art, whatever one thought of its racist politics, by light-years" (190). Harvey Green elaborates in *Everyday Life:* "As a part of cinematic history, Griffith's motion picture deserves attention because it was the first feature-length film. It also broke free from the conventions of the stage: Griffith used long distance shots, switchbacks, fade-outs, close-ups and panoramas," thus disseminating virulent racism in an avant-garde cinematic package destined to reach about fifty million viewers (4).
62. "The Hydra," *The Half-Century Magazine* 12.5 (May-June 1922): 3.
63. Johnson, 243.
64. Gatewood, 186, 269, 23.
65. "Of the Coming of John" is the short story that comprises the penultimate chapter of Du Bois's *The Souls of Black Folk* (1903; New York: Penguin, 1989). When John returns to the small town of Altamaha, Georgia, after a classical education and a brief sojourn in New York City, he attempts to establish a

school for the black children. When he is promptly dismissed after being accused of sedition, he determines to return to the North. He is practically on his way out of town when he is forced to defend his sister from an attempted rape and takes the life of her white antagonist in the process. The story ends ambiguously, with John either sitting on a tree stump, musing while awaiting and then rising to meet the approaching lynch mob, or leaping from the seaside cliff once the mob surrounds him.

66. Quoted in McDowell, 99.
67. "An Opportunity for Negro Writers," *Opportunity* 2.21 (September 1924): 1.
68. Frazier, "The New Negro Middle Class," 262.
69. Larsen, *Quicksand*, 80.
70. Paula Baker, "The Domestication of Politics: Women and American Political Society, 1780–1920," in *Unequal Sisters: A Multi-Cultural Reader in U.S. Women's History*, ed. Vicki L. Ruiz and Ellen Carol DuBois (New York: Routledge, 1994), 85–110. Baker argues that by the beginning of the nineteenth century, before women acquired political power in the public sphere, they routinely used their positions within the home—especially their maternal function—as a means of "translating moral authority into political influence," (87). In *Domestic Allegories of Political Desire*, Claudia Tate contends that "for roughly a decade—the 1890s—black women writers of the post-Reconstruction era reaffirmed in novels their belief that virtuous women like themselves could reform society by domesticating it" (19). In this way, the black novelists were participating in a tradition of using domestic sentimentalism to promote a specific political agenda.
71. Tate, 7.
72. Ralph Ellison, "Twentieth-Century Fiction and the Black Mask of Humanity," 1953. *The Sound and the Fury*, by William Faulkner (1929; New York: Norton, 1987), 260–61.
73. Jessie Fauset, foreword to *The Chinaberry Tree* (1931; Boston: Northeastern University Press, 1995), xxxi.
74. Earl Lewis, "Work, Family, and the African-American Experience: Some Questions Historians Have Failed to Ask" (paper presented at the Center for the Education of Women/Family Care Resources Program lecture series on the family, University of Michigan, Ann Arbor, 25 Sept. 1997).
75. Billingsley, 28.
76. Billingsley, 28.

2. Revising the Victorian Maternal Ideal in Jessie Fauset's *There Is Confusion*

1. Thadious Davis, foreword to *There Is Confusion* (1924; Boston: Northeastern University Press, 1989), v-vi.
2. More extensive descriptions of the Civic Club Dinner are given in Davis's foreword to *There Is Confusion*, xxiii-xxiv, Cheryl Wall, *Women of the Harlem Renaissance* (Bloomington: Indiana University Press, 1995), 69–71, and Steven Watson, *The Harlem Renaissance: Hub of African-American Culture, 1920–1930* (New York: Pantheon Books, 1996), 27–29. As all three scholars note, while Fauset and the publication of *There Is Confusion* may have served as the purported rationale for the gathering, she was largely relegated to the sidelines of what became a networking affair to showcase the younger generation of black writers and endorse Alain Locke as the spokesperson of the fledgling movement. For the purposes of my argument, it is enough that it was Fauset's first novel that provided the occasion for the celebration. The quote is from Watson.
3. "The Debut of the Younger School of Negro Writers," *Opportunity* 2.17 (May 1924): 143.
4. Fauset, Nella Larsen, and Walter White collectively decided to write novels after discussing their impressions of *Birthright* (1922), a novel by the white writer T. S. Stribling, which featured an educated black protagonist. They expressed their dissatisfaction with contemporary literary depictions of black characters and their determination to represent black people in fiction accurately.
5. Fauset facilitated the careers of these writers in a much more concrete fashion as well. As literary editor of *The Crisis* from 1919 to 1926 she encouraged, promoted, and printed the work of several young black writers. In his autobiography, *The Big Sea*, Langston Hughes rendered the often-quoted opinion that Fauset had "midwifed" the Renaissance into existence.
6. Montgomery Gregory, "The Spirit of Phyllis [*sic*] Wheatley," *Opportunity* 2.18 (June 1924): 181.
7. Gregory, 181.
8. "The Debut of the Younger Generation of Negro Writers," 143.
9. Many critics have noted that black writers who fashioned what Liveright perceived as "impossibly good fiction types" had legitimate reasons for doing so, principally to refute the abundance of pseudo-scientific theories of intrinsic black inferiority. Common authorial practices included featuring black characters indistinguishable from white people, asserting the desirability of belonging to the black race by having these accomplished black people choose to work for the advancement of their race rather than assimilate into the white public, and displaying the achievable talents of black people to provide positive role

models for other black people to follow and instill a racial pride despite the proliferation of denigrating stereotypes. See Hazel Carby, *Reconstructing Womanhood: The Emergence of the Afro-American Woman Novelist* (New York: Oxford University Press, 1991), 88–91; Ann duCille, *The Coupling Convention: Sex, Text, and Tradition in Black Women's Fiction* (New York: Oxford University Press, 1993), 7–8, 18; Kevin Kelley Gaines, *Uplifting the Race: Black Leadership, Politics and Culture in the Twentieth Century* (Chapel Hill: The University of North Carolina Press, 1996), 221.

10. Dorothy West, "An Unimportant Man," in *The Richer, the Poorer: Stories, Sketches, and Reminiscences* (New York: Anchor Books, 1995), 150.

11. Jessie Fauset, *Comedy: American Style* (1931; New York: G.K. Hall & Co., 1995), 81. Further references to this novel will be cited parenthetically in the text.

12. Idlewild, Michigan, was the premier black resort of the 1920s. Prominent black individuals such as W. E. B. Du Bois and Charles Chesnutt owned vacation property there.

13. St. Clair Drake and Horace R. Cayton, *Black Metropolis: A Study of Negro Life in a Northern City* (New York: Harcourt, Brace, and Company, 1945), 530–31.

14. Drake and Cayton, 531.

15. The motto is a corruption of that of the white Byes, the Quaker family who owned Peter's ancestors as slaves in the eighteenth century and retained them as servants after their manumission. The white Bye family motto was "By their fruits ye shall know them," (24).

16. Gatewood, 345.

17. Gaines, 221.

18. Of course, many other white writers, most notably James Fenimore Cooper in *Last of the Mohicans*, contributed to this unyielding cultural expectation of white-skinned heroines, but Stowe supplied the model figures of Eliza, Cassy, and Emmeline in *Uncle Tom's Cabin* (1852; New York: Bantam Books, 1981); all three women look white, speak standard English, and enjoy the advantages of a white upbringing until the evil institution of slavery claims them from their privileged existence. Clearly, white audiences were enabled to identify with these characters in ways they were not able to with those dialect-speaking, self-deprecating, "unadulterated" racial types such as Uncle Tom's wife Aunt Chloe (the "glossy" black cook who refers to her own sons as "you niggers"), or Topsy ("one of the blackest of her race"), whose childish antics serve as a narrative foil to Little Eva. In fact, Eliza became one of the leading cultural icons of the era, as her flight to freedom carrying her son over the Ohio River ice floes was an indispensable scene in the immensely popular stagings of the novel lasting well into the twentieth century.

19. Claudia Tate, *Domestic Allegories of Political Desire: The Black Heroine's Text at the Turn of the Century* (New York: Oxford University Press, 1992), 63.

20. W. E. B. Du Bois, "The Superior Race," *Smart Set*, April 1923, in *Writings by W. E. B. Du Bois in Periodicals Edited by Others, vol. 2 1910–1934*, ed. Herbert Aptheker (Millwood, NY: Kraus-Thomson Organization Limited, 1982), 184. Du Bois goes on to comment that "Hair is a matter of taste. Some will have it drab and stringy and others in a gray, woven, unmoving mass. Most of us like it somewhere in between, in tiny tendrils, smoking curls, and sweeping curves. I have loved all these varieties in my day. I prefer the crinkly kind, almost wavy, in black brown and glistening. In faces I hate straight features; needles and razors may be sharp—but beautiful, never."
21. Fauset, *Comedy: American Style*, 77.
22. Hazel Carby, *Reconstructing Womanhood: The Emergence of the Afro-American Woman Novelist* (New York: Oxford University Press, 1987), 34.
23. Carby, *Reconstructing Womanhood*, 143.
24. Charles W. Chesnutt, *The Marrow of Tradition* (1901; Ann Arbor: The University of Michigan Press, 1969), 261.
25. In *Women of the Harlem Renaissance*, Cheryl Wall perceives the chinaberry tree as a symbol of "the legacy of slavery" which "shadow[s]" Sal and Halloway and prevents them from being able to marry (79).
26. Wall, 79.
27. Hodges, *Black Society*, 269.
28. McLendon, 56.
29. McLendon, 56.
30. McLendon, 56.
31. Clearly, Lee's decision to marry Janet was not induced entirely by the color of her skin. Surely, there was no epidemic shortage of women of his social standing with skin as pale as Janet's. However, part of the problem with his choice of Janet, like Junius Murray's choice of Mattie, has to do with the men's implied belief that such women somehow did not belong in domestic service—as if their similitude to "real" white women made them better than their darker-skinned counterparts and undeserving of the same fate. Lee's freedom to marry below his class position also speaks to the gender inequities inherent in a social order in which the family's status is determined primarily by the occupation of the husband/father. The point I want to make here is that wives were often viewed as mere accoutrements to men, and having a light-skinned wife strengthened a man's claim to class prestige, regardless of her background, whereas the converse did not apply.
32. Anna Julia Cooper, *A Voice from the South* (1892; New York: Oxford University Press, 1988), 22.
33. Cooper, 29.
34. James Oliver Horton, *Free People of Color: Inside the African American Community* (Washington, DC: Smithsonian Institution Press, 1993), 105.
35. Horton, 116.

36. Sarah L. Delany and A. Elizabeth Delany with Amy Hill Hearth, *Having Our Say: The Delany Sisters' First 100 Years* (New York: Bantam Doubleday Dell, 1993), 157.
37. Delany et al., 157–58.
38. Quoted in Angus McLaren, *A History of Contraception: From Antiquity to the Present Day* (Oxford: Basil Blackwell, 1990), 206.
39. I am indebted to Sandra Gunning of the University of Michigan, Department of English Language and Literature, for suggesting this race-conscious way of interpreting Roosevelt's injunction.
40. Ross Brown, *Afro-American World Almanac: What Do You Know about Your Race, with Unusual Historic Facts about Prominent People of African Descent from A to Z* (Chicago: Bedford Brown Edition, 1942). James Weldon Johnson, *Black Manhattan* (1930; New York: Da Capo Press, 1991), 246.
41. Johnson, 238.
42. Quoted in Johnson, 239.
43. Nella Larsen, *Quicksand, An Intimation of Things Distant: The Collected Fiction of Nella Larsen* (New York: Doubleday, 1992), 132.
44. McLaren, 242.
45. In a quote taken from *The Coupling Convention*, duCille is referring specifically to the criticisms made by several critics, among them Houston Baker, Barbara Christian, and Alice Walker, of the "tragic mulatta" heroine type featured in many early black novels. "Such criticisms seem to me ahistorical in the degree to which they chide early African American writers for not being 100 to 150 years ahead of their times. These early authors who ... battled slavery, institutionalized racism, and illiteracy, as well as the discriminatory practices of the publishing industry, are condemned for writing through and against the dominant racial and sexual ideologies of their times, rather than out of the enlightened, feminist vision of ours" (18).
46. DuCille, 99.
47. Gatewood, 190–91.
48. Joel is later credited with the plan of convincing Peter and Joanna to live in the family home after their marriage (290), but because this takes place shortly following the death of Philip, and Joanna is constantly acknowledged as her father's favorite, the same implications do not attend his contrivance.
49. Quoted in Darlene Clark Hine, *Hine Sight*, 75.
50. Mary F. Sisney, "The View from the Outside: Black Novels of Manners," in *Reading and Writing Women's Lives: A Study of the Novel of Manners*, ed. Bege K. Bowers and Barbara Brothers (Ann Arbor: UMI Research Press, 1990), 173. Sisney argues that Fauset's use of marriage as the vehicle for women's engagement with society makes her the direct literary descendent of Jane Austen. This claim simultaneously insinuates that Fauset's characters are essentially white in a figurative blackface and exhibits a textual blindness to the frequent moments in Fauset's narratives that operate to undermine an allegedly

idealized domesticity. In her categorization of Fauset's work within the rubric of novels of manners, Sisney may adhere too strictly to literary theorist Fredric Jameson's definition of genres as "essentially literary institutions, or social contracts between a writer and a specific public, whose function is to specify the proper use of a particular cultural artifact." [Jameson, *The Political Unconscious: Narrative as a Socially Symbolic Act* (Ithaca, NY: Cornell University Press, 1981), 106.] In her adherence to the "social contract" implied by the conventional novel of manners, Sisney appears to overlook the fact that her claim of an Austen-like order provided by marriage at the close of Fauset's narratives is contradicted by the problematic endings that undermine an implied optimism.

51. Wall, 67.
52. Fauset, *The Chinaberry Tree*, 157.
53. Nina Miller, "Femininity, Publicity, and the Class Division of Cultural Labor: Jessie Redmon Fauset's *There Is Confusion*," *African American Review* 30.2 (summer 1996): 217.
54. Miller, 217.
55. Abe C. Ravitz, *Imitations of Life: Fannie Hurst's Gaslight Sonatas* (Carbondale: Southern Illinois University Press, 1997), 131. Prominent euthenicists included Fannie Hurst and Clarence Darrow, both very publicly acknowledged "friends" to the African American.
56. McCoy, 114–15.
57. Robert C. Toll, *Blacking Up: The Minstrel Show in Nineteenth-Century America* (New York: Oxford University Press, 1974), 32.
58. Toll, 28.

3. Elite Rejection of Maternity in Nella Larsen's *Quicksand* and Passing

1. Du Bois opened "The Forethought" to his 1903 polemic *The Souls of Black Folk* (1903; New York: Penguin Group, 1989) with the statement: "Herein lie buried many things which if read with patience may show the strange meaning of being black here in the dawning of the Twentieth Century. This meaning is not without interest to you, Gentle Reader; for the problem of the Twentieth Century is the problem of the color-line" (1).
2. Nella Larsen, *Quicksand, An Intimation of Things Distant: The Collected Fiction of Nella Larsen*, ed. Charles R. Larson (1928; New York: Doubleday, 1992), 56. All subsequent quotations will be cited parenthetically in this chapter.
3. Ann E. Hostetler claims that Helga's father is a "black jazz musician," but I have not been able to locate the textual evidence to support her assertion.

Hostetler, "The Aesthetics of Race and Gender in Nella Larsen's *Quicksand*," *PMLA* 105.1 (January 1990): 35.

4. Not only does Helga fling this bit of information at Dr. Anderson in her exit interview from Naxos, where some critics have noted she may be exaggerating the shock value of her personal history in an effort to shame the school's principal, but she also is startled into the admission by her Uncle Peter's newlywed wife, who is clearly displeased by Helga's connection to her husband. When the woman asks her directly whether her parents had ever been married, Helga is compelled to acknowledge her lack of certainty (61).

5. Martha J. Cutter, "Sliding Significations: Passing as a Narrative and Textual Strategy in Nella Larsen's Fiction," *Passing and the Fictions of Identity*, ed. Elaine K. Ginsberg (Durham: Duke University Press, 1996), 84.

6. Nella Larsen, *Passing, An Intimation of Things Distant*. Clare attributes part of her rationale for passing into the white world to her desire for equal status with Irene and other middle-class black people: "[W]hen I used to go over to the South Side, I used almost to hate all of you. You had all the things I wanted and never had had. It made me all the more determined to get them, and others," (188–89).

7. In a discussion of this particular aspect of my argument, Marlon Ross of the Department of English Language and Literature at the University of Michigan suggested to me that this may indeed be precisely Larsen's point, that what the Redfields represent *is* the typical middle-class household. I agree that Larsen displayed intense cynicism regarding the degree to which healthy companionate relationships existed behind the façade of the happy middle-class family, and this is likely the message that Larsen as author is intending to convey. However, I would also contend that Irene as a character believes in an ideal of domestic harmony which clearly deviates from the reality of her situation; even if her parents are exceptional and represent a household model rarely achieved, Irene has deluded herself into the conviction that she has managed to resolve the problems plaguing her marriage and has restored her family to that idealized status.

8. This observation is not meant to imply that all women inevitably possess a maternal instinct. However, I think it is important to the thematics of the narrative that we accept that Helga does because it provides the motivational context to explore the implications of the conflict between her desire for children and her discomfort with the social climate to which she would be subjecting them.

9. Larsen used the same device to create a pen name for herself which she used to publish short stories before she began her career as a novelist. Under the name "Allen Semi," the reverse of her married name, Nella Imes, she wrote two stories, "The Wrong Man" and "Freedom," for *Young's Magazine* in 1926. In his introduction to *An Intimation of Things Distant*, Charles Larson suggests that Larsen may have chosen to use a pseudonym in an effort to obscure her

authorship of what she perceived as unremarkable, utilitarian "hack writing," (xiii).

10. Darlene Clark Hine, "Female Slave Resistance: The Economics of Sex," *Hine Sight: Black Women and the Re-Construction of American History* (Brooklyn: Carlson Publishing, 1994), 34–35, 30. In this chapter Hine chronicles several documented accounts of slave women who engaged in postponed marriages, abortion, and infanticide in order to evade raising children doomed to slavery.
11. See introduction for a detailed explanation as to why this was the case.
12. Marita Golden, introduction to *An Intimation of Things Distant*, by Nella Larsen, vii.
13. Charles Larson, foreword to *An Intimation of Things Distant*, xiv.
14. Deborah E. McDowell, "'That nameless ... shameful impulse': Sexuality in Nella Larsen's *Quicksand* and *Passing*," *Black Feminist Criticism and Critical Theory*, ed. Joe Weixlmann and Houston A. Baker, Jr. (Greenwood, FL: Penkevill, 1988), 147.
15. McDowell, 141–46.
16. McDowell, 146.
17. Richard Wright, *Uncle Tom's Children* (New York: HarperCollins, 1993), 129.
18. Claudia Tate, *Psychoanalysis and Black Novels: Desire and the Protocols of Race* (New York: Oxford University Press, 1998), 9.
19. Tate, 122.
20. David L. Blackmore has argued that this passage lends itself to the interpretation of Brian as a closet homosexual. He explicates the quote from Irene with the following statement: "Early in the novel, Irene expresses concern about [Brian's] sexual drive." Among the other evidence Blackmore provides is "Again and again she uses the word *queer* in reference to her husband, and particularly his desire to escape to South America," and "Her fear that he might be perceived as at all feminine betrays her subconscious concern that he is perhaps not the conventional 'man' he is supposed to be." Blackmore, "'That Unreasonable Restless Feeling': The Homosexual Subtexts of Nella Larsen's *Passing*," *African American Review* 26.3 (1992): 476–78. I would argue, however, that an alternative, equally viable reading would consider that just as Irene has deluded herself about other aspects of her marriage, she has deluded herself into the belief that her husband has homosexual tendencies. Not only would this deflect his lack of sexual attraction to her onto a source external to her personal desirability, but it would also explain Irene's anxiety about Brian's borderline womanish appearance, her absolute certainty in his sexual fidelity—demonstrated both by her response to Jack Bellew's crass attempt at humor and her lack of concern about sending her husband out alone with Clare to various social functions she for some reason cannot attend, and her inattention to the early signs of a budding relationship between Clare and Brian—especially their numerous dances at the Negro Welfare League affair and Brian's suggestion afterwards that he drop Irene off first and then

drive Clare home. As with her conviction that she has competently mended all of the loose threads of their marriage, this is a situation where Irene would rather believe her concocted fictions than the obvious truth.
21. Fauset, *Comedy: American Style*, 37.
22. This is also another clue to the probability of an affair between Clare and Brian, because while Ted takes after his mother in appearance, his disposition is an exact replica of his father's. Larsen includes this frank disclosure of the intensity of Ted's feelings for Clare to suggest that Brian would have responded to her in kind.
23. Larsen also uses the symbolism of slumber and lateness to indicate that Irene is insensible to most of what is going on around her. While a substantial amount of the action of the novel is taking place, Irene is absent because she is asleep or for some reason detained. Besides the considerable time the boys spend with their father before Irene even wakes up in the mornings, Irene is often napping while Brian is engaged in other activities she never knows anything about. Irene does not witness the scene of the first meeting between Brian and Clare because she "com[es] downstairs a few minutes later than she had intended" (233). Irene is also sleeping (which will cause her to be late) immediately before the tea party that begins shortly after her realization that there is something more than innocent friendship going on between Brian and Clare. Irene is late getting downstairs before she, Brian, and Clare depart for Felise Freeland's party the night Clare is killed, and remains in the Freelands' apartment after all the other guests have rushed downstairs following Clare's plunge from the casement window, delaying her appearance on the accident (or murder) scene.
24. Kate Chopin, *The Awakening*, *The Awakening and Selected Stories* (1899; New York: Penguin Books, 1984), 171.
25. My reading contradicts one provided by Charles Larson in *Invisible Darkness: Jean Toomer and Nella Larsen* (Iowa City: University of Iowa Press, 1993), which hinges on "Brian's absence from the final scene." Larson contends that "Irene faints and is lifted up by strong arms, belonging to someone other than her husband" (86). His interpretation of someone else lifting Irene is likely based on the fact that the following paragraph (the last in the book) talks about Irene hearing the voice of "the strange man." However, this "strange man" is not a reference to the man who picks her up, but to the "official and authoritative" "strange man" of three paragraphs earlier who is evidently in charge of the investigation into Clare's death (275, 274). Brian is unquestionably among "the little group shivering in the small hallway" in the final scene of the novel (274). He is mentioned by name five different times and actively participates in the denouement through both speech and action.

4. The Stereotypical Mammy in Fannie Hurst's *Imitation of Life*

1. Charlotte Mason, an extremely wealthy elderly widow known as "Godmother" to conceal her identity per her request, is typically used to demonstrate the more disturbing dimensions of white "beneficence" toward the Renaissance artists. According to Steven Watson, author of *The Harlem Renaissance,* Mason "expended nearly $75,000—over a half million dollars by current valuation" on the artists she supported, principally Hurston and Langston Hughes, "but her patronage exacted the more debilitating tolls of dependency, control, and infantilization." Mason drew up contracts that placed Hurston and Hughes on monthly stipends which were paid on the condition that they fulfilled certain obligations to her, including detailing their daily activities, expenses, and, in Hurston's case, obtaining Mason's consent before submitting any writing for publication. Watson, *The Harlem Renaissance: Hub of African-American Culture, 1920–1930* (New York: Pantheon Books, 1995), 146–50.
2. Quoted in Gay Wilentz, "White Patron and Black Artist: The Correspondence of Fannie Hurst and Zora Neale Hurston," *Library Chronicle of the University of Texas* 35 (1986): 32.
3. The correspondence is held by the Harry Ransom Humanities Research Center at the University of Texas at Austin in the Fannie Hurst collection.
4. See Wilentz, 35–37 for a fuller discussion of this incident and the impact it had on Hurston's career. Also see Cheryl A. Wall, *Women of the Harlem Renaissance* (Bloomington: Indiana University Press, 1995), 201–2. The most complete account is in Robert Hemenway, *Zora Neale Hurston: A Literary Biography* (Urbana: University of Illinois Press, 1977), 319–23.
5. Fannie Hurst, *Anatomy of Me: A Wonderer in Search of Herself* (Garden City, NY: Doubleday & Co., 1958), 350. Hereafter, quotations from this autobiography will be cited parenthetically in the text.
6. My point here is not to endorse Hurst as a sincere ally to black people. She also agitated on behalf of the "working girl" and was an outspoken activist for several other political causes. As occurred during the abolition movement, it is obviously entirely possible to advocate civil rights while harboring a belief in a strict racial hierarchy. Hurst did not necessarily have to consider black people her social equals in order to promote their fair treatment, and her status as "friend" could easily have coexisted with prejudicial attitudes. My purpose is to consider a reading of *Imitation of Life* consistent with Hurst's articulated aspiration to denounce racial injustice.
7. Quoted in Wilentz, 39.
8. Dorothy West, *The Living Is Easy* (1948; Boston: The Feminist Press, 1982), 74.

9. Jon Halliday, "Sirk on Sirk," *Imitation of Life: Douglas Sirk, Director,* ed. Lucy Fischer (New Brunswick, NJ: Rutgers University Press, 1991), 228.
10. Quoted in Beverly Guy-Sheftall, *Daughters of Sorrow: Attitudes Toward Black Women, 1880–1920* (Brooklyn, NY: Carlson Publishing, 1990), 83.
11. W. E. B. Du Bois, "The Black Mother," Quoted in Guy-Sheftall, *Daughters of Sorrow,* 83.
12. Paula Giddings, *When and Where I Enter: The Impact of Black Women on Race and Sex in America* (New York: Bantam Books, 1984), 232
13. Quoted in Giddings, 237.
14. Guy-Sheftall, 81–82.
15. Quote appears in Dorothy Burnham, "The Life of the Afro-American Woman in Slavery," *Black Women in American History,* vol. 1, ed. Darlene Clark Hine (Brooklyn, NY: Carlson Publishing, 1990), 205.
16. Tillie Olsen, ed., *Mother to Daughter, Daughter to Mother, Mothers on Mothering: A Daybook and Reader* (Old Westbury, NY: The Feminist Press, 1984), 181.
17. Olsen, 182.
18. Olsen, 182.
19. *Half-Century Magazine* 7.3 (September 1919): 11. "Mammy Sue" appears in 9.4 (October 1920): 5, 12. Page references will be noted in the text.
20. The relevant scripture is found in Ephesians 6:5–8. "[5]Slaves, obey your earthly masters with fear and trembling, in singleness of heart, as you obey Christ; [6]not only while being watched, and in order to please them, but as slaves of Christ, doing the will of God from the heart. [7]Render service with enthusiasm, as to the Lord and not to men and women, [8]knowing that whatever good we do, we will receive the same again from the Lord, whether we are slaves or free." *The New Student Bible, New Revised Standard Version* (Grand Rapids, MI: Zondervan Publishing House, 1994), 1070.
21. Berlant, 114.
22. Bea's reflection, incorporating the status of the women as possible "what nots" to the black working-class men of the town, also seems to insinuate that the potential housekeepers are preeminently concerned about the viability of their sex lives, disreputable though they are.
23. Excerpt from the film review appears in the original trailer to Stahl's film.
24. See Berlant for a fuller discussion of the implications of the conflation of "Aunt Delilah" with the Aunt Jemima phenomenon, 122–28.
25. Jane Caputi and Helene Vann, "Questions of Race and Place: Comparative Racism in *Imitation of Life* (1934) and *Places in the Heart*" *Cineaste* 15.4 (1987): 18.
26. Caputi and Vann, 18.
27. Smith, 45.
28. The "incantation" Delilah uses to subdue Peola's tooth cutting through before Jessie's: "Doan' talk—go ter sleep! / Eyes shut an' doan' you peep! /

Keep still, or he jes' moans, / 'Raw Head an' Bloody Bones!'" is perhaps one of the moments of "authenticity" which critics believed were due to Hurst's association with Zora Neale Hurston.

29. Fauset, *Comedy: American Style*, 52. Subsequent references cited in text by page number.
30. Lucy Fischer, "Three-Way Mirror: Imitation of Life," in *Imitation of Life: Douglas Sirk, Director*, ed. Lucy Fischer (New Brunswick, NJ: Rutgers University Press, 1991), 28.
31. As the ceremony proceeds, "The Order of the Sisters of the Rising Star spread a banner the size of a wall, and two hundred marching members of the Amalgamated Lodges of the Sons and Daughters of David, turned out in caps with visors and spears tipped with tin foil" (Hurst, 325).
32. Jesus speaks these words to his disciples in Mark 9:35. *Holy Bible, New Revised Standard Version*.
33. In a discussion of this phase of my argument, Marlon Ross, Professor of English at the University of Michigan, suggested that this statement might be taken to contradict my earlier supposition that Hurst herself believed these to be faithful and accurate representations of realistic black characters. My point here, however, is that Delilah and Peola demonstrate the extremes to which black women are pushed in their attempt to accommodate American repression and dominant social expectations. Delilah submits to the prevailing doctrine but liberates herself by constructing via her religious convictions an alternative hierarchical value scheme that enables her to accept her earthly degradation without complaint. Because Peola is superficially indistinguishable from the white majority, she is not compelled to adhere to the societal demands that she accept her designated place. As she herself argues in her rationalization of her choice to pass in her final scene with her mother, "It might be easier if I was out-and-out black like you. Then there wouldn't be any question" (297). As it stands, though, Peola does have an option, and she opts to be considered white. The most severe indictment is of the social conditions that push the women into such behavioral stances.

Bibliography

Primary Literature

Cable, George Washington. *Old Creole Days.* New York: Charles Scribner's Sons, 1879.
Chesnutt, Charles. *The Conjure Woman and Other Conjure Tales.* 1899. Durham, NC: Duke University Press, 1993.
———. *The Wife of His Youth and Other Stories of the Color Line.* 1899. Ann Arbor: The University of Michigan Press, 1968.
———. *The House Behind the Cedars.* 1900. New York: Penguin Books, 1993.
———. *The Marrow of Tradition.* 1901. Ann Arbor: The University of Michigan Press, 1969.
Chopin, Kate. *The Awakening and Selected Stories.* 1899, 1892–98. New York: Penguin Books, 1984.
Cooper, Anna Julia. *A Voice from the South.* 1892. New York: Oxford University Press, 1988.
Crane, Stephen. "The Monster." 1899. *Maggie and Other Stories.* New York: Washington Square Press, 1960.
Davis, Elizabeth Lindsay. *Lifting as They Climb.* 1933. New York: G.K. Hall & Co., 1996.
Dixon, Thomas. *The Clansman: An Historical Romance of the Ku Klux Klan.* New York: Doubleday, Page & Co., 1905.
Du Bois, W. E. B. *Darkwater: Voices from Within the Veil.* 1920. New York: Schocken Books, 1969.
———. *The Souls of Black Folk.* 1903. New York: Penguin Books, 1989.
Dunbar, Paul Laurence. *Folks from Dixie.* New York: Dodd, Mead, & Co., 1898.
Fauset, Jessie Redmon. *The Chinaberry Tree.* 1931. Boston: Northeastern University Press, 1995.

———. *Comedy: American Style*. 1933. New York: Simon & Schuster Macmillan, 1995.

———. *Plum Bun*. 1928. Boston: Beacon Press, 1990.

———. *There Is Confusion*. 1924. Boston: Northeastern University Press, 1989.

Gray, Leona. "Mammy Sue." *The Half-Century Magazine* 9.4 (October 1920): 5,12.

Harper, Frances E. W. *Iola Leroy*. Philadelphia: Garrigues Bros., 1893.

Hopkins, Pauline. *Contending Forces*. Boston: Colored Co-operative Publishing Co., 1900.

Hughes, Langston. *Not Without Laughter*. 1930. New York: Simon & Schuster, 1995.

———. *The Ways of White Folks*. 1934. New York: Random House, 1990.

Hurst, Fannie. *Anatomy of Me: A Wonderer in Search of Herself*. Garden City, NY: Doubleday & Co., 1958.

———. *Imitation of Life*. New York: Harper & Brothers, 1933.

Hurston, Zora Neale. *The Complete Stories*. New York: HarperCollins, 1995.

———. *Dust Tracks on a Road*. Philadelphia: J. B. Lippincott, 1942.

———. *Their Eyes Were Watching God*. 1937. New York: Harper & Row, 1990.

Imitation of Life. Dir. John Stahl. Perf. Claudette Colbert, Louise Beavers, Fredi Washington. Universal, 1934.

Imitation of Life. Dir. Douglas Sirk. Perf. Lana Turner, Juanita Moore, Susan Kohner. Universal, 1959.

Jacobs, Harriet [Linda Brent]. *Incidents in the Life of a Slave Girl*. 1861. *The Classic Slave Narratives*. Ed. Henry Louis Gates, Jr. New York: Penguin Books, 1987.

Johnson, James Weldon. *The Autobiography of an Ex-Coloured Man*. 1912. New York: Random House, 1989.

———. *Black Manhattan*. 1930. New York: Da Capo Press, 1991.

Jones, Gayl. *Corregidora*. 1975. Boston: Beacon Press, 1986.

Larsen, Nella. *An Intimation of Things Distant: The Collected Fiction of Nella Larsen*. New York: Doubleday, 1992.

Little, Benilde. *Good Hair*. New York: Simon & Schuster, 1996.

Stowe, Harriet Beecher. *Uncle Tom's Cabin*. 1852. New York: Bantam Doubleday Dell, 1981.

Terrell, Mary Church. *A Colored Woman in a White World*. 1940. Salem, NH: Ayer Co., 1986.

Toomer, Jean. *Cane*. 1923. New York: Liveright, 1975.

Washington, Booker T. *Up from Slavery*. 1901. New York: Penguin, 1986.

West, Dorothy. *The Living Is Easy*. 1948. New York: The Feminist Press, 1982.

———. *The Richer, the Poorer*. New York: Doubleday, 1995.

———. *The Wedding*. New York: Doubleday, 1995.

White, Walter. *A Man Called White: The Autobiography of Walter White*. New York: Viking Press, 1948.

Wright, Richard. *Uncle Tom's Children*. 1940. New York: HarperCollins, 1993.

Secondary Sources

Aptheker, Herbert, ed. *The Correspondence of W. E. B. Du Bois*. Amherst: The University of Massachusetts Press, 1973.

———. *Writings by W. E. B. Du Bois in Periodicals Edited by Others, Vol. 2, 1910–1934*. Millwood, NY: Kraus-Thomson Organization Limited, 1982.

Armstrong, Nancy. *Desire and Domestic Fiction: A Political History of the Novel*. New York: Oxford University Press, 1987.

Baker, Paula. "The Domestication of Politics: Women and American Political Society, 1780–1920." *Unequal Sisters: A Multi-Cultural Reader in U.S. Women's History*, edited by Vicki L. Ruiz and Ellen Carol DuBois. New York: Routledge, 1994.

Baskin, Alex. *Margaret Sanger, the Woman Rebel and the Rise of the Birth Control Movement in the United States*. New York: Archives of Social History, 1976.

Bassin, Donna, Margaret Honey, and Meryle Mahrer Kaplan, eds. *Representations of Motherhood*. New Haven, CT: Yale University Press, 1994.

Bell, Bernard W. *The Afro-American Novel and Its Tradition*. Amherst: The University of Massachusetts Press, 1987.

Bennett, Juda. *The Passing Figure: Racial Confusion in Modern American Literature*. New York: Peter Lang Publishing, Inc., 1996.

Berg, Allison Brooke. *Mothering the Race: Women's Narratives of Reproduction, 1899–1928*. Ph.D. Diss., Indiana University, 1992.

Berlant, Lauren. "National Brands/National Body: Imitation of Life." In *Comparative American Identities: Race, Sex, and Nationality in the Modern Text*, edited by Hortense Spillers. New York: Routledge, 1991.

Bernardi, Daniel, ed. *The Birth of Whiteness: Race and the Emergence of U.S. Cinema*. New Brunswick, NJ: Rutgers University Press, 1996.

Berzon, Judith R. *Neither White nor Black: The Mulatto Character in American Fiction*. New York: New York University Press, 1978.

Billingsley, Andrew. *Black Families in White America*. Englewood Cliffs, NJ: Prentice-Hall, 1968.

Blackmore, David L. "'That Unreasonable Restless Feeling': The Homosexual Subtexts of Nella Larsen's *Passing*." *African American Review* 26.3 (1992): 475–84.

Bogle, Donald. "Black Beginnings: From *Uncle Tom's Cabin* to *The Birth of a Nation*." *Representing Blackness: Issues in Film and Video*, edited by Valerie Smith. New Brunswick, NJ: Rutgers University Press, 1997.

———. *Toms, Coons, Mulattoes, Mammies, and Bucks: An Interpretive History of Blacks in American Films*. New 3rd ed. New York: The Continuum Publishing Company, 1994.

Bone, Robert. *Down Home: Origins of the Afro-American Short Story*. New York: Columbia University Press, 1975.

Bourdieu, Pierre. *Distinction: A Social Critique of the Judgment of Taste*. Trans. Richard Nice. 1979. Cambridge, MA: Harvard University Press, 1984.

Brodhead, Richard. *Cultures of Letters: Scenes of Reading and Writing in Nineteenth-Century America*. Chicago: The University of Chicago Press, 1993.

Brody, Jennifer DeVere. "Clare Kendry's 'True' Colors: Race and Class Conflict in Nella Larsen's *Passing*." *Callaloo* 15.4 (fall 1992): 1053–65.

Brown, Ross. *Afro-American World Almanac: What Do You Know about Your Race, with Unusual Historic Facts about Prominent People of African Descent from A to Z*. Chicago: Bedford Brown Edition, 1942.

Brown-Guillory, Elizabeth. "Disrupted Motherlines: Mothers and Daughters in a Genderized, Sexualized, and Racialized World." *Women of Color: Mother-Daughter Relationships in 20th-Century Literature*, edited by Elizabeth Brown-Guillory. Austin, TX: University of Texas Press, 1996.

Burnham, Dorothy. "The Life of the Afro-American Woman in Slavery." *Black Women in American History*, Vol. 1. edited by Darlene Clark Hine. Brooklyn, NY: Carlson Publishing, 1990.

Buschman, Richard. *The Refinement of America: Persons, Houses, Cities*. New York: Alfred A. Knopf, 1992.

Caputi, Jane, and Helene Vann. "Questions of Race and Place: Comparative Racism in *Imitation of Life* (1934) and *Places in the Heart* (1984)." *Cineaste* 15.4 (1987): 16–21.

Carby, Hazel. *Reconstructing Womanhood: The Emergence of the Afro-American Woman Novelist.* New York: Oxford University Press, 1987.

Collins, Patricia Hill. *Black Feminist Thought: Knowledge, Consciousness, and the Politics of Empowerment.* Boston: Unwin Hyman, 1990.

———. "Shifting the Center: Race, Class, and Feminist Theorizing about Motherhood." In *Representations of Motherhood*, edited by Donna Bassin, Margaret Honey, and Meryle Kaplan. New Haven, CT: Yale University Press, 1994.

Conroy, Marianne. "No Sin in Lookin' Prosperous." In *The Hidden Foundation: Cinema and the Question of Class*, edited by David E. James and Rick Berg. Minneapolis: University of Minnesota Press, 1996.

Cutter, Martha J. "Sliding Significations: Passing as Narrative and Textual Strategy in Nella Larsen's Fiction." In *Passing and the Fictions of Identity*, edited by Elaine K. Ginsberg. Durham, NC: Duke University Press, 1996.

Daly, Brenda O., and Maureen T. Reddy, eds. *Narrating Mothers: Theorizing Maternal Subjectivities.* Knoxville: The University of Tennessee Press, 1991.

Davis, Thadious M. Introduction to *Passing*, by Nella Larsen. New York: Penguin Books, 1997.

———. *Nella Larsen, Novelist of the Harlem Renaissance: A Woman's Life Unveiled.* Baton Rouge: Louisiana State University Press, 1994.

"The Debut of the Younger School of Negro Writers." *Opportunity* 2.17 (May 1924): 143.

Degler, Carl N. *At Odds: Women and the Family in America from the Revolution to the Present.* New York: Oxford University Press, 1980.

Delany, Sarah L., and A. Elizabeth Delany with Amy Hill Hearth. *Having Our Say.* New York: Bantam Doubleday Dell, 1993.

Douglas, Ann. *The Feminization of American Culture.* 1977. New York: Doubleday, 1988.

———. *Terrible Honesty: Mongrel Manhattan in the 1920s.* New York: Farrar, Straus, and Giroux, 1995.

Drake, St. Clair, and Horace R. Cayton. *Black Metropolis: A Study of Negro Life in a Northern City.* New York: Harcourt, Brace, and Company, 1945.

duCille, Ann. *The Coupling Convention: Sex, Text, and Tradition in Black Women's Fiction.* New York: Oxford University Press, 1993.

Felski, Rita. *Beyond Feminist Aesthetics: Feminist Literature and Social Change.* Cambridge, MA: Harvard University Press, 1989.

Fischer, Lucy, ed. *Imitation of Life: Douglas Sirk, Director*. New Brunswick, NJ: Rutgers University Press, 1991.

———. "Three-Way Mirror: *Imitation of Life*." In *Imitation of Life: Douglas Sirk, Director*, edited by Lucy Fischer. New Brunswick, NJ: Rutgers University Press, 1991.

Flitterman-Lewis, Sandy. "Imitation(s) of Life: The Black Woman's Double Determination as Troubling 'Other.'" *Literature and Psychology* 34.4 (1988): 44–57.

Frazier, E. Franklin. *On Race Relations: Selected Writings*. Chicago: University of Chicago Press, 1968.

Gaines, Kevin Kelley. *Uplifting the Race: Black Leadership, Politics and Culture in the Twentieth Century*. Chapel Hill: The University of North Carolina Press, 1996.

Gatewood, Willard. *Aristocrats of Color*. Bloomington: Indiana University Press, 1990.

Giddings, Paula. *In Search of Sisterhood: Delta Sigma Theta and the Challenge of the Black Sorority Movement*. New York: William Morrow, 1988.

———. *When and Where I Enter: The Impact of Black Women on Race and Sex in America*. New York: Bantam Books, 1984.

Gilroy, Paul. *The Black Atlantic: Modernity and Double-Consciousness*. Cambridge, MA: Harvard University Press, 1993.

Goldsmith, Meredith. "Edith Wharton's Gift to Nella Larsen." *Edith Wharton Review* 11.2 (fall 1994): 3–5, 15.

Grayson, Deborah R. "Fooling White Folks." *Bucknell Review* 39.1 (1995): 27–37.

Green, Harvey. *The Uncertainty of Everyday Life: 1915–1945*. New York: HarperCollins, 1992.

Gregory, Montgomery. "The Spirit of Phyllis [*sic*] Wheatley: A Review of 'There Is Confusion' by Jessie Redmon Fauset." *Opportunity* 2.18 (June 1924): 181–82.

Guy-Sheftall, Beverly. *Daughters of Sorrow: Attitudes Toward Black Women, 1880–1920*. Brooklyn, NY: Carlson Publishing, Inc., 1990.

Halliday, Jon. "Sirk on Sirk." In *Imitation of Life: Douglas Sirk, Director*, edited by Lucy Fischer. New Brunswick, NJ: Rutgers University Press, 1991.

Hare, Nathan. *The Black Anglo-Saxons*. Chicago: Third World Press, 1965.

Haynes, George E. "Negro Migration: Its Effect on Family and Community Life in the North." *Opportunity* 2.22 (October 1924): 303–5.

Herrera, Andrea O'Reilly. "'Herself Beheld': Marriage, Motherhood, and Oppression in Brontë's *Villette* and Jacobs's *Incidents in the Life of a*

Slave Girl." In *Family Matters in the British and American Novel*, edited by Andrea O'Reilly Herrera, Elizabeth Mahn Nollen, and Sheila Reitzel Foor. Bowling Green, OH: Bowling Green State University Popular Press, 1997.

Hine, Darlene Clark. *Hine Sight: Black Women and the Re-Construction of American History*. Brooklyn, NY: Carlson Publishing, 1994.

Hirsch, Marianne. "Maternity and Rememory: Toni Morrison's *Beloved*." In *Representations of Motherhood*, edited by Donna Bassin, Margaret Honey, and Meryle Kaplan. New Haven, CT: Yale University Press, 1994.

———. *The Mother/Daughter Plot: Narrative, Psychoanalysis, Feminism*. Bloomington: Indiana University Press, 1989.

Horton, James Oliver. *Free People of Color: Inside the African-American Community*. Washington, DC: Smithsonian Institution Press, 1993.

Horton, Merrill. "Blackness, Betrayal, and Childhood: Race and Identity in Nella Larsen's *Passing*." *College Language Association Journal* 28.1 (September 1994): 31–45.

Hostetler, Ann E. "The Aesthetics of Race and Gender in Nella Larsen's *Quicksand*." *PMLA* 105.1 (January 1990): 35–46.

Huggins, Nathan Irvin. *Harlem Renaissance*. New York: Oxford University Press, 1971.

Hutchinson, George. *The Harlem Renaissance in Black and White*. Cambridge, MA: Harvard University Press, 1995.

"The Hydra." *The Half-Century Magazine* 12.5 (May-June 1922): 3.

Jameson, Fredric. *The Political Unconscious: Narrative as a Socially Symbolic Act*. Ithaca, NY: Cornell University Press, 1981.

Johnson, James Weldon. *Black Manhattan*. 1930. New York: Da Capo Press, 1991.

Jones, Jacqueline. *Labor of Love, Labor of Sorrow: Black Women, Work, and the Family from Slavery to the Present*. New York: Basic Books, 1985.

Kaplan, E. Ann. *Motherhood and Representation: The Mother in Popular Culture and Melodrama*. New York: Routledge, 1992.

Kramer, Victor A., ed. *The Harlem Renaissance Re-Examined*. New York: AMS Press, 1987.

Landry, Bart. *The New Black Middle Class*. Berkeley: University of California Press, 1987.

Larson, Charles R. *Invisible Darkness: Jean Toomer and Nella Larsen*. Iowa City: University of Iowa Press, 1993.

Lattin, Patricia Hopkins. "Childbirth and Motherhood in *The Awakening*." In *Approaches to Teaching Chopin's* The Awakening, edited by Bernard

Koloski. New York: The Modern Language Association of America, 1988.

Levine, Lawrence W. *Highbrow/Lowbrow: The Emergence of Cultural Hierarchy in America.* Cambridge, MA: Harvard University Press, 1988.

Lewis, David Levering. *When Harlem Was in Vogue.* New York: Knopf, 1981.

Lewis, Earl. "Work, Family, and the African-American Experience: Some Questions Historians Have Failed to Ask." Paper presented at the Center for the Education of Women/Family Care Resources Program lecture series on the family, University of Michigan, Ann Arbor, 25 Sept. 1997.

Lott, Eric. *Love and Theft: Blackface Minstrelsy and the American Working Class.* New York: Oxford University Press, 1993.

Madigan, Mark J. "Miscegenation and 'The Dicta of Race and Class': The Rhinelander Case and Nella Larsen's *Passing*." *Modern Fiction Studies* 36.4 (winter 1990): 523–29.

Major, Geraldyn Hodges. *Black Society.* Chicago: Johnson Publishing Co., 1976.

McCoy, Beth A. "'Is This Really What You Wanted Me to Be?': The Daughter's Disintegration in Jessie Redmon Fauset's *There Is Confusion*." *Modern Fiction Studies* 40.1 (spring 1994): 101–17.

McDowell, Deborah E. "The Neglected Dimension of Jessie Redmon Fauset." In *Conjuring: Black Women, Fiction, and Literary Tradition*, edited by Marjorie Pryse and Hortense Spillers. Bloomington: Indiana University Press, 1985.

———. Introduction to *Quicksand and Passing*, by Nella Larsen. New Brunswick, NJ: Rutgers University Press, 1986.

———. "'That nameless ... shameful impulse': Sexuality in Nella Larsen's *Quicksand* and *Passing*." In *Black Feminist Criticism and Critical Theory*, edited by Joe Weixlmann and Houston A. Baker, Jr. Greenwood, FL: The Penkevill Publishing Co., 1988.

McLaren, Angus. *A History of Contraception: From Antiquity to the Present Day.* Oxford: Basil Blackwell Ltd., 1990.

McLendon, Jacquelyn. *The Politics of Color in the Fiction of Jessie Fauset and Nella Larsen.* Charlottesville, VA: University Press of Virginia, 1995.

Miller, Nina. "Femininity, Publicity, and the Class Division of Cultural Labor: Jessie Redmon Fauset's *There Is Confusion*." *African American Review* 30.2 (summer 1996): 205–20.

Morrison, Toni. *Playing in the Dark: Whiteness and the Literary Imagination.* New York: Random House, 1993.

———. "Unspeakable Things Unspoken: The Afro-American Presence in American Literature." In *Criticism and the Color Line*, edited by Henry B. Wonham. New Brunswick, NJ: Rutgers University Press, 1996.

Motz, Marilyn Ferris, and Pat Browne, eds. *Making the American Home: Middle-Class Women and Domestic Material Culture, 1840–1940*. Bowling Green, OH: Bowling Green State University Popular Press, 1988.

Olsen, Tillie, ed. *Mother to Daughter, Daughter to Mother, Mothers on Mothering: A Daybook and Reader*. Old Westbury, NY: The Feminist Press, 1984.

Peiss, Kathy, and Christina Simmons, eds. *Passion and Power: Sexuality in History*. Philadelphia: Temple University Press, 1989.

Ravitz, Abe C. *Imitations of Life: Fannie Hurst's Gaslight Sonatas*. Carbondale: Southern Illinois University Press, 1997.

Rhines, Jesse Algeron. *Black Film/White Money*. New Brunswick, NJ: Rutgers University Press, 1996.

Richards, Larry. *African American Films Through 1959: A Comprehensive, Illustrated Filmography*. Jefferson, NC: McFarland & Company, Inc., 1998.

Robinson, William J. *Fewer and Better Babies: Birth Control, or the Limitation of Offspring by Prevenception*. 1916. New York: Eugenics Publishing Co., Inc., 1931.

Rodrique, Jessie. "The Black Community and the Birth Control Movement." In *Passion and Power: Sexuality in History*, edited by Kathy Peiss and Christina Simmons. Philadelphia: Temple University Press, 1989.

Rueschmann, Eva. "Sister Bonds: Intersections of Family and Race in Jessie Redmon Fauset's *Plum Bun* and Dorothy West's *The Living Is Easy*." In *The Significance of Sibling Relationships in Literature*, edited by JoAnna Stephens Mink and Janet Doubler Ward. Bowling Green, OH: Bowling Green State University Popular Press, 1993.

Ryan, Pamela. "A Woman's Place: Motherhood and Domesticity in Literature." *Unisa English Studies* 29.1 (April 1991): 24–34.

Sampson, Henry T. *Blacks in Black and White: A Source Book on Black Films*. Metuchen, NJ: The Scarecrow Press, 1977.

Samuels, Shirley, ed. *The Culture of Sentiment: Race, Gender, and Sentimentality in Nineteenth-Century America*. New York: Oxford, 1992.

Sanchez-Eppler, Karen. *Touching Liberty: Abolition, Feminism, and the Politics of the Body*. Berkeley: The University of California Press, 1993.

Sanger, Margaret. *Motherhood in Bondage*. New York: Brentano's, 1928.

Selig, Michael E. "Contradiction and Reading: Social Class and Sex Class in *Imitation of Life.*" *Wide Angle: A Film Quarterly* 10.4 (1988): 13–23.

Shaw, Stephanie J. *What a Woman Ought to Be and to Do: Black Professional Women Workers During the Jim Crow Era.* Chicago: The University of Chicago Press, 1996.

Shockley, Ann Allen. *Afro-American Women Writers 1746–1933: An Anthology and Critical Guide.* New York: Penguin, 1988.

Silverman, Debra B. "Nella Larsen's *Quicksand*: Untangling the Webs of Exoticism." *African American Review* 27.4 (winter 1993): 599–614.

Simmons, Christina. "Modern Sexuality and the Myth of Victorian Repression." In *Passion and Power: Sexuality in History*, edited by Kathy Peiss and Christina Simmons. Philadelphia: Temple University Press, 1989.

Singh, Amritjit, William S. Shiver, and Stanley Brodwin, eds. *The Harlem Renaissance: Revaluations.* New York: Garland Publishing, 1989.

Sisney, Mary F. "The View from the Outside: Black Novels of Manners." In *Reading and Writing Women's Lives: A Study of the Novel of Manners*, edited by Bege K. Bowers and Barbara Brothers. UMI Research Press, 1990.

Smith, Valerie. "Reading the Intersection of Race and Gender in Narratives of Passing." *diacritics* 24.2 (summer-fall 1994): 43–57.

———, ed. *Representing Blackness: Issues in Film and Video.* New Brunswick, NJ: Rutgers University Press, 1997.

Smith-Rosenberg, Carroll. *Disorderly Conduct: Visions of Gender in Victorian America.* New York: Alfred A. Knopf, 1985.

Snitow, Ann, Christine Stansell, and Sharon Thompson, eds. *Powers of Desire: The Politics of Sexuality.* New York: Monthly Review Press, 1983.

Stallybrass, Peter, and Allon White. *The Politics and Poetics of Transgression.* Ithaca, NY: Cornell University Press, 1986.

Stovall, Tyler. *Paris Noir: African Americans in the City of Light.* New York: Houghton Mifflin Company, 1996.

Sundquist, Eric. *To Wake the Nations: Race in the Making of American Literature.* Cambridge, MA: Harvard University Press, 1993.

Sylvander, Carolyn Wedin. *Jessie Redmon Fauset, Black American Writer.* Troy, NY: The Whitson Publishing Co., 1981.

Tate, Claudia. *Domestic Allegories of Political Desire: The Black Heroine's Text at the Turn of the Century.* New York: Oxford University Press, 1992.

———. "Nella Larsen's *Passing*: A Problem of Interpretation." *Black American Literature Forum* (1980): 142–46.

———. *Psychoanalysis and Black Novels: Desire and the Protocols of Race.* New York: Oxford University Press, 1998.

Thurer, Shari L. *The Myths of Motherhood: How Culture Reinvents the Good Mother.* Boston: Houghton Mifflin Co., 1994.

Toll, Robert. *Blacking Up: The Minstrel Show in Nineteenth Century America.* New York: Oxford University Press, 1974.

Van Doren, Carl. "The Younger Generation of Negro Writers." *Opportunity* 2.17 (May 1924): 144–45.

Wade-Gayles, Gloria. "The Truths of Our Mothers' Lives: Mother-Daughter Relationships in Black Women's Fiction." *SAGE: A Scholarly Journal on Black Women* 1.2 (fall 1984): 8–12.

Wall, Cheryl A. *Women of the Harlem Renaissance.* Bloomington: Indiana University Press, 1995.

Warren, Kenneth. *Black and White Strangers: Race and American Literary Realism.* Chicago: The University of Chicago Press, 1993.

Washington, Mary Helen, ed. *Invented Lives: Narratives of Black Women, 1860–1960.* Garden City, NY: Doubleday, 1987.

Watson, Steven. *The Harlem Renaissance: Hub of African-American Culture, 1920–1930.* New York: Pantheon Books, 1995.

Wilentz, Gay. "White Patron and Black Artist: The Correspondence of Fannie Hurst and Zora Neale Hurston." *Library Chronicle of the University of Texas* 35 (1986): 20–43.

Wintz, Cary D. *Black Culture and the Harlem Renaissance.* Houston: Rice University Press, 1988.

Wonham, Henry B., ed. *Criticism and the Color Line: Desegregating American Literary Studies.* New Brunswick, NJ: Rutgers University Press, 1996.

Index

A

Abolitionist rhetoric, 14
Anatomy of Me (Hurst), 112
Aristocrats of color (*see* Black elite)
Aristocrats of Color (Gatewood), 68
Aunt Jemima, 113, 124
Awakening, The (Chopin), 108

B

Baltimore Afro-American, The, 116
Beavers, Louise, 121
Berlant, Lauren, 120
Billingsley, Andrew, 23, 38
Birth control, 17
Birth of a Nation, 34–35, 119
Birthright (Stribling), 35
Black elite, 22–24, 31–32
Black Mammy Association, 116
Black Mammy Memorial Institute, 116
Black Metropolis: A Study of Negro Life in a Northern City (Drake & Cayton), 22, 24–25
Boni & Liveright, 39, 76
Brent, Linda (*see* Jacobs, Harriet)
"Bronzeville," 24–25
Brown, Sterling, 112–13

C

Cane (Toomer), 31, 39
Caputi, Jane, 123–24
Carby, Hazel, 9, 54–55
Cayton, Horace R., 22, 24–25, 48
Chesnutt, Charles, 20, 40–41, 52, 55–56, 61
Childlessness, 12, 15, 17, 20–21, 62–64, 76, 89, 91, 95, 135–36
Chinaberry Tree, The (Fauset), 7, 40, 53, 56–57, 72, 74–75; origins of primary characters, 47
Chopin, Kate, 108
Clansman, The (Dixon), 34
Class distinctions, 24–26
Collins, Patricia Hill, 13, 15
Colored American Magazine, 62
Comedy: American Style (Fauset), 3 6, 8, 19–20, 30, 40, 45, 58–59, 72, 104, 126, 129; origins of primary characters, 47
"Coming of John, Of the" (Du Bois), 35
Contending Forces (Hopkins), 55
Cooper, Anna Julia, 13, 61
Corregidora (Jones), 21
Craft, Ellen, 89
Craft, William, 89
Crisis magazine, 32
Cullen, Countee, 39
Cutter, Martha J., 83

Index

D

"Damnation of Women, On the" (Du Bois), 13
Daughters of the Confederacy, 116
Davis, Thadious, 9, 46, 72
Delany, Bessie, 63
Detroit Study Club, 70
Dixon, Thomas, 34
Douglas, Ann, 32–33
Douglass, Frederick, 14
Drake, St. Clair, 22, 24–25, 48
Du Bois, W. E. B., 13, 32, 33, 35, 53, 81, 116; opposition to Booker T. Washington, 32, 115
duCille, Ann, 9, 65, 67

E

Ellison, Ralph, 37
Eugenics, 76, 90
Euthenics, 76

F

Fatherhood, 18, 20, 42–47, 103–4
Fauset, Annie Seamon, 62
Fauset, Bella Huff, 62
Fauset, Jessie Redmon, 2, 8–9, 11, 15, 21, 23, 29–30, 35, 36, 39–79 passim, 81; biography, 31–32, 62; *Chinaberry Tree, The,* 7, 40, 47, 53, 56–57, 72, 74–75; criticism of, 71, 74; *Comedy: American Style,* 3–6, 8, 19–20, 30, 40, 45, 47, 58–59, 72, 104, 126, 129; critique of black elite, 28; euphemisms for black elite, 27; literary concerns of, 61; literary goals of, 37; *Plum Bun,* 21, 40, 47, 53, 72; reason for becoming a novelist, 35; representation of maternity, 12, 62; resistance to light-skin privilege, 52; resistance to racial hierarchy, 26; *There Is Confusion,* 5–8, 15, 19–20, 23, 29, 39–53 passim, 59–60, 65–79, 133; typical character types, 47; viewed as elitist, 32
Fisk University, 87, 115
Frazier, E. Franklin, 22, 26, 36
Freedom's Journal, 62

G

Gaines, Kevin Kelley, 16, 33, 52
Gatewood, Willard, 52, 68
Giddings, Paula, 29
Glasgow, Ellen, 116
Golden, Marita, 93
Good Hair, 1–2
Grant, Madison, 17
Gray, Leona, 2, 117, 120
Great Migration, 22
Gregory, Montgomery, 40–42
Griffith, D. W., 34–35, 119–20
Grimké, Angelina Weld, 13–14, 21

H

Half-Century Magazine, The, 34, 117
Hampton University, 115
Harlem Renaissance, 9, 11, 15, 22, 30, 32, 111; attitude toward black elite, 31; attitude toward sexuality, 94; goals of, 35, 37; link to literary precursors, 36; origins of, 39–40;

reason for failure, 36; target audience, 36–37
Harper, Frances E. W., 36, 40, 52, 54, 93
Harris, Herbert, 62
Hellman, Lillian, 116
"Her Virginia Mammy" (Chesnutt), 61
Hine, Darlene Clark, 17, 89
Hirsch, Marianne, 12
Hopkins, Pauline, 36, 40, 52, 55
Horton, James Oliver, 62–63
Howard University, 115
Hughes, Langston, 31, 39, 40
Hurst, Fannie, 2–3, 9, 11, 15, 21, 27–28, 30, 110; *Imitation of Life,* 2–3, 8–9, 16, 19, 21, 27, 111–37 passim; representation of maternity, 12; resistance to racial hierarchy, 26
Hurston, Zora Neale, 15, 20, 36, 40, 111–13

I

Idlewild, 47, 103
Imes, Elmer, 32
Imitation of Life (Hurst), 2–3, 8–9, 16, 19, 21, 111–37 passim; class distinction in, 27
Imitation of Life (Sirk), 9, 114, 132–33
Imitation of Life (Stahl), 9, 114, 123, 132–33
Incidents in the Life of a Slave Girl (Jacobs), 14
Iola Leroy (Harper), 54–55

J

Jacobs, Harriet, 14
Jocasta, 12
Johnson, Alice, 57
Johnson, Charles, 39
Johnson, James Weldon, 34, 88
Johnson, Lillian E., 70
Jones, Gayl, 21

L

Landry, Bart, 22–26
Langston, John Mercer, 31
Larsen, Nella, 2–3, 9, 11, 15, 18, 21, 23–24, 30–31, 35, 36, 40, 79; biography, 32, 94–95; criticism of, 71; critique of black elite, 28; euphemisms for black elite, 27; *Quicksand,* 4, 9, 16, 18, 36, 81–110 passim; *Passing* (Larsen), 3–4, 8–9, 16, 24, 81–110 passim, 126–29, 131–36; representation of maternity, 12, 81–110 passim; resistance to racial hierarchy, 26; viewed as elitist, 32
Larson, Charles, 93
Lewis, Earl, 37–38
Lindsay, Ben, 76
Little, Benilde, 1
Liveright, Horace, 41–42
Living Is Easy, The (West), 18–19, 24, 28, 114
"Long Black Song" (Wright), 95

M

Mammy, 9, 35, 61, 110, 112–37 pas-

sim, 133, 137; attributes of, 2, 119–20, 127; critique of, 113; historical significance, 114–20; marketability of, 125; recuperative reading of, 118; revulsion toward, 124, 126–27; white female dependence on, 116, 120–26, 131, 136
"Mammy Sue" (Gray), 2, 117
Marrow of Tradition, The (Chesnutt), 55–56
McCoy, Beth, 76, 79
McDowell, Deborah, 9, 93–94
McLendon, Jacquelyn, 9, 58
Miller, Nina, 75–76
Minstrelsy, 117
Miscegenation, 16, 34, 54–58, 59–60, 75, 82–83, 84–85, 86, 88, 89–90, 93, 94–95, 96–97, 98–99, 102, 118–119, 129–30, 135
Morrison, Toni, 15, 30
Motherhood, 15–17, 19,; American birth rates, 63; as bridge between the races, 13; children vs. career, 16, 90–91; conditions under slavery, 14–15, 89; cultural expectations of, 64–65, 67, 70; and domestic service, 28; and entrapment, 18, 92, 99, 101–10, 126; flawed, 3–4, 8, 17–18, 86, 90, 105–06; influence on character, 15; literary standard, 7–8; and marital sex, 96–98; and middle-class identity, 16, 21, 108; positive models, 5–6, 122; and "race suicide," 17; rejection of (*see* Childlessness); representational significance, 11, 17; and self-sacrifice, 130; separate spheres, 20; skin color consciousness, 19–20; as theoretical construct, 12; as trope of social exclusion, 81–82; as uplift strategy, 6, 15; and white supremacy, 131

M

NAACP (National Association for the Advancement of Colored People), 34, 35, 67
Narrative of the Life of Frederick Douglass, an American Slave, Written by Himself (Douglass), 14
Negro in American Fiction, The (Brown), 113
New Black Middle Class, The, 22
New York Daily News, The, 121

O

Opportunity magazine, 40; literary contests, 36, 112

P

Passing (Larsen), 3–4, 8–9, 16, 24, 81–110 passim, 126–29, 131–36; and class concerns, 81; marital relationship, 85–86; maternal alienation, 83–84
Passing (for white), 4, 29–30, 53–54, 58, 71–72, 96, 107
Passing of the Great Race, The (Grant), 17
Pinchback, P. B. S., 31
Plum Bun (Fauset), 21, 40, 53, 72; origins of primary characters, 47

Q

Quicksand (Larsen), 4, 9, 16, 18, 36,

81–110 passim, and class concerns, 81; and maternal alienation, 82; and maternal rejection, 86–92; religion in, 91–92

R

Rachel (Grimké), 13–14, 21
Racial uplift, 16
Red Summer of 1919, 33
Regional tension, 28, 30, 35
Revolt of Modern Youth, The (Lindsay), 76
Rhinelander case, 16
Rice, Thomas D., 78
Rich, Adrienne, 117
Roosevelt, Theodore, 63—64

S

Sanger, Margaret, 17
Sexuality, 93–101, 115, 118–120
Sirk, Douglas, 114
Sisney, Mary F., 71
Skin color: consciousness of, among blacks, 19–20
Smith, Valerie, 9, 127
Spillers, Hortense, 12
Stahl, John, 114, 121, 123
Story of the Negro, The, Vol. II (Washington), 115
Stowe, Harriet Beecher, 52, 135
Stribling, T. S., 35

T

Tate, Claudia, 9, 14, 30, 36, 52, 100–01

Their Eyes Were Watching God (Hurston), 15, 111
There Is Confusion (Fauset), 5–8, 15, 19–20, 23, 42–53 passim, 65–66, 70–79, 133; class and color, 59–60; domestic servants, 29; feminine ideal in, 65–66; maternal influence in, 66–71; origins of primary characters, 47; performing arts in, 77–79; physical description of Joanna, 53; publication reception, 39, repudiation of light-skin privilege, 53; role in literary tradition, 40
Thurer, Shari, 17
Toll, Robert, 78
Toomer, Jean, 31, 39
Tragic mulatto/a, 3, 52–61 passim, 93
Truth, Sojourner, 77
Tubman, Harriet, 77
Tuskegee Institute, 87, 115

U

Uncle Tom's Cabin (Stowe), 52, 135
"Unimportant Man, An" (West), 44
Urban League, 36–37

V

Vann, Helene, 123
Voice from the South, A (Cooper), 13

W

Wade-Gayles, Gloria, 12, 19
Wall, Cheryl, 56, 72

Index

Walrond, Eric, 39
Washington, Booker T., 87, 114–15, 118–19; opposition to W. E. B. Du Bois, 32
Watson, Steven, 31
West, Dorothy, 2, 18, 23–24, 36, 40, 44, 114; depiction of Southern stereotypes, 28; euphemisms for black elite, 27
Wheatley, Phillis, 40, 77
White, Walter, 35, 40
Williams, Daniel Hale, 57
Williams, John Sharp, 116
Wilson, Woodrow, 33–34
World War I (the Great War), 33, 45, 78, 95, 135–36
World War II, 112
World's Columbian Exposition (1893), 113
Wright, Richard, 95

New Approaches

Yoshinobu Hakutani, *General Editor*

The books in this series deal with many of the major writers known as American realists, modernists, and post-modernists from 1880 to the present. This category of writers will also include less known ethnic and minority writers, a majority of whom are African American, some are Native American, Mexican American, Japanese American, Chinese American, and others. The series might also include studies on well-known contemporary writers, such as James Dickey, Allen Ginsberg, Gary Snyder, John Barth, John Updike, and Joyce Carol Oates. In general, the series will reflect new critical approaches such as deconstructionism, new historicism, psychoanalytical criticism, gender criticism/feminism, and cultural criticism.

For additional information about this series or for the submission of manuscripts, please contact:

> Peter Lang Publishing
> P.O. Box 1246
> Bel Air, MD 21014-1246

To order other books in this series, please contact our Customer Service Department at:

> 800-770-LANG (within the U.S.)
> (212) 647-7706 (outside the U.S.)
> (212) 647-7707 FAX

Or browse online by series at:

> www.peterlangusa.com